Cisco IOS Releases: The Complete Reference

Mack M. Coulibaly

CISCO SYSTEMS
CISCO PRESS

Cisco Press
201 West 103rd Street
Indianapolis, IN 46290 USA

Cisco IOS Releases: The Complete Reference

Mack M. Coulibaly

Published by:
Cisco Press
201 West 103rd Street
Indianapolis, IN 46290 USA

Printed in the United States of America 1 2 3 4 5 6 7 8 9 0

Library of Congress Cataloging-in-Publication Number: 99-64087

ISBN: 1-57870-179-1

Warning and Disclaimer

This book is designed to provide information about **Cisco IOS Releases**. Every effort has been made to make this book as complete and as accurate as possible, but no warranty or fitness is implied.

The information is provided on an "as is" basis. The author, Cisco Press, and Cisco Systems, Inc. shall have neither liability nor responsibility to any person or entity with respect to any loss or damages arising from the information contained in this book or from the use of the discs or programs that may accompany it.

The opinions expressed in this book belong to the author and are not necessarily those of Cisco Systems, Inc.

Trademark Acknowledgments

All terms mentioned in this book that are known to be trademarks or service marks have been appropriately capitalized. Cisco Press or Cisco Systems, Inc. cannot attest to the accuracy of this information. Use of a term in this book should not be regarded as affecting the validity of any trademark or service mark.

Feedback Information

At Cisco Press, our goal is to create in-depth technical books of the highest quality and value. Each book is crafted with care and precision, undergoing rigorous development that involves the unique expertise of members from the professional technical community.

Readers' feedback is a natural continuation of this process. If you have any comments regarding how we could improve the quality of this book, or otherwise alter it to better suit your needs, you can contact us through email at ciscopress@mcp.com. Please make sure to include the book title and ISBN in your message.

We greatly appreciate your assistance.

Publisher	J. Carter Shanklin
Executive Editor	Alicia Buckley
Cisco Systems Program Manager	Jim LeValley
Managing Editor	Patrick Kanouse
Contributing Editor	Marla Reece-Hall
Project Editor	Jennifer Nuckles
Copy Editor	Scott MacLean
Technical Editors	John Branigan
	Joe Fianco
	Peter Long
Team Coordinator	Amy F. Lewis
Book Designer	Gina Rexrode
Cover Designer	Louisa Klucznik
Compositor	Gina Rexrode
Indexer	Tim Wright

About the Author

Mack M. Coulibaly has more than ten years of experience in software and hardware system design, including five years of network administration comprised of Cisco IOS software. Mr. Coulibaly is currently the IOS Serviceability Program Manager at Cisco Systems where he develops customer-focused IOS defect resolution, feature integration, release processes, and general serviceability guidelines. He is a contributor to the development of the latest Cisco IOS release process and created the popular white paper "Cisco IOS Reference Guide" and the Cisco IOS Roadmap, both of which are available at www.cisco.com.

Formerly, Mr. Coulibaly worked as a research consultant engineer at the multinational consortium Intelsat, where he developed simulation system software for the Intelsat VII telecommunication satellite. He then joined Standard Microsystems Corporation (SMC) as development engineer and Alpha Test manager, after which he worked at Cable & Wireless as senior network engineer. Before he began working at Cisco Systems in 1997, he was on the Cisco router configuration management team at Citicorp Global Technology Infrastructure, responsible for configuring and managing more than 3000 Cisco routers.

In addition to higher education in mathematics and physics from Université Du Benin, Mr. Coulibaly also holds a B.S. in electrical engineering from the University of the District of Columbia.

About the Contributing Editor

Marla Reece-Hall is a freelance writer, editor, and publishing consultant. During her tenure at Macmillan Publishing USA, she worked as copy and developmental editor on several dozen computer-related titles, focusing particularly on database titles for the Sams and Que imprints. Her current work includes providing market research and manuscript analysis for publishers and a variety of writing projects, including poetry, fiction, and assignments for non-profit and philanthropic organizations. She lives with her husband and three children in Indiana. You can contact Marla through her website at www.reece-hall.com.

About the Technical Reviewers

John Branigan currently works for Total Network Solutions (TNS), an international professional services firm providing internetworking services. Mr. Branigan has held this position for the past two years. Previously, Mr. Branigan spent 15 years involved with networking at Citibank.

Joe Fianco has worked for 21 years in the telecommunications industry, holding positions with ITT Worldcom, supporting subscriber voice and data transmission trouble resolution, and Citicorp, where he initially supported the international switched X.25 data network and T-1/E-1 based backbone. Mr. Fianco then transitioned to internetworking support, and, finally, became responsible for network design review, implementation, and third-level support for operations. Mr. Fianco is currently employed at EBS Dealing Resources. EBS utilizes Cisco Systems products to provide an electronic currency trading platform servicing financial institutions worldwide.

Peter Long is Director of Marketing at Cisco Systems and is responsible for worldwide marketing of Cisco IOS software. He has been working in the networking and communications industry for 20 years. Before joining Cisco, Mr. Long worked as a consultant to Telstra in Australia. Earlier he held technical, marketing, and management positions with various networking companies. Mr. Long holds a B.Sc. degree with first-class honors in computer science from the University of Melbourne and an M.B.A. degree from Monash University, both in Australia.

Dedications

I would like to thank Cisco's management, particularly Terry Mar and Gwynne Roshon-Larsen of Serviceability Design and Dixie Garr of Customer Success Engineering, for their support and continued leadership.

To my best friend, companion, and wife, Bimlesh L. Singh, whose love and continued support provided the energy to complete this book, I would like to give thanks and express my unrestricted love. Finally, I dedicate this book to my soon-to-be-born child, whose arrival we are impatiently awaiting in April 2000.

Acknowledgments

Writing a book containing such a plethora of information is rarely the work of one person. Indeed, the long process of making this book received direct and indirect contributions from numerous Cisco employees. Indirect contributions were made through documents and web pages developed by functional teams responsible for managing particular aspects of Cisco IOS Software release processes. In fact, some paragraphs of this book borrow from publications and training material previously developed by Cisco. I would like to acknowledge those who contributed to these materials through their teams: the IOS Release Operation team, the IOS Release Marketing team, the IOS Source Management team, the IOS Program Management team, the IOS development engineers and my own team, the IOS Serviceability team. Furthermore, I would like to recognize the following Cisco employees for their contribution to the development and/or improvement of the broad Cisco IOS release processes.

- Alan Newman
- Gene Peterson
- Chris Kolberg
- Mary Emerson
- Tom Johndrew
- Ann De Jesus
- Dani Abou-Chedid
- Dan Oberrotman
- Tim Dimacchia
- Lorie Reilly
- Kuan-Li Ong
- Robert Beckett
- Cindy Method
- Gabrielle Capolupo
- Matthew Munoz
- Ed Nelson
- Joe Novak

I would also like to thank Lynette Quinn, Amy Lewis, and Alicia Buckley for helping with the development of this book. Additional thanks go to Marla Reece-Hall who provided excellent editorial services. Further, the quality of this book would be diminished without the technical review of Peter Long, Joe Fianco, John Branigan, Kim Dion, Ken Trader, and Bill Warren.

Contents at a Glance

Table of Contents

Introduction

Cisco Internetwork Operating System (Cisco IOS™) software is an operating system that tightly integrates a broad range of Internet and enterprise network hardware. Network hardware evolves with the introduction of new generations of design techniques, processors, switching modules, and memory components. The Cisco IOS software, however, provides the unifying thread that connects otherwise disparate networks to build a scalable global infrastructure.

Since 1990, Cisco routers and switches have been considered the de facto standard for the Internet and enterprise networks. Cisco Systems hardware, powered by sophisticated, feature-full Cisco IOS software, became the system of choice for the Internet backbone. In fact, by 1998 more than 85% of the worldwide Internet traffic was handled by hardware built by Cisco Systems, Inc.

The Purpose of This Book

This book is designed to help network professionals responsible for designing, implementing, or supporting a network containing Cisco IOS-supported routers and switches. In this book, you will learn to select (among other things) the best Cisco IOS software releases for your network, techniques to identify the content of a Cisco IOS software image, and how to plan and predict software fixes that affect mission-critical applications. Chapter 8, "Hardware Architectures and Cisco IOS Software," is dedicated to how the Cisco IOS software maps the physical attributes of hardware to a logical structure that maximizes distributed computing resources and increases availability of services. This comprehensive spectrum of information is concisely presented to help the network engineer efficiently design, implement, and manage world-class network infrastructures powered by Cisco IOS software.

The purpose of this book is three-fold:

- It explains the background, context, and structure of the Cisco IOS Release processes as they have evolved over time.
- It describes how to identify an individual release, its features, and its relationship to the larger picture of Cisco IOS software releases.
- It provides a comprehensive set of resources, Cisco IOS Software versioning, binary image naming conventions, Cisco IOS software product numbering systems, and feature set definitions. These elements result in a powerful reference library for any network professional.

Together, these three facets of information should enable you to do the following:

- Identify any existing Cisco IOS image, including its release name, feature set, supported platforms, life cycle, and its placement in the scale of existing releases.
- Determine the way in which Cisco IOS uses or transforms hardware resources of a given platform.
- Determine possible upgrade paths for existing releases.
- Select current or future releases based on business needs for long-term stability versus short-term growth.
- Select current or future releases based on feature sets and platforms.

Who Should Read This Book?

The information in this book does not assume significant prior knowledge of Cisco IOS software, but it does assume that readers have one or more of the following:

- Network or system administration background, preferably with Cisco routers or switches running Cisco IOS software.

- Theoretical understanding of the role of integrated system software on hardware such as routers and switches.
- Business understanding of internetwork operations for the purpose of making executive-level decisions.
- Familiarity with the Cisco family of products.

In this era of fast-paced technology, it is often difficult to slow down to search for information. This book serves as an indispensable, easy-to-use reference tool for the following professionals:

- Network designers
- Network administrators and information technology professionals
- Network consultants
- Systems and sales engineers
- Individuals with an aspiration to networking careers

This book does not cover or include information on how to install or configure Cisco IOS software, routers, and so on. However, it does provide numerous cross-references to sites on Cisco Connection Online (CCO), www.cisco.com, which provide a variety of additional details.

How This Book Is Organized

The core of this book, and the part to which you are most likely to refer repeatedly appears in Part II, "Specification of Cisco IOS Releases." However, to fully understand the terminology and the implications of any release or its relationship to hardware or network services, you will need to refer to the information in Part I, "What Every Network Administrator Should Know."

Part I describes the progress of the software architecture. This evolution is the result of Cisco's response to changes in the networking marketplace with the expansive growth of the Internet. Chapter 1, "Evolution of the Cisco IOS System Architecture," and Chapter 2, "An Overview of The Evolution of Cisco IOS Release Models," explain the architectural changes and evolution of the Cisco IOS release models. Chapter 3, "Characteristics of Cisco IOS: Definitions, Naming Convention, Versioning, Numbering, and Feature Packaging," defines the various characteristics found in Cisco IOS releases. These include release types, life cycle milestones, naming, and numbering conventions.

These three chapters approach the "Why?" factor in the evolution of Cisco IOS software development and deployment strategies. In other words, they answer the following crucial questions and more:

- What are different release models?
- Why did the number of major releases in one model change in the next?
- What do all the portions of a release name mean, and how long is my version of Cisco IOS software supported by Cisco Systems?

Additionally, Chapter 3 defines the categories of information found in the IOS specifications tables in Part II.

Part II of this book includes Chapter 4, "Early Cisco IOS Software Releases: The Classic Phase of the Cisco IOS Release Process," Chapter 5, "Cisco IOS Releases during the NGRP Phase," Chapter 6, "Cisco IOS Releases 11.3/11.3T and Related STED: The Beginning of the Technology Release Model," and Chapter 7, "Current Cisco IOS Releases: Extension of the Technology Model". Part II briefly describes the specific release model of the grouping and then lists the various Cisco IOS releases, their main features, platforms, milestones, migration recommendations, and so on. The chapters in Part II follow the evolution of the release models, and range from major releases to minor releases. Because the list of features can often be quite extensive, not all features are listed. However, the target market provides the reader with an indication of the type of technology features that can be expected in that release. Additionally, a reference to more information on the CCO is provided with each release.

Part III, "The Hardware-Software Relationship," contains reference material on one of the major components with which Cisco IOS software interacts: hardware or platforms. Chapter 8, "Hardware Architectures and Cisco IOS Software," lists the physical resources of numerous platforms and the way in which Cisco IOS software utilizes hardware physical resources. This information should prepare system administrators for ways in which they can understand and improve resource management and performance.

Finally, Appendix A, "Cisco IOS Image Name Reference," provides a comprehensive list of images to help you determine the features and characteristics of a given release. This reference section applies to the information in Chapter 2 on how to determine the contents of an IOS image. Appendix B, "Cisco IOS Software Product Numbering System," contains examples of product numbers that contain information to help the customer identify the platform, the feature set, the maintenance revision number, and the IOS release train. Appendix C, "New Features of Cisco IOS 12.0T," contains the newest features of the latest IOS release. Also, a glossary of terms and feature abbreviations appears at the end of the book. For purposes of brevity in the release templates of Part II, feature names, protocols, technologies, and so on, appear in their abbreviated forms. The reader should refer to the glossary for further description.

Conventions Used in This Book

The conventions used in this book are relatively self-explanatory. The key to the naming conventions is explained in Chapter 3. The general guideline, however, is that italics indicates a placeholder. Additionally, a lowercase "x" is a placeholder for a digit, such as in 9.x, 10.x, or 12.0(x)T. An uppercase "X" is not a placeholder, but instead indicates a short-lived early deployment release, as described in Chapter 3.

PART I

What Every Network Administer Should Know

CHAPTER 1

Evolution of the Cisco IOS System Architecture

Cisco IOS is the original brand name for Cisco's routing software. As Cisco's technology offerings expanded, IOS diversified and became a series of tightly linked internetworking software products. Although its brand name might still equate to routing software, the continuing evolution of IOS has seen the software migrate to support LAN, ATM, xDSL, and WAN switches as well as provide important functionality for network applications such as network security, network management, DHCP, and web scaling services. This chapter defines Cisco IOS, the evolution of its architecture, and the goals and benefits of this architecture. This background information helps explain the formation and evolution of the various Cisco IOS software releases described in this book.

Cisco IOS Definition

The Cisco IOS software is a sophisticated operating system optimized for internetworking. It provides an architecture that is dissociated from hardware, enabling adaptation to changing network technologies through dynamic feature integration and upgrade.

In short, Cisco IOS can be thought of as a highly intelligent internetworking administrator that manages and controls complex distributed network resources and functions.

Because of the dynamic nature of Cisco IOS, the software has taken a progressive form of development and deployment, evolving with the market it serves. Cisco engineers have successively adapted the underlying architecture of Cisco IOS to enable multidimensional growth and frequent incorporation of new features and developments. Key to this growth and market benefit are the following two related aspects of the Cisco IOS architecture:

- A transition from a monolithic foundation to a more modular structure
- The underlying division of Kernel (General) services from Network services

This evolution has thus far culminated in the capability of Cisco IOS engineers to develop interoperable, independent features sets for various networking solutions.

Move Toward Modularity

From an early inclination toward a monolithic architecture, Cisco IOS software moved to a more modular architecture. This structure allows two fundamental opportunities:

- Compartmentalized, interchangeable code modules that access core services separately, decreasing or eliminating interdependencies and making the software easier to port.
- Multiple-track, feature development based on business units, which is the core of current Cisco IOS development strategies. This enables multiple, feature- or platform-specific releases that are all based on the same original source code.

The upcomimg sections provide more details about these features.

Division of Kernel and Network Services

The IOS architecture can be represented as two separate fundamental services: Kernel services and Network services. IOS Kernel services provide all functions necessary for IOS multiplatform portability and scalability. IOS Network services represent all functionality built on top of Kernel services to deliver IOS internetworking features. By disconnecting the two categories of services from each other, Cisco IOS software can offer feature sets that provide specific network solutions in modules that can be separately integrated into different platforms.

Development History

Understanding the development history of the Cisco IOS software helps to explain the underlying causes of the release models discussed in Chapter 2, "An Overview of the Evolution of Cisco IOS Release Models."

The evolution of the release models from 9.x to 12.0T and beyond is more or less related to the architectural changes described in this section.

The Early System Architecture

As mentioned earlier in this chapter, Cisco IOS has evolved from a monolithic architecture to a more modular architecture. The early releases of IOS (prior to version 9.21) formed a singular, monolithic system. The software was arranged as a set of procedures, enabling any procedure(s) to call any other. This monolithic structure did not enforce data hiding; most of its operating code had structural and operational interdependencies.

This architecture obviously did not scale very well and made the introduction of new features and platforms a more drastic process.

Evolution to Modular Architecture

Cisco IOS releases 9.21 through 11.2 represent engineering efforts to redesign Cisco IOS into modular components or subsystems. Figure 1-1 illustrates this architectural evolution.

Figure 1-1 *The IOS Modular Structure Creates Separable, Yet Linked, Subsystems [Feature Set]*

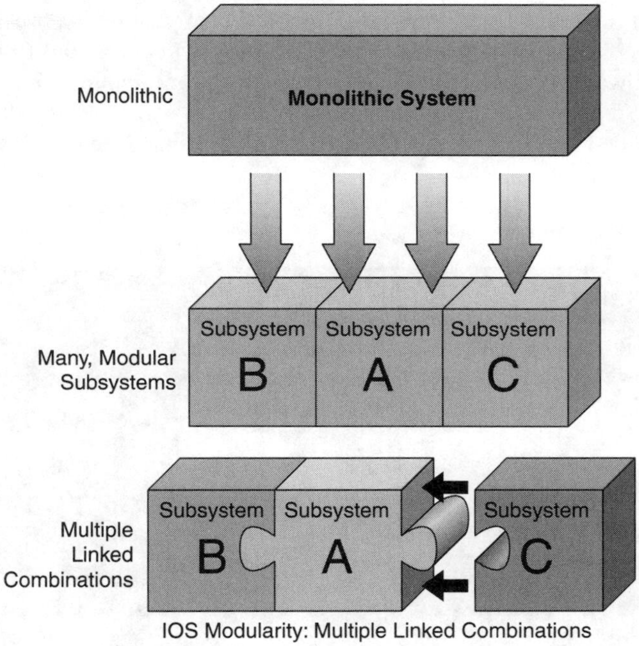

Organized as a set of layers, each subsystem in the modular architecture provides an independent entry point into the system code. The subsystems themselves are defined as discrete modules that support various functions within the embedded (Kernel) system. This layered subsystem design has enabled engineering to partition Cisco IOS into more manageable and easily scalable feature sets.

This evolution of the IOS architecture facilitated the formation of the multiple-track release processes dubbed as the next generation of release process (NGRP), described in Chapter 2.

The focus of NGRP was to separate the development of new hardware platforms and new software features from the original source code. This prevented the main software code (also known as the main release train) from being adversely impacted by new development changes. Both the IOS software architecture and the release process were further refined in the technology release process, described later in this book.

Solid State Architecture—IOS Feature Sets as Network Solutions

Cisco IOS feature sets became possible because many specific Network services have been decoupled from the IOS Kernel.

For example, although today Cisco offers such feature sets as enterprise and desktop feature sets, these are prepackaged solutions limited by IOS Kernel and subsystem dependencies. As solution sets evolve, they attain still finer levels of granularity. Solution sets evolve as feature-specific entities rather than Kernel or subsystem definitions (by default, however, there will always be some level of subsystem definition). Figure 1-2 summarizes IOS evolution to feature sets. The complete list of currently available Cisco IOS software feature sets is provided in Appendix A, "Cisco IOS Image Name Reference," at the end of this book.

Figure 1-2 *Cisco IOS Feature Set Packaging*

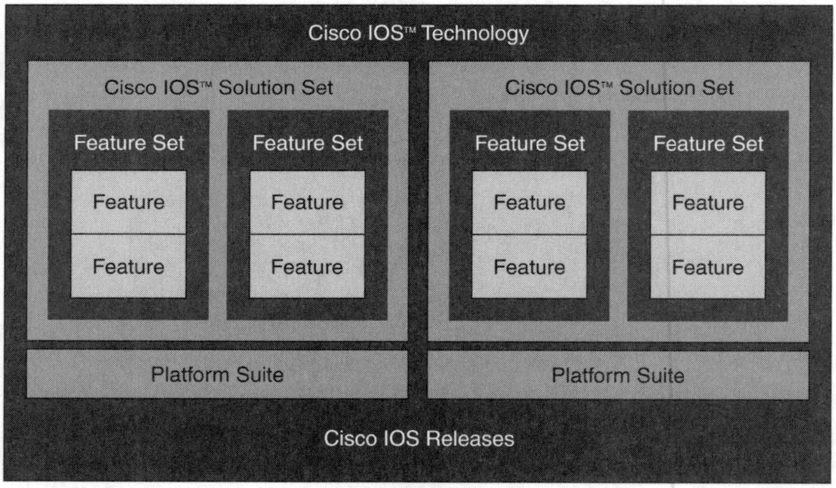

Cisco IOS Solution Sets

Cisco IOS feature sets can be logically viewed as providing three categories of services: Kernel services, Network services, and Application services (not always present). For the purpose of clarity, this introduction focuses on the Kernel and Network services. Kernel services can be viewed as providing the base IOS engineering reference platform, while Network services comprise all value-added features that reside on top of the operating system. Figure 1-3 logically illustrates the separation in Network and Kernel services.

Figure 1-3 *Cisco IOS Services*

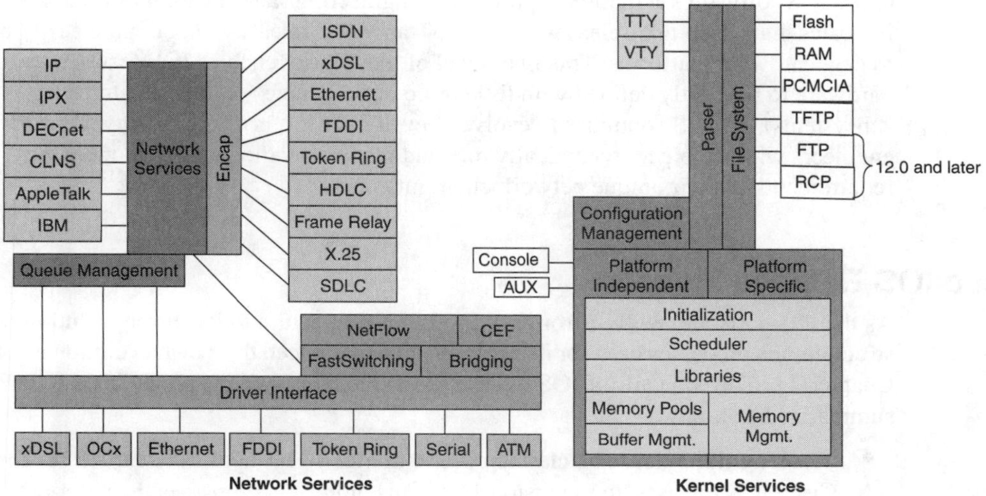

Chapter 7, "Current Cisco IOS Releases: Extension of the Technology Model," lists this category of services in greater detail, and Chapter 8, "Hardware Architectures and Cisco IOS Software," lists both general and specific categories of network features in greater detail as they appear in the Cisco IOS context.

Summary of Cisco IOS Engineering Efforts

The following sections summarize the evolution of Cisco IOS Engineering building blocks.

Monolithic Code

The early releases of Cisco IOS grew into a singular, monolithic system, which was fundamentally router centric. It was arranged as a set of procedures, enabling any procedure to call any other procedure with highly structural and operational interdependencies.

Modular Structure

Starting with IOS version 9.21 and continuing through IOS version 11.2, IOS was redesigned into modular components or subsystems. Defined as a discrete module that supports various functions, each subsystem now provides an independent entry point to the system code. This layered subsystem design enables Cisco to package IOS images into more manageable and scalable feature sets.

Port-Ready Modularity

Cisco IOS software's evolution to port-ready engineering started with IOS version 11.3 and indicates that Cisco IOS releases 11.3, 11.3T and later releases can be more easily ported to new hardware platforms. This finer level of modularity enables IOS features and hardware to be tightly defined with little or no dependencies on other features (or subsystems). As IOS continues to evolve to even finer levels of modularity, network engineers will be able to dynamically mix and match specific features to meet the requirements of their unique network environments.

Cisco IOS Release Models

As the IOS software evolved from a monolithic architecture to its current solution set structure, the processes used for its deployment experienced their own evolutionary stages. Chapter 7 provides details of IOS release processes. For now, the processes can be summarized as follows:

- **The singular release or classic release model**—This applies to earlier versions of Cisco IOS releases up to version 11.1. This model encompasses the monolithic structure and the majority of the modular development stage (as mentioned previously, the modular structure includes releases up to 11.2). Part III of this book, "The Hardware-Software Relationship," lists the timing, features, and technical specifications of each of the IOS releases during this period.
- **The next generation of release process (NGRP)**—Cisco IOS releases 11.2, 11.2P, and 11.2F mark the beginning of the NGRP, which is characterized by the following:
  - — A main release, 11.2, which targets high stability by providing only incremental fixes.
  - — A platform release, 11.2P, which targets support for most hardware platforms, port adapters, and interface processors. 11.2P is the recipient of newly developed hardware.
  - — A feature release, 11.2F, which receives all of the commits of 11.2P by way of software synchronization. Additionally, 11.2F directly receives newly developed software features.

  The advent of this set of major releases also marks the transition from a model with one Cisco IOS release to a model with simultaneous multiple Cisco IOS releases. Part II of this book, "Specification of Cisco IOS Releases," describes the effect of the expansion of the Internet on the NGRP and provides detailed specifications of the Cisco IOS software versions during this period.
- **The technology release process**—This covers Cisco IOS releases 11.3, 11.3T, 12.0, 12.0T, and related early deployment releases. The introduction of 11.3 and 11.3T marks the departure from three simultaneous major releases of the NGRP era and the

beginning of the streamlined technology model, which enables two simultaneous major Cisco IOS releases. Although some changes or improvements to the process are expected, this model is expected to continue with 12.1 and 12.1T. Chapter 7 elaborates on the significance of the technology releases and the driving force behind the multiplicity of today's Cisco IOS software releases.

Benefits of Cisco IOS Software

The current architecture and engineering strategies of Cisco IOS software offer a number of benefits for growth and diversity. The following list outlines not only the benefits of Cisco IOS, but also helps to explain the strategy behind the evolution of its release processes.

- **Flexibility**—The IOS software architecture provides an extendible medium for integrating new capabilities as requirements and technologies evolve. Additionally, as new technologies emerge, these can be integrated into future releases that are based on proven source code.
- **Scalability**—Cisco IOS supports network expansion and incorporation of new technologies by employing features such as filtering, protocol termination and translation, smart broadcasts, helper address services, multimedia, and voice services. Cisco IOS provides connectivity and interoperability for data protocol standards, media access methods, and services from leading network vendors.
- **Interoperability**—IOS supports a wide array of standards-based, physical, and logical protocol interfaces. The support ranges from twisted copper pairs to optical fiber and broadband wireless; and from LAN to WAN media. It integrates network protocols such as TCP/IP, Novell NetWare, AppleTalk, DECnet, SNA, and many others.
- **Manageability**—The IOS software is one of Cisco's vehicles for building embedded intelligence into network devices. Management interfaces such as the IOS diagnostic interface, as well as agent software for intelligent network-aware applications, enable users to troubleshoot and monitor a wide array of network appliances. Cisco IOS software also serves as a key technology component for Cisco Systems as it moves toward large-scale deployment of intelligent agents and policy-based automated management.

Summary

Cisco IOS software provides support for a large number of network protocols and runs on multiple platforms while retaining design criteria that are independent of hardware. The IOS software architecture provides flexibility with an extendible platform on which Cisco can integrate new capabilities as requirements and technologies evolve.

The list of features, combined with the number of platforms and interfaces currently supported by the Cisco IOS software, demonstrate the flexibility of this complex internetworking software solution. The current feature set expansion of IOS software is the result of an evolution in both directly marketable innovations and software development methodologies over a period of several years. For more information, visit Cisco Connection Online (CCO) at http://www.cisco.com.

The next few chapters expand on the guidelines that governed early Cisco IOS releases. Understanding the limitations and benefits of each of these releases helps you make informed decisions during the planning, design, and implementation of network infrastructures.

CHAPTER 2

An Overview of the Evolution of Cisco IOS Release Models

Perhaps the most noticeable characteristic of the Cisco IOS releases is that there are dozens of release versions listed either in CCO or in other Cisco literature. This raises questions such as Why are there so many releases? What do they all do? and What does 12.0(1)XA mean? Despite the apparent complexity of this software release strategy, this chapter will attempt to concisely explain its logic, the reasons behind each variation, and logical connections from the earliest versions of IOS releases to the latest 12.10 releases.

Figure 2-1 graphically depicts the parent-child relationship between current Cisco IOS releases.

Figure 2-1 *Relationship between Current IOS Releases*

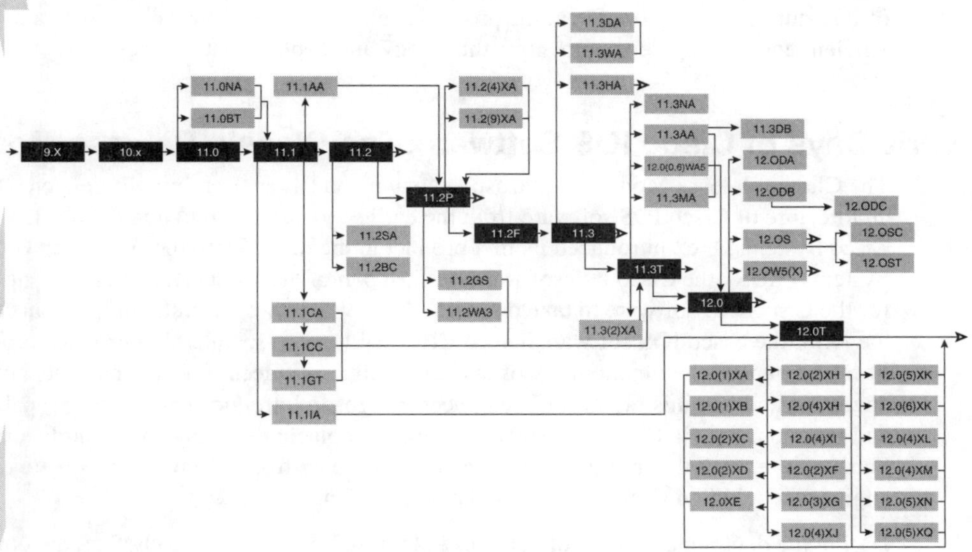

The lines between the boxes, as well as the boxes themselves, indicate types of releases and relationships. The basic distinctions are as follows:

- The dark boxes with a simple *n.n* or *n.nl* numbering scheme are *major releases.*
- Lighter colored boxes are Early Deployment (ED), including Short-Lived, Early Deployment (XED) releases, Consolidated Early Deployment Releases, and Specific Technology/Market Early Deployment Releases.

  The lines indicate parent-child relationships and possible migration paths.
- Open arrows indicate that a release deployed successive maintenance revisions.
- A *release train* comprises multiple interim and maintenance revisions.

This chapter introduces the evolution of Cisco IOS release processes.

The Cisco IOS Software Release Models

As mentioned in Chapter 1, "Evolution of the Cisco IOS System Architecture," Cisco IOS releases evolved through three phases of engineering development and release strategy:

- The Classic Release Process
- The Next Generation Release Process
- The Technology Release Process

The differences among the models of these processes reflected the underlying architecture of IOS during that period. Then, the process itself was refined to accommodate a more efficient engineering development methodology and deployment strategy.

The Early Days of Cisco IOS Software: The Classic Release Model

The Classic Release Model was retrospectively named as such. It initially reflected the architecture of Cisco IOS software from the earliest versions through version 9.1. When Cisco Systems, Inc., introduced its first product in the mid-1980s, the Advanced Gateway Systems (AGS), the Cisco IOS software was just part of the product and there was no intent for the Cisco IOS software to take on a life of its own. However, following the success of the AGS, the Cisco IOS software helped Cisco Systems to seamlessly introduce product lines and expand the functionality of existing products. Indeed, for the first time, network engineers and administrators could engineer designs to introduce new routing capability and functionality via Cisco IOS software without replacing existing Cisco hardware. Furthermore, with the introduction of each new product from Cisco Systems, network engineers could find a familiar user and command line interface.

During the deployment phase of versions 9.2 through 11.1, the Cisco IOS architecture evolved into a more modular design. The end of this period coincides with the appearance of the first early deployment (ED) releases, such as 11.0BT and 11.0NA.

The purpose of ED releases is defined fully in the "Categories of Releases" section in Chapter 3, "Characteristics of Cisco IOS: Definitions, Naming Convention, Versioning, Numbering, and Feature Packaging." However, the basic design of ED releases corresponds roughly with the plan to develop specialized features based on a copy of a major Cisco IOS software branch. The separated branch can closely focus on the development of the new technologies independently from the original major branch, which continues to deliver more mature technologies.

With the deployment of the first ED releases also came a new issue—how to integrate new features of the ED releases back into the major releases. As the new technology of the ED releases matured, it was necessary to integrate them into major IOS releases to maintain continuity and to avoid dispersion and divergence.

Chapter 4, "Early Cisco IOS Software Releases: The Classic Phase of the Cisco IOS Release Process," provides detailed specifications of the software versions deployed during the classic release era.

Next Generation of Release Process (NGRP)

The expansion of computer networks in the corporate world coupled with the explosive growth of the public Internet quickly required a new Cisco IOS release strategy. Cisco Systems needed to provide software releases to meet the varying demands of the growing and diversified marketplace. The next generation of the Cisco IOS release process was designed to service this multiplicity of the networking market theatres. It provided three concurrent and closely related major IOS releases: 11.2, 11.2P, and 11.2F (see Figure 2-2). The following synopsis provides the simplest explanation of this model.

- Cisco IOS 11.2 main release (or main line) is the unification of features of prior proven technologies. It contains only proven technologies and stable code. The NGRP model calls for only incremental defect fixes and no new features on the main release. It serves as the basis for the other major releases of the NGRP model.
- Release 11.2P focused on new hardware platform development. The separation from the base code of 11.2 main line enabled development teams to integrate newly developed hardware-specific features to meet the vast needs and rapid changes experienced by corporate networks and the Internet.
- Release 11.2F assumed the responsibility of deploying new software features. In addition to the specific features directly introduced in this release, it also inherited any commits made to 11.2P or bug fixes applied to 11.2 main line. Cisco IOS release 11.2F constituted the superset of both 11.2 and 11.2P.

Figure 2-2 *Cisco IOS NGRP Model*

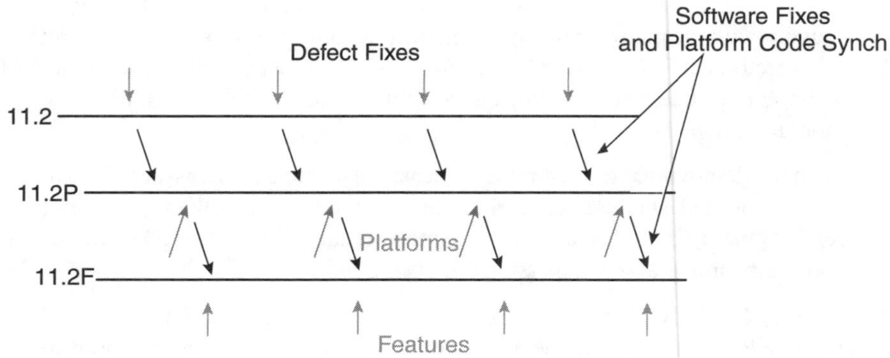

The NGRP model quickly exhibited some engineering coordination deficiencies, especially at the 11.2F level. Less than a year after the implementation of NGRP, Cisco IOS release 11.2F stopped shipping because it failed to meet Cisco quality requirements. Regular code conflicts between the features directly committed 11.2F, and those synced from 11.2P raised questions about the effectiveness of the NGRP. While 11.2 main line and 11.2P continued to provide successive maintenance releases, the IOS release team was at work developing an engineering method to smoothly transition out of the NGRP. The current technology release process emerged as a result.

Overview of the Current Cisco IOS Release Model: The Technology Release Process

The current Cisco IOS release process was developed as a result of the experience gained through the 11.2F release train. The first release of the technology era is based in Cisco IOS 11.2(7)F. Let's first see how this came about.

The End of Cisco IOS Software Release 11.2F and the Beginning of 11.3

During the NGRP phase, the 11.2 main release train received no new functionality. Successive maintenance revisions of 11.2 only received incremental bug fixes. While new hardware platform was committed to 11.2P, new software features went to 11.2F. Furthermore, periodic software sync provided 11.2F with the platform features that had been directly committed to 11.2P. This meant that software and hardware features which were separately committed and tested in distinct releases needed to coexist in 11.2F.

Using 11.2F in this way greatly increased both its value and its complexity. Unfortunately, the latter proved too difficult to manage effectively, and the release stopped shipping at

11.2(4)F. It was, however, still the only source of many IOS features and represented a great deal of engineering effort.

An engineering task force worked to bring 11.2F in line with the quality specifications that are expected of Cisco Systems, while the release team set about developing the new IOS technology release process. By late 1997, Cisco IOS version 11.2(7)F (a non-shipping version) was fully functional and ready to be used as the basis for the initial deployment of 11.3 and 11.3T. At the same time that 11.2F was taken off the market [(11.2(4)F to 11.2(7)F], the Cisco development machine continued to produce new software features to meet customer demands and the changing market. These newly developed features had to be committed to a release other than 11.2F in order to avoid new software conflicts. The new features were committed in 11.2P and in specific technology early deployment releases such as 11.1CA, 11.1CC, 11.1CT, 11.2BC, 11.2GS, and 11.2WA.

Figure 2-3 shows the transition from 11.2(7)F to the 11.3/11.3T pair.

Figure 2-3 *The Making of 11.3/11.3T Release Pair*

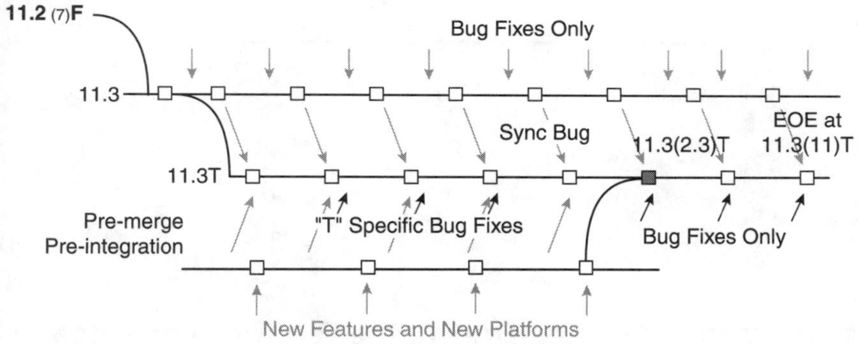

The Initial Implementation Plans of the Transition to 11.3/11.3T

In an effort to converge software and hardware features from 11.1CA, 11.1CC, 11.1CT, 11.2P, and 11.2GS, the release team devised a short- and long-term plan.

The short-term plan was centered around transitioning 11.2F to 11.3/11.3T releases. This phase, which marks the beginning of the technology release process, was to last approximately one year. That time was deemed sufficient to enable a development strategy to bring together features dispersed in the Cisco IOS early deployment releases.

The long-term plan was the ultimate unification of the early deployment releases into a new pair of major releases: Cisco IOS releases 12.0 and 12.0T.

The Highlights of the Technology Release Process

The major noticeable change from NGRP to the technology release process is the transition from three concurrent IOS major releases to two concurrent major releases. The technology model sanctions a main release (11.3) and a technology release (11.3T). The main line release maintains the same characteristics as the main line release of the NGRP era. However, the "T" release combines both the characteristics of 11.2P and 11.2F. Indeed, with the technology release process, both platform-specific features and software-specific features share a common release vehicle called the "T" release.

Figure 2-4 shows the transition to two concurrent major releases, IOS versions 11.3 and 11.3T.

Figure 2-4 *Cisco IOS Technology Release Process: Major Releases 11.3 and 11.3T*

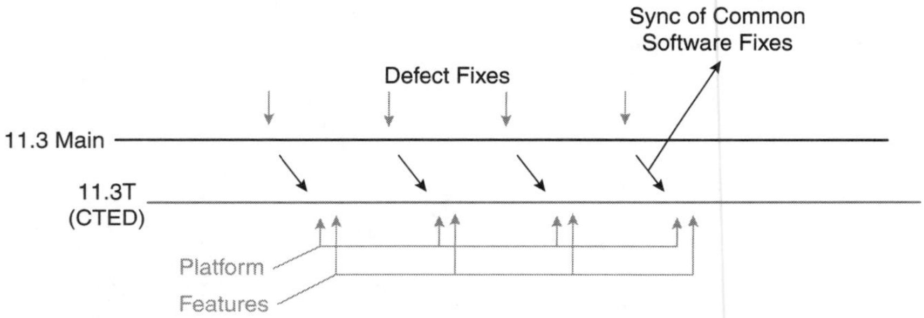

Early Deployment Releases During the Technology Release Process

In addition to the major Cisco IOS release trains, the technology release model also includes several categories of early deployment releases. Early deployment releases closely align with technology market theatres and serve as vehicles to quickly introduce engineering efforts to the market. Field-proven features of ED releases are periodically converged into the "T" release. The "T" release evolves and matures into the next main line release.

Cisco IOS ED releases, which are described in detail in Chapter 3, fall into the following categories:

- Consolidated Technology Early Deployment (CTED) releases (also known as the "T" release or the "T" train)
- Specific Technology Early Deployment (STED) releases
- Specific Market Early Deployment (SMED) releases
- Short-Lived Early Deployment Releases, also known as X Releases (XED)

The following bullets summarize the development and deployment relationship among Cisco IOS releases:

- Common code bug fixes are applied to the main line release. The fix is periodically synced to the consolidated release train (CTED) which syncs to any parented active STED releases.
- Specific Technology or Specific Market ED releases are parented to either the main release or the CTED release and remain active for as long as the parent is active. They receive new features and enhancements as well as inherit common code fixes from either the main line release or the CTED via periodic sync.
- X releases (XED) or Short-Lived releases are rooted in the CTED. They provide the Cisco development team a vehicle for quickly bringing new technologies to market. Cisco IOS XEDs are quickly synced back to the CTED release train. Once the features of the XED are released with the CTED, the XED usually becomes obsolete and reaches the end of engineering—hence the name short-lived release.
- Proven technologies introduced in the first six maintenance revisions of the CTED are carried forward to form the basis for the next main line release.

Figure 2-5 illustrates the relationship between Cisco IOS XED and CTED.

Figure 2-5 *Relationship of Cisco IOS XED to CTED*

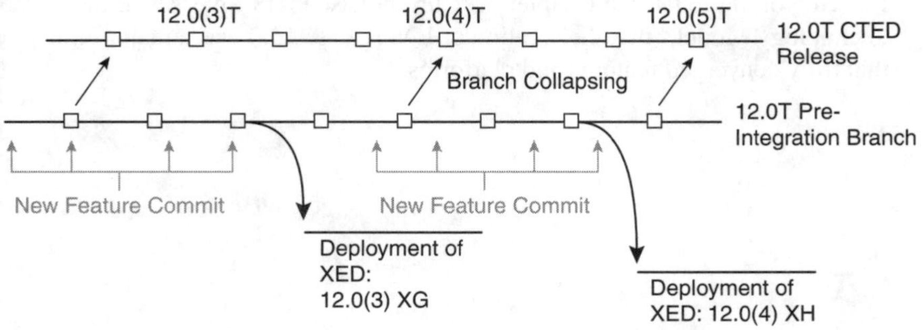

Chapter 3 provides detailed information on the current technology release process, including expanded coverage of the early deployment releases.

Importance of Unifying the Releases

The culmination of Cisco's effort is to generate timely and marketing-sensitive support for new features, making certain that all releases are eventually unified into a highly stable IOS release train. This good intention has not always materialized. In fact, prior to the release of IOS 12.0 and parented early deployment releases, the Cisco IOS software had substantially diverged, as shown in Figure 2-6.

Figure 2-6 *Divergence of Cisco IOS ED Releases*

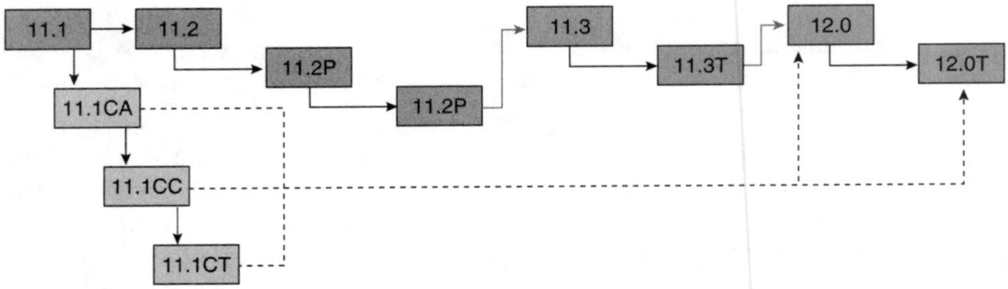

This divergence explains why a certain Cisco IOS release might not support a given feature when it seems logical that it should by virtue of its placement in the IOS release tree. For example, the port adapter PA-4E1G is supported in 11.1CA but not in 11.2, 11.2P, or 11.2F. This discrepancy can be explained by the dispersion of features during the transition from 11.2F to 11.3. This feature and a few others previously committed to other Specific Technology releases during the transition phase were finally ported to the 12.0 releases. Although this presented a limitation for anyone with the need for features and platforms developed during the time from 11.2(4)F to 11.3(1)T, network administrators can overcome the potential deficiencies by migrating to the 12.0-based releases.

Indeed, you'll see later in Chapter 7, "Current Cisco IOS Releases: Extension of the Technology Model," that the creation of IOS release 12.0 was a major unification process that truly converged features and platforms.

CHAPTER 3

Characteristics of Cisco IOS: Definitions, Naming Convention, Versioning, Numbering, and Feature Packaging

As with any software product, Cisco IOS software has certain characteristics common to each release. Chapter 1, "Evolution of the Cisco IOS System Architecture," and Chapter 2, "An Overview of the Evolution of Cisco IOS Release Models," of this book have provided an overview of the software architecture and release processes used for software deployment. This chapter shows how these two factors and the overall goals of Cisco Systems influence the characteristics of Cisco IOS releases. The information in this chapter will help you decipher a given Cisco IOS release by decoding information contained in the release's name, the IOS software image name, or the banner generated by the **show version** command line interface.

The Influence of Cisco's Business Unit Structure

As mentioned in Chapter 2, the current structure of Cisco IOS releases mirrors the structure of Cisco Systems, Inc. This connection is helpful in understanding the source, purpose, and target market of a specific release. Furthermore, the correlation between the structure of the company and that of IOS software outlines the manner in which various IOS releases are organized and controlled.

Cisco is structured by line of businesses (LOBs), and each line of business supports multiple business units (BUs). For example, the service provider line of business (SPLOB) includes the network user business unit (NUBU), the multi-service access business unit (MSABU), and the network and service management business unit (NSMBU) among others.

Adjacent to the LOBs and other business functions is the IOS Technology Division (ITD). Similar to LOBs, ITD includes service units such as the IP internet service unit (IPISU), which develops Cisco's Internet scaling devices such as Local Director, Distributed Director, and Cache Engine. IPISU also architects the underlying infrastructure for IP protocols enhancement such as quality of service (QoS), Virtual Private Network, IP Multicasting, and other IP scaling services.

The Cisco IOS Technologies Division works closely with every LOB, BU, and functional organization within Cisco to support the company's initiative to deliver new technology to the marketplace. Figure 3-1 illustrates the business unit organization and its support for the various services of IOS software.

Figure 3-1 *Cisco IOS Service Structure Supported by Business Units*

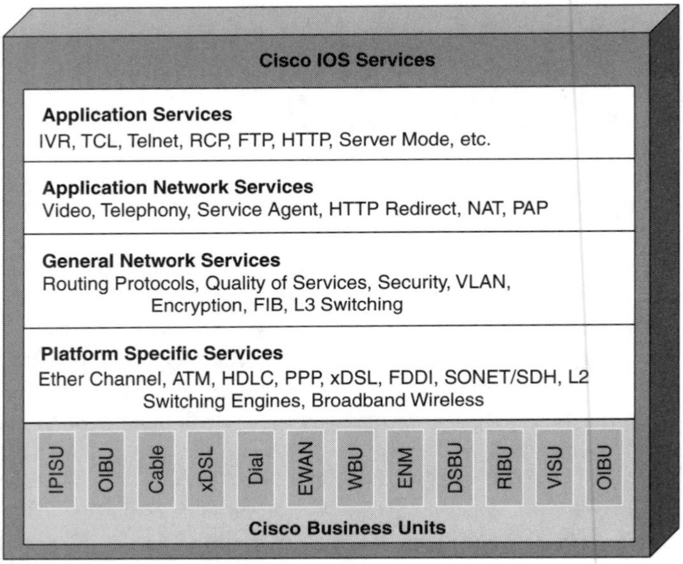

Categories of Cisco IOS Releases

Cisco IOS releases are defined in two high-level groups: major releases and minor releases. Figure 3-2 shows a grid of Cisco IOS release types.

Figure 3-2 *Types of Cisco IOS Releases*

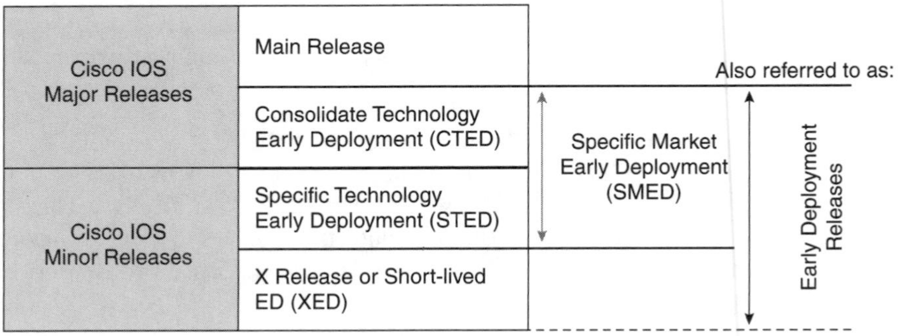

To understand the characteristics of each release category definition, you should familiarize yourself with a few terms associated with the release type.

- **Deployment categories**—These are, in respective order:
  - — **Limited deployment (LD)**—This refers to Cisco IOS main releases which have not reached general deployment certification. The release may be in its initial stages, or is intentionally limited in life span so it never reaches general deployment (GD).
  - — **Candidate for general deployment**—Any main line IOS release is a potential candidate for GD. However, not all main line IOS releases attain the GD certification.
  - — **General deployment (GD)**—This refers to the point at which Cisco declares the release essentially stable on all platforms, in all network environments. GD certification is attained only if certain quality criteria are met. Among the criteria are customer surveys of the release, the number of severity 1 and severity 2 defects, and the normalized trend of customer-found defects in the release over the previous four maintenance releases. A customer advocacy GD certification cross functional team composed of TAC, GSE, NSA engineers, System Test Engineering, IOS Engineering, and others is formed to evaluate every outstanding defect of the release. This team gives the final blessing for general deployment.
  - — **Maintenance releases**—These are also called maintenance revisions, and are successive software revisions of a release train. They combine incremental fixes integrated over several interim releases. Maintenance revisions of ED releases integrate new functionality as well as software fixes. Maintenance releases are fully tested and typically deployed every seven to eight weeks, unless the release is in mature maintenance mode. In which case, maintenance revisions are deployed every 13 to 14 weeks.
  - — **Interim releases**—These are work-in-process Cisco IOS images (typically built weekly) that are built between maintenance releases to integrate the latest round of bug fixes (and new features in case of ED releases). Because only limited testing is performed on interim releases, customers should use them with caution. Cisco IOS interim builds are engineering vehicles that integrate new incremental software modules or software bug fixes. The aggregation of those fixes appears in the next fully tested maintenance release.
- **Release train**—This refers to a Cisco IOS release, including all its interim and maintenance revisions.

- **Major releases**—Cisco IOS major releases are those controlled by ITD. Typically, IOS major releases provide the foundation for any other type of IOS release. Example of major releases include 11.2, 11.2P, and 11.2F. With the current technology release process, the main line and the "T" (or CTED) constitute the major releases. For example, 12.0 main and 12.0T are the major releases of Cisco IOS 12.0.

Definitions of other terms used in the descriptions of the release types appear in the glossary of terms at the end of the book.

Cisco IOS Main Releases

The IOS Technology Division manages Cisco IOS main releases. They consolidate features, platforms, functionality, technology, and host proliferation from the preceding set of early deployment releases. In other words, main line releases are general-purpose IOS software that seeks to achieve greater stability and quality. For this reason, the contents of main line releases do not change with successive maintenance revisions. Maintenance revisions provide incremental bug fixes leading to greater software quality. Examples of main releases are 11.2, 11.3, 12.0, and 12.1.

The first few maintenance revisions of a Cisco IOS main release are qualified as LD. At some point during the release life cycle, the main release might achieve GD certification, which marks a quality milestone. Once a GD, every subsequent revision of the release is also a GD. For that reason, once a release is declared GD, it automatically enters a phase called *restricted maintenance phase*. While in this phase, engineering modification of the code, including bug fixes with major code rework, is strictly limited and controlled by a program manager. This ensures that no adverse bug is reintroduced to a GD certified Cisco IOS release.

Early Deployment Releases

Early deployment (ED) releases take several forms. However, the one thing EDs undoubtedly have in common is the introduction of new software and hardware features into successive maintenance revisions. Cisco IOS EDs are the avenues of exploration and enhancement, which adapt to current market needs and growth. ED releases are categorized as Consolidated Technology releases (CTED), Specific Technology (STED), Specific Market (SMED), and Short-Lived or X releases (XED).

The Consolidated Technology Release of 12.0 and Beyond

The Consolidated Technology release train was introduced with the technology release process and can be easily identified by the "T" appended to the major release number. Examples are 11.3T, 12.0T, and 12.1T. Consolidated Technology releases are the unified Cisco IOS release vehicles which introduce diversified new technologies to the marketplace. They are called Consolidated Technology because they transcend the internal BU and LOB definitions. Software images of the CTED release, just like images of main releases, are built for current and active Cisco hardware platforms, regardless of the business unit originator.

By design, the technology train is extremely rich in hardware and software features (WIC, Port adapters, interface processors, and so forth.) If you have Cisco gear and you've been looking for an IOS release that supports a certain combination of hardware and features, chances are you'll find them in the latest "T" release.

Because the code of the Cisco IOS CTED is constantly changing to accommodate the addition of new features, the CTED might experience a higher rate of defects than its parent main line release. In order to reduce this risk factor, the CTED usually accepts new functionality for about 12 to 14 months (the first six maintenance revisions). Thereafter, the code is closed to new additions and the branch is relabeled to a name that conforms to the next main release train. For example, Cisco IOS release 12.0T will become Cisco IOS 12.1 after the sixth maintenance revision—12.0(7)T (12.0(6)T was skipped). However, for some early technology adapters, time-to-market flexibility and the abundance of features in the IOS CTED software usually outweigh the occasional stability factor.

Figure 3-3 shows the evolution of the CTED into the next main line release and the maintenance revisions in between.

Figure 3-3 *The CTED for 12.0 and Beyond (12.0T, 12.1T, and so on) Becomes the Next Main Line Release*

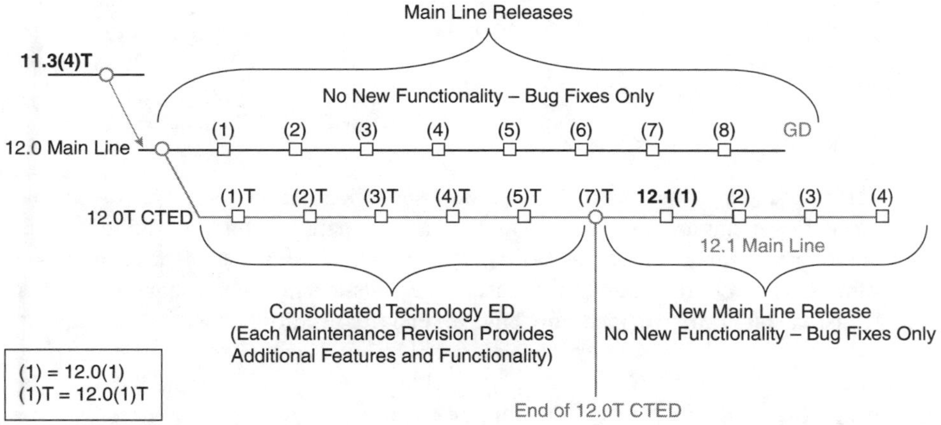

Figure 3-3 illustrates how the new main line release is the previous "T" release and therefore has all the features and hardware support that were once part of the preceding CTED release train.

Consolidated Technology Release of 11.3

Cisco IOS 11.3T marked the initial implementation of CTED releases. As stated earlier, this was a transitional phase to get to a unified Cisco IOS release marked by the advent of 12.0. For that reason, 11.3T was open to new features for only three maintenance releases. Beginning with 11.3(3.2)T, it officially stopped accepting new features to prepare for the consolidation and unification with other ED releases, which led to the birth of 12.0. A Cisco IOS ED release is said to have reached mature maintenance (MM) phase once it stops accepting new features. (For more information, see "Cisco IOS Software Life Cycle Milestones," later in this chapter.) Hence, 11.3T entered mature maintenance phase at 11.3(4)T (maintenance revision after 11.3(3.2)T). Immediately after the MM milestone, a branch of 11.3T was collapsed into the pre-integration branch of 12.0. This assured that features of 11.3T are fully carried in to 12.0. Figure 3-4 depicts this relationship.

Figure 3-4 *CTED of 11.3, Leading to 12.0 Major Releases*

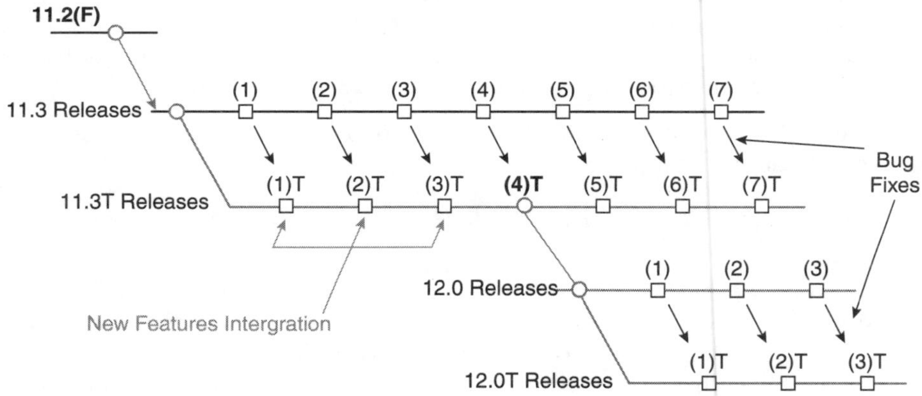

It is important to note that in the preceding scenario, the technology release train continued to coexist in mature maintenance mode with the main line release. While in mature maintenance mode, the CTED (11.3T) feature and platform acceptance characteristics were similar to that of the main line release, 11.3. This meant that subsequent maintenance revisions of 11.3T provided only bug fixes with no additional new functionality.

Specific Technology Release and Specific Market Release

As the name indicates, Specific Technology ED releases have similar feature commit characteristics to CTED releases. Except for the fact that Specific Technology releases (STEDs) are limited in scope by focusing on specific technology or market theatre, the two types of releases have comparable development and deployment characteristics. Additionally, STEDs are always released on a limited set of hardware platforms and are under the sole supervision of a Cisco business unit. The business unit owner of a

Specific Technology release follows a number of guidelines, among which the following are worth noting:

- Regular synchronization with the parent IOS major release
- Regular scheduled maintenance revisions
- Convergence to the next IOS main release

Aside from these restrictions, the business unit freely manages the STED to meet the targeted market requirements.

STED are identified by using two character letters appended to the major release version. Cisco IOS Releases 11.1CA, 11.1CC, 11.1CT, 11.3NA, 11.3MA, 11.3WA, and 12.0DA are all examples of Specific Technology releases.

The growth of the telecommunication industry and the increased partitioning of technologies into market segments have greatly influenced the evolution of Cisco IOS Specific Technology releases. As a consequence, a hybrid form of Cisco IOS STED has emerged, Specific Market Early Deployment releases (SMED). Although they are managed exactly as STED, SMEDs transcend Specific Technology barriers to achieve business solutions for a given market theatre. This means that SMEDs also cross over Cisco's business unit boundaries. In that sense, they are more like the CTED. On the other hand, they are built for limited and specific hardware platforms of relevance to the targeted market. This latter characteristic is similar to that of an STED—hence, the hybrid nature of SMED releases.

As an example, Cisco IOS Release 12.0S is an SMED release targeted at the Internet service provider market. It delivers an array of cross business unit technology solutions that is of primary interest to Internet service providers. Moreover, the Cisco IOS software binaries of 12.0S are only developed and built for selected hardware platforms such as the gigabit switch router 12000 series and the 7500 and the 7200 series routers.

Because of this hybrid nature, SMED are identified by only one alphabetic character appended to the major release version; for example, 12.0S and 12.1E.

As a general rule, STED and SMED Cisco IOS releases provide new features and/or hardware support with each maintenance revision. Because the code base is essentially the same as the major Cisco IOS release from which it is rooted, the STED frequently syncs with its parent to inherit bug fixes that have been applied to the parent. In addition to sync bug fixes, maintenance and interim revisions provide bug fixes specific to the STED/SMED (the portion of the code that is different from the parent's code base). Figure 3-5 shows an example of an STED release and how specific features were integrated into it. Figures 3-5 and 3-6 show the bug sync and feature integration process for an STED/SMED release based respectively on 11.3 and 12.0 major releases. Please note that both STED and SMED follow the same bug fix and new feature integration process.

Figure 3-5 *Origin and Characteristics of Cisco IOS 11.3NA STED (prior to 12.0)*

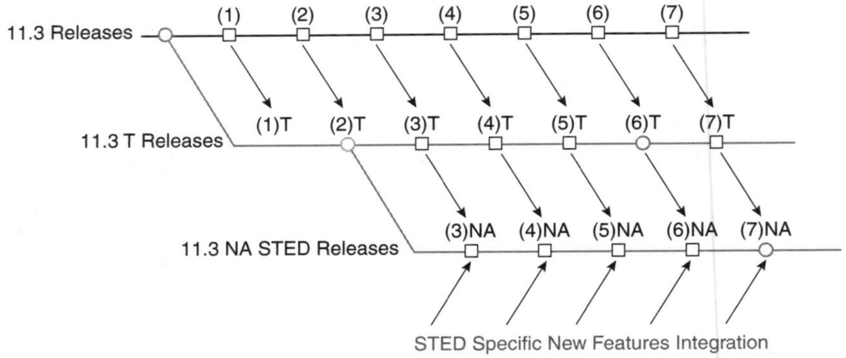

Figure 3-6 *Bug Sync and Feature Integration Process of STED/SMED Releases Based on 12.0 Major Releases*

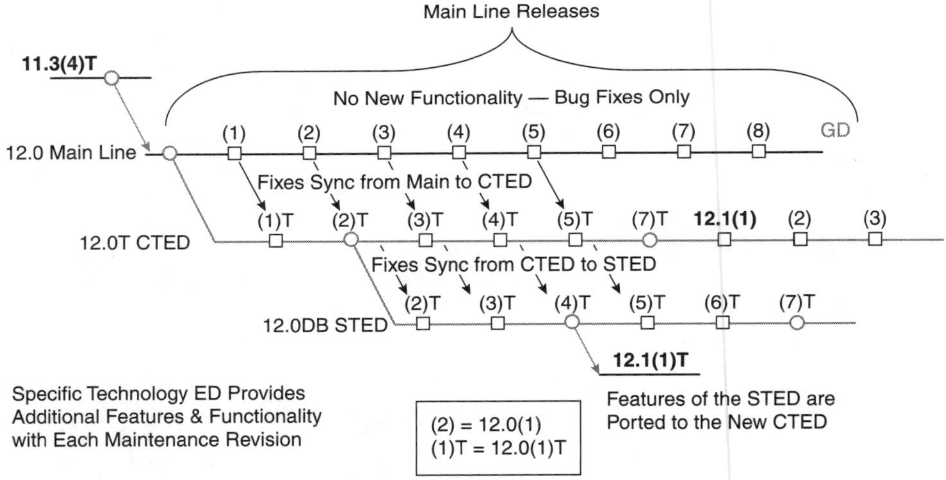

Cisco IOS X Releases

Although Cisco IOS X release early deployments (XED) have, to a small degree, existed since 11.2, they are a significant part of the current release model and development strategy. Beginning with the redefinition of the Cisco IOS release model, which was implemented to coincide with the release of Cisco IOS version 12.0, XEDs have been heavily used to meet critical time-to-market requirements. The current release model dissociates Cisco IOS early deployment names from their parent business unit and aligns them with the underlying technology for which they are created. This change was necessary to better prepare Cisco

IOS software to support the rapid growth of the company's product lines. Indeed, from 1998 to 1999, the amount of hardware and new technology (software features) introduced in Cisco IOS has more than quadrupled. With that kind of growth rate, it was necessary to find a way to allow the corporation to freely expand while maintaining the integrity of the IOS software. The X releases provided such a vehicle.

This model allowed any single or multiple business units (with similar or complementary technology focus) to pull a private branch of the Cisco IOS CTED for the purpose of developing targeted new technologies. This flexibility enabled timely delivery of new technologies without compromising the integrity of the IOS CTED release train. After successful field deployment, the feature/technology delivered by the X release is immediately ported to one of the next CTED maintenance revisions, which carries it into the main stream of Cisco IOS major releases (See Figure 3-7. Also, see Figure 2-5 for more detail.)

Cisco IOS XEDs are Short-Lived releases that only exist for as long as it takes to release their features with the next maintenance revision of the CTED to which they are rooted. They do not provide software maintenance revisions nor do they provide regular software interim builds.

The Cisco IOS XED releases follow a sequential naming convention. The first character of an X-release name is obviously always an "X". The second character is a sequentially generated alpha character to differentiate one X release from another. If a catastrophic software defect is found in an XED release prior to its convergence with the next CTED, a software rebuild is initiated and a number is appended to the name. 12.0(4)XB1 and 12.0(4)XB2 are examples of 12.0(4)XB rebuilds. This convention is explained further in the next section.

Figure 3-7 *Cisco IOS XED Release Deployment and Integration Process*

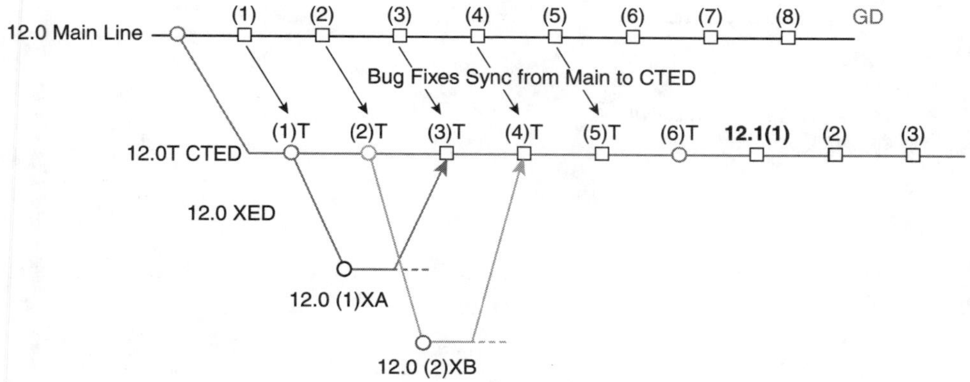

Cisco IOS Release Naming Conventions

The name of Cisco IOS early deployment releases such as 11.3NA, 12.0DA, 12.0W5, 12.1E, and so forth follow a well-defined naming convention. The release naming process was slightly modified so that the alphanumeric letter or group of letters appended to the numbers of the release name now indicate the type of core technology (or specialty) targeted by the release. It should be noted that Cisco IOS main line releases are simply identified by the major release number (with no alphanumeric suffix) whereas the CTED is always identified by a "T" suffix. (Cisco IOS main releases are sometimes identified with an "M" appended to the major number, such as 12.0M.) For example, 12.1 or 12.1M is a main line release and 12.1T is a CTED.

Cisco IOS release names are composed of the following:

- The major release number of the release (for example, 11.3 or 12.0).
- The sync point to the parent major release revision level. That is, the maintenance revision of the parent release where the early deployment is rooted. For example, 12.0(5)DA is based on 12.0(5) maintenance revision of the major release 12.0.
- The type of releases (that is STED, SMED, or XED). The alphanumeric letter or set of letters makes this differentiation. STED have two alphanumeric letters, SMED contain one alphanumeric letter, and XED have two alphanumeric letters, the first of which is always an "X".

Figure 3-8 shows an example of an STED rooted in the CTED.

Figure 3-8 *The Initial Release of 12.0NA STED Is Based on 12.0(2)T*

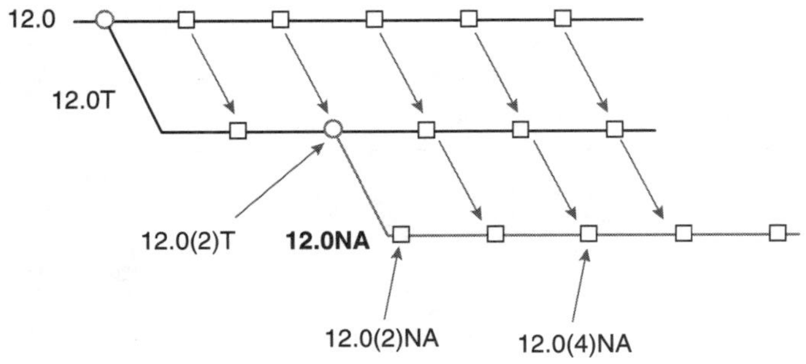

Before going any further, let's define the letters that make up Cisco IOS early deployment release names.

Letter Definitions for Major ED Releases

A single letter appended to the major release number indicates major ED releases or SMED such as 11.2P, 11.3T, and 12.0S. These are ED releases directly rooted in the main line code. The following letter definitions apply to them:

E = Enterprise-specific release (for example, 12.1E)
F = Feature-specific enhancements (applies only to 11.2F)—part of NGRP
P = Platform features (applies only to 11.2P)—part of NGRP
S = Service provider (for example, 12.0S)
T = Consolidated Technology release identifier (for example, 12.0T)

Multiple Letter Definitions for STED and XED Releases

Two letters appended to the major release number identify an STED or XED release. Except for an "X" in the first position, the first letter identifies the targeted technology. The second letter serves as a differentiation for multiple releases targeting the same technology (for example, 12.0DA, 12.0DB, 12.0DC)—an exception is noted below. The following definitions apply to letters in the first position of a Cisco IOS ED name:

A = Access server/dial technology (for example, 11.3AA)
C = Core routers (11.1CA, 11.1CT, 11.1CC)
D = xDSL technology (for example, 11.3DA)
G = Gigabit switch routers (11.2GSR)
H = SDH/SONET technology (for example, 11.3HA)
N = Voice, Multimedia, Conference (for example, 11.3NA)
W = ATM/LAN Switching/Layer 3 Switching (for example, 12.0W5)
X = A short-lived, one-time release (for example, 12.0XA)
Y = A short-lived, one-time release (when Xs are exhausted)

New letters may be defined for the purpose of creating new releases.

Cisco IOS XEDs Based on STED Releases

As a general rule, Cisco IOS XEDs are based on CTEDs. However, there can be time-to-market reasons for which the business unit's IOS release team might need to introduce an XED rooted in an STED. In an effort to clearly show that the upgrade migration path for such an XED is to the parent STED, the first letter of the STED is maintained while the second letter is changed to an X or Y. For example, 12.0(4a)WX5(11a) is based on 12.0W5 STED release. The rule can be summarized as this: an "X" or "Y" in the second position of the release name identifies a Short-Lived Early Deployment release (XED) based on (or rooted in) the STED which is identified by the first letter. This is illustrated in Figure 3-9.

Figure 3-9 *Example of an XED Rooted in an STED*

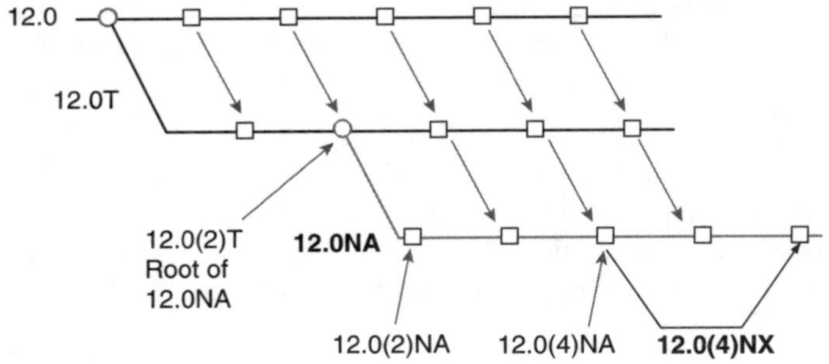

Cisco IOS XED Names—Sequential but Independent

It is important to note that Cisco IOS XED are discrete independent releases whose features migrate back into their parent release. A later XED is not necessarily the upgrade migration path for an earlier XED. For example, 12.0(2)XC might introduce a new module on the 3600 while 12.0(1)XB introduces the new Cisco 800 platform series. It should be clear that 12.0(2)XC is not a logical migration path for 12.0(1)XB. In this particular case, 12.0(1)XB's migration path is to 12.0(3)T while 12.0(2)XC's migration path is to 12.0(4)T.

Figure 3-10 shows the way two sample Cisco IOS XED releases pulled from the 12.0T branch converge back into later maintenance revisions of 12.0T. Since they both introduce completely different hardware, the second letter (A and B) is used to differentiate them.

Figure 3-10 *Two Cisco IOS XED Releases Deployed from and Integrated Back into the 12.0T Release Train*

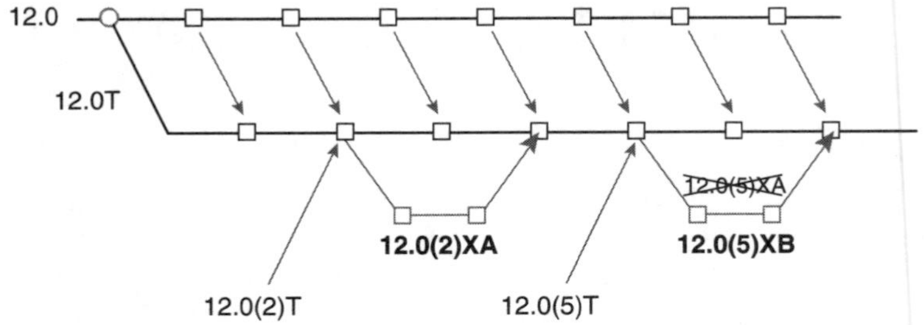

Cisco IOS Maintenance and Interim Version Numbering Conventions

After the IOS software release name is selected, software images are delivered to customers by using a successive maintenance and interim revision numbering scheme. The figures in this section are somewhat self-explanatory, but some points and exceptions should be mentioned. Figures 3-11 and 3-12 show the version numbering for a main release and a CTED release. Figures 3-13 and 3-14 show the maintenance and interim numbering schemes for the STED "Wx" releases, which differ slightly from the general rule. Figures 3-15 and 3-16 show STED maintenance revisions and interim numbering schemes.

As noted earlier in the release definitions, Cisco IOS XED releases do not provide interim builds. Therefore, the Cisco IOS software interim numbering convention does not apply to XED releases. However, it's important to note that only Cisco Customer Support Engineers (Technical Assistance Center or TAC engineers) are officially allowed to distribute Cisco IOS interim builds as a temporary fix for customer-impacting defects. Only maintenance revision software images are officially shipped and/or publicly sold to customers. If you are using an IOS interim build, it is strongly recommended that you upgrade to the next fully tested maintenance revision image. For information on whether a specific release receives maintenance releases or interim builds, check the release's spec table in Chapters 4 through 7.

Figure 3-11 *Cisco IOS Main Releases Interim Builds and Maintenance Revisions Numbering Convention*

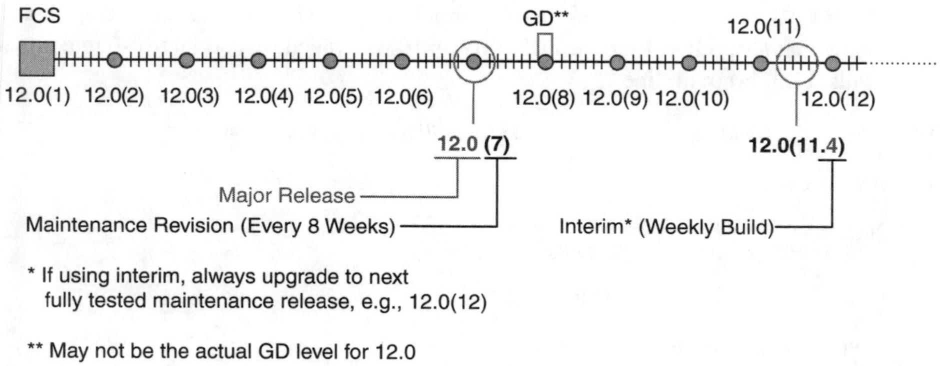

Figure 3-12 *Cisco IOS CTED Maintenance and Interim Numbering Convention*

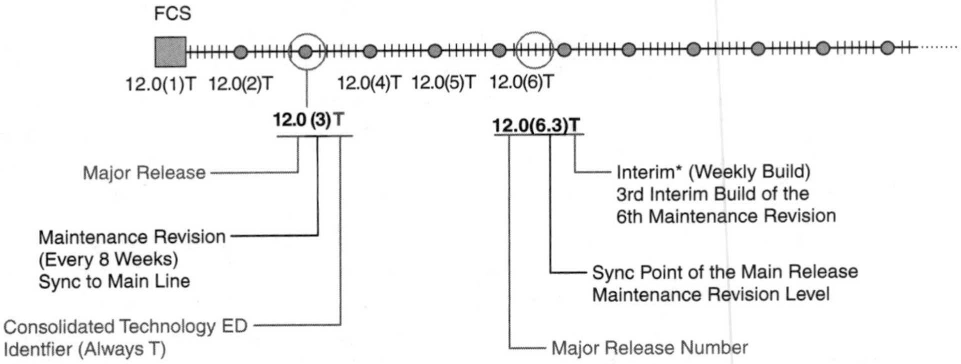

The numbering processes shown in Figures 3-13 and 3-14 are a slight departure from the general practice and apply only to Cisco IOS Releases 11.2WA3, 11.3WA4, and 12.0W5. It is worth noting that the "Wx" releases do not regularly synchronize to their parent release. However, the numbering system always shows the last synchronization point, indicated by the leading major release numbers. For example, if the following "Wx" release example was synchronized to 11.3(4a), then the maintenance number would be 11.3(4a)WA4(6). The major release number indicated by 11.3(4a) is clearly identified to show that Cisco IOS Release 11.3(4a)WA4(6) is synced to, and bug-to-bug compatible with, 11.3(4a) main line.

Figure 3-13 *Cisco IOS Wx Maintenance Releases Have a Slightly Different Numbering System*

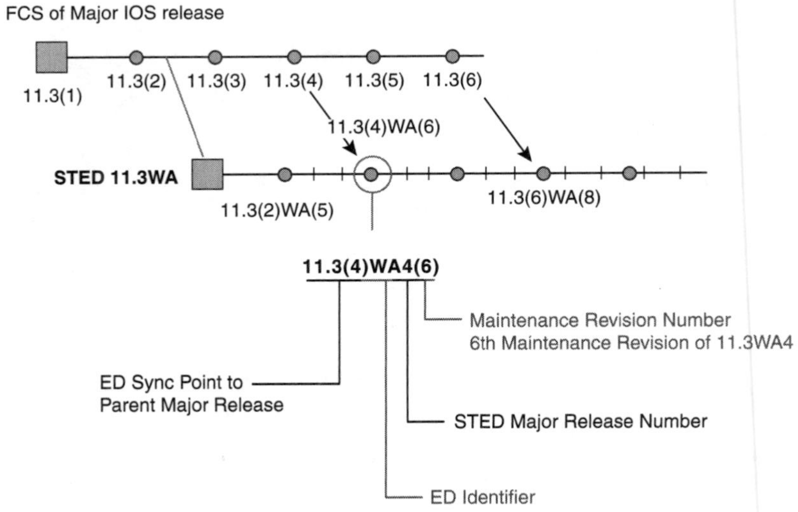

Figure 3-14 *The Exception: Cisco IOS Wx Interim Numbering System*

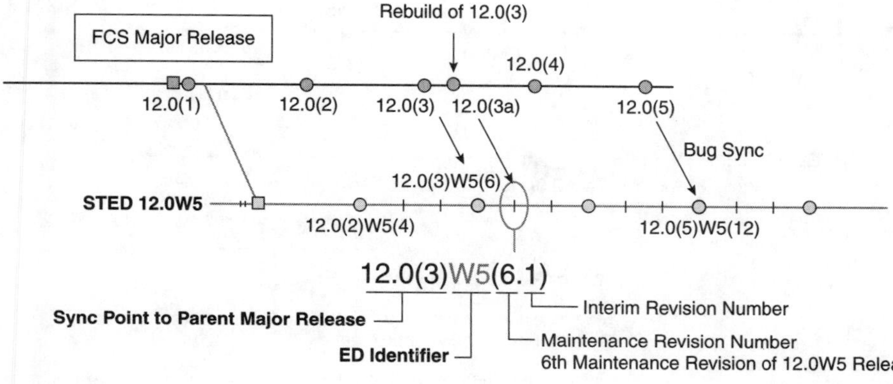

Figure 3-15 *STED Maintenance Release Numbering Convention*

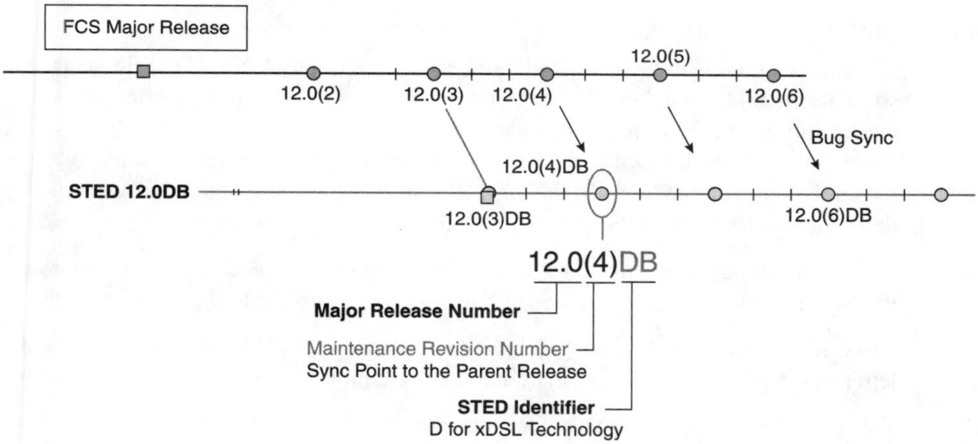

Figure 3-16 *STED Interim Release Numbering Convention*

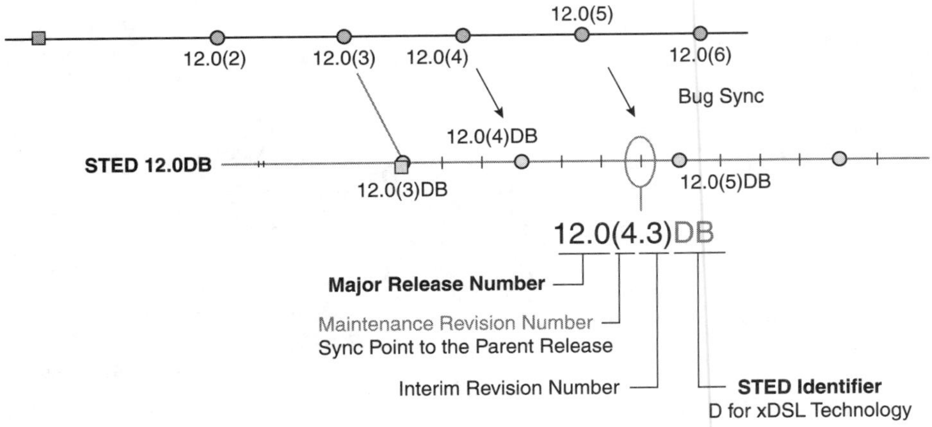

Cisco IOS Software Rebuild Numbering Convention

The final elements in the name and number scheme of any Cisco IOS release are the software rebuild indicators. On occasion, continuous internal testing after public availability of the IOS images can uncover network-impacting software defects. Under those circumstances, Cisco usually decides to defer (remove the maintenance releases from CCO) the defective images. In that case, the software defect is quickly fixed, and the deferred software revision is rebuilt.

The rebuilt image is technically identical to the deferred images. The difference between the two images is the software defect fixes that were applied to the rebuilt images.

Cisco IOS main releases distinguish the rebuild by appending a lowercase alphanumeric letter to the maintenance version number. For example, 12.0(3a) is the rebuild of 12.0(3).

Two rules apply to early deployment releases:

- If the defect is specific to the ED release, then the rebuild occurs on the ED release branch. In that case, a decimal number is appended to the ED identifier. For example 12.0(5)T1 is the rebuild of 12.0(5)T. Similarly, 12.0(5)DA1 is the rebuild of 12.0(5)DA.
- If the defect was found on the common code of the major release branch, then it is fixed on the main line branch and the fix is synced to all parented ED releases. The sync point of the ED maintenance number will then show the rebuild indicator. For example, 12.0(3a)T or 12.0(3a)W5(8) are maintenance releases of 12.0(3)T and 12.0(3)W5, both of which are based on the rebuild of 12.0(3) main release.

Figure 3-17 and Figure 3-18 show the most common uses for rebuild numbering for main releases and a CTED release, respectively. Figure 3-19 depicts the STED rebuild numbering process. This process is used to annotate a release, which is parented to a maintenance revision. Figure 3-20 depicts the same release parented to a rebuild. Figure 3-21 again shows the "Wx" use of a slightly modified version of the rules of this numbering scheme.

Note that there could be several rebuilds of the same maintenance revisions. For example, 12.0(4b) is the rebuild for 12.0(4a). Similarly, 12.0(5)T3 is the rebuild of 12.0(5)T2, which, in turn, was the rebuild of 12.0(5)T1. In this example, the affected defective software images of 12.0(4a), 12.0(5)T, 12.0(5)T1, and 12.0(5)T2 would have all been deferred and removed from public reach.

Figure 3-17 *Cisco IOS Main Release Rebuild Numbering Scheme*

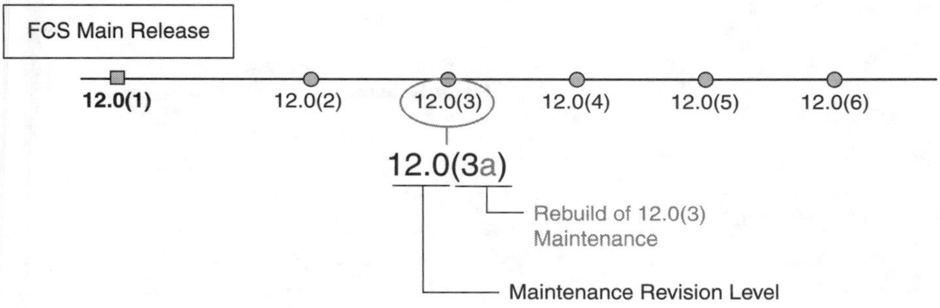

Here again, there could be several Cisco IOS rebuilds where 12.0(3b) would be the rebuild for 12.0(3a).

Figure 3-18 *Cisco IOS CTED Rebuild Numbering Scheme*

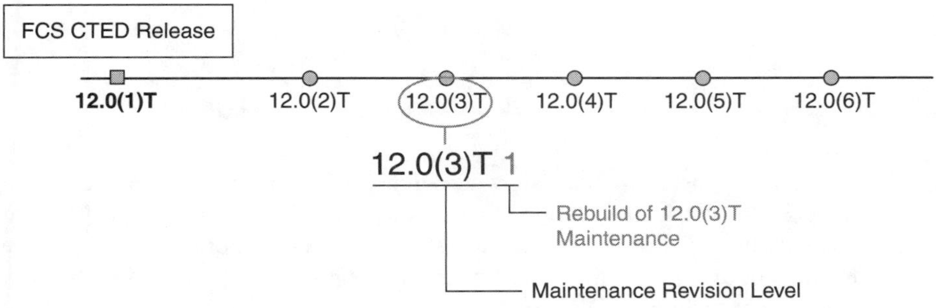

Similar to the main line, there could be several rebuilds on a particular maintenance revision of the CTED. For example, 12.0(3)T2 is the rebuild of 12.0(3)T1 and 12.0(5) XE4 is the rebuild of 12.0(5) XE3.

Figure 3-19 *Cisco IOS STED Rebuild Numbering Convention*

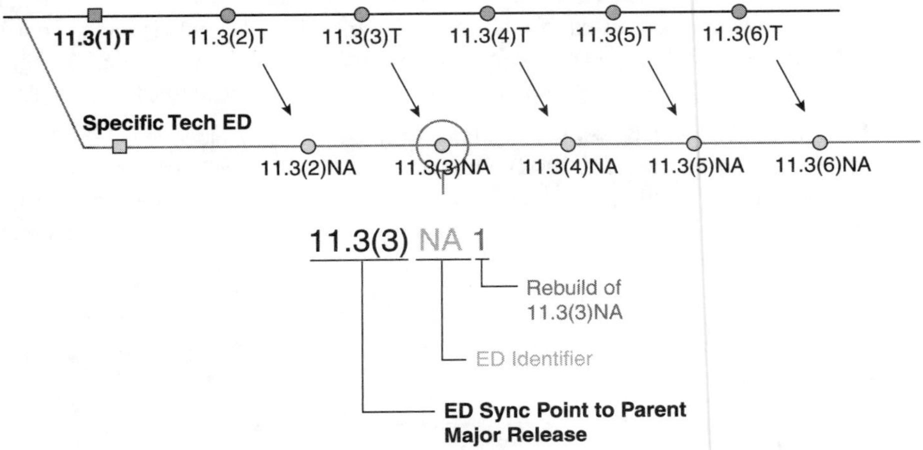

Figure 3-20 *Numbering of an STED Parented to a Rebuild*

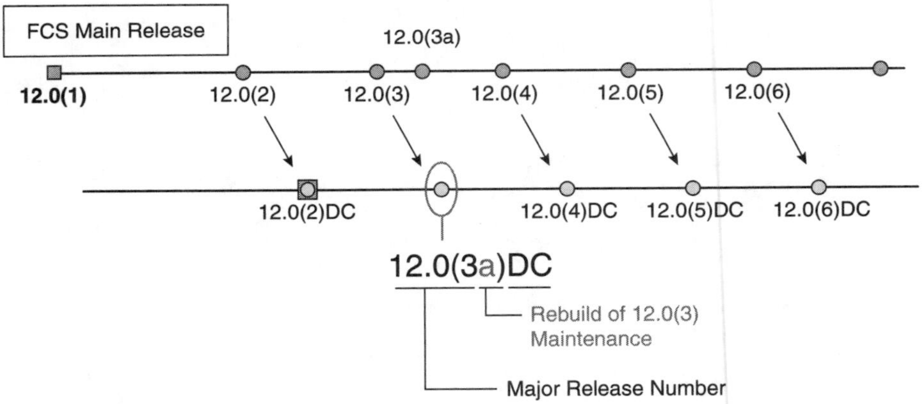

The rebuild numbering process shown in Figure 3-21 applies to Cisco IOS Releases 11.2WA3, 11.3WA4, and 12.0W5. Note that these STEDs do not regularly synchronize to the parent release; however, they always show the last sync point, indicated by the leading numbers. For example, if the preceding example was synced to 11.3(4a), then the number would have been 11.3(4a)WA4(6).

Figure 3-21 *A Wx STED Interim Showing the Sync Point to a Rebuild Maintenance Revision*

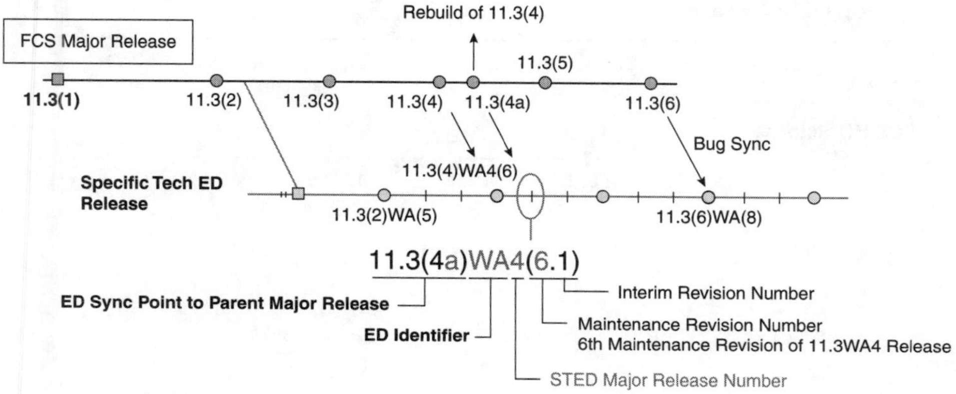

Figures 3-22 and 3-23 show the XED release rebuild numbering scheme. Although Cisco IOS XEDs are one-time releases and do not provide regular maintenance revisions, software image rebuilds are sometimes necessary to fix major defects on XED branches.

A decimal number is appended to the XED identifier to differentiate the rebuild from the original build.

Figure 3-22 *Rebuild Numbering Scheme for XED Releases*

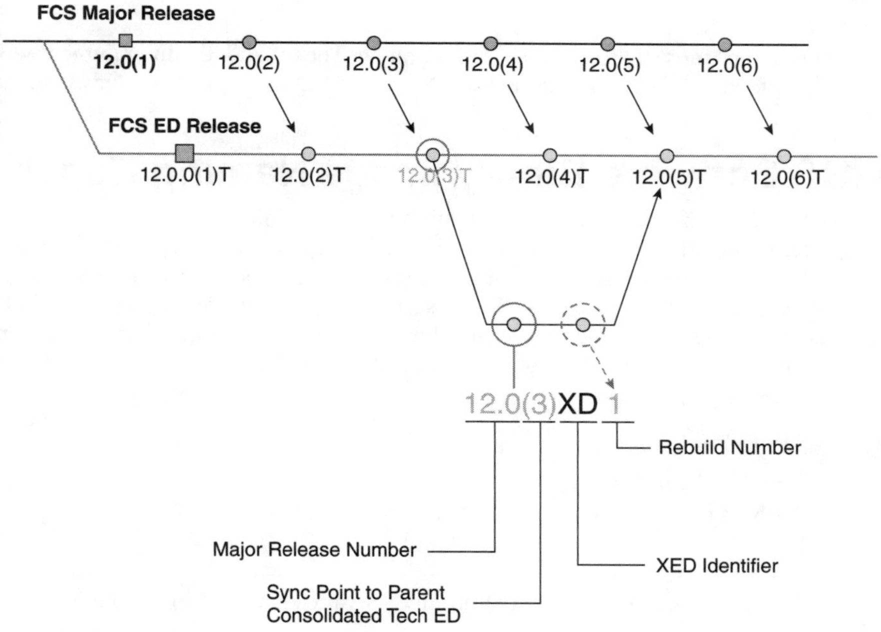

Figure 3-23 *Numbering of Multiple Rebuilds*

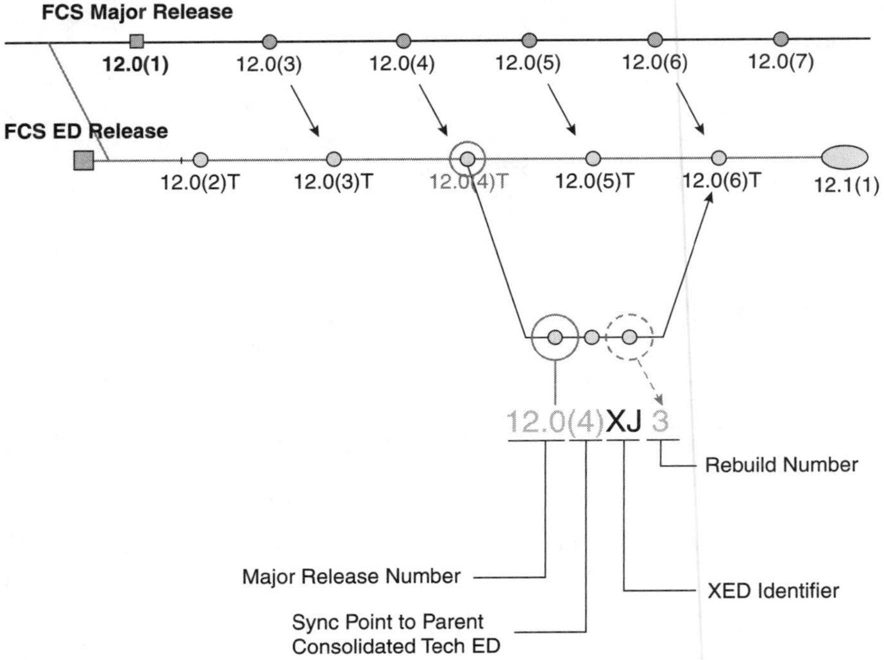

There can be more than one rebuild on a branch. The rebuild identifier number will continue to increment as shown in Figure 3-23. Note that 12.0(6)T was not released to the public.

Cisco IOS Software Binary Image Naming Convention

As another useful resource of information for determining image specifications, Cisco Systems and other vendors who use Cisco IOS on routers, switches, and boards utilize a well-defined convention for naming software images. The convention identifies the platform or board for which the binary software is built, the feature-content package of the image, and the area of memory utilized by the image at run time. The image name follows the following three-part format, illustrated in Figure 3-24:

PPPPP-FFFF-MM

PPPPP = Platform

FFFF = Features
MM = Run-time memory and compression format

NOTE S is the "plus" feature set. The definition of S varies per platform and per IOS release.

Figure 3-24 *Cisco IOS Binary Image Naming System*

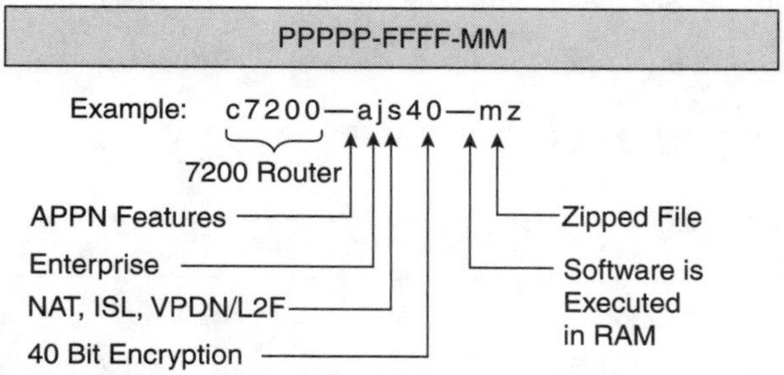

The image c7200-ajs40-mz in the preceding example can be broken down into the following individual components.

NOTE The complete feature set definition is provided in Appendix A, "Cisco IOS Image Name Reference."

---

c7200 = 7200 router
a = APPN features
j = Enterprise feature package
s = NAT, ISL,VPDN/L2F (plus package)
40 = 40 bit encryption
m = Software is executed in RAM
z = Zipped file

The next several subsections help identify the feature content of a particular Cisco IOS image through indicators in the naming convention. Several references will be made to sections in Appendix A.

The Platform Identifiers

The first part of the image name (PPPP) indicates the platform for which the image is built. Please note that if the platform is a system board, the image is named differently.

The complete list of platform identifiers is provided in the Appendix A table "IOS Image Platforms (PPPP) and Board Definitions."

System Board Identifiers

Cisco IOS images built for system boards follow a three-part naming convention, separated by dashes: BBB-PPPP-MM.

The parts are defined as:

BBB = Board
PPPP = Platform

MM = Memory area utilized at execution. Also indicates the compression method of the image (See the section "The Memory Space" in Chapter 8 for a complete description.)

Figure 3-25 illustrates the system boards IOS image naming system.

Figure 3-25 *System Boards IOS Image Naming System*

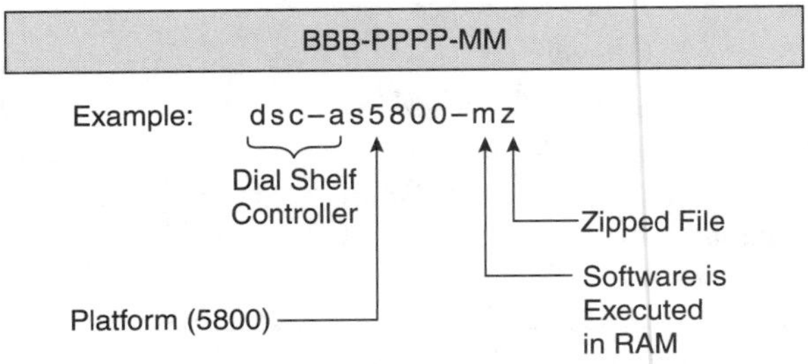

The preceding example identifies the IOS image of the dial shelf system board as dsc-as5800-mz. The breakdown is as follows:

dsc = Dial shelf controller
as5800 = Platform (5800)
m = Software is executed in RAM
z = Zipped file

NOTE The complete list of platform and system board designators is tabulated in Appendix A.

IOS Feature Set Content

The second part of the image name (FFFF) identifies the feature content of the image (also referred to as IOS feature set).

For example, c7200-ajs56-mz is an image name where "a", "j", "s" and "56" designate the feature package of that particular image. (See Appendix A tables for designator definitions.)

Reference to the feature designator table in Appendix A shows that "a" stands for APPN features, "j" is for enterprise features (desktop + all routing protocols), "s" is for the plus features such as NAT, ISL, L2F, and VPDN, and "56" stands for 56-bit encryption.

The letters are always specified in alphabetical order and the definition is fairly constant across the products on which the features exist. The content of a particular feature set can be augmented with new features. However, the content is never reduced.

Cisco IOS Software Run-Time Memory Space

The third part of the image name designation, MM, is composed of two alphabetic characters. The first letter identifies the memory area where the IOS image is executed at runtime. The second letter indicates the method used to compress the IOS binary image. Let's look at our previous example again: c7200-ajs56-mz. As Table 3-1 shows, "m" indicates that the software image runs in RAM and "z" indicates that the code is zip compressed.

Table 3-1 *IOS Execution Area*

Image Name Designator	Execution Area
f	Image runs in Flash memory
m	Image runs in RAM
r	Image runs in ROM
l	Image is relocated at run time

Zipped IOS images are self-unzippable so the users do not need to run extra commands to run the software. A user only needs to get the image into the router flash or ROM. At runtime the image automatically "unzips" itself and relocates itself in the area of memory from which it is intended to run. No further action is necessary from the system administrator. The compression identifiers are listed in Table 3-2.

Table 3-2 *IOS Image Compression Identifiers*

Compression Identifier	Action
z	Image is Zip compressed (lowercase z)
x	Image is Mzip compressed
w	Image is "Stac" compressed

Cisco IOS Software Image File Type Extensions

Whenever necessary, IOS images are accompanied by readme-types of files. Those files have a suffix file extension designator such as Tar or HTML.

- **Tar**—This utility is used for packaging files together. These files are compressed by using gzip or the Unix compress utility. These files are release notes or special instruction files that are provided to instruct customers of special handling.

- **HTML**—These are separate files containing information relevant to the IOS image. They can be viewed by using a web browser.

How to Identify an IOS Release from a Running Router

The **show version** command issued on running Cisco IOS software generates the Cisco IOS banner that contains a wealth of information.

Cisco IOS image banners are strings that display information regarding the type of build from which the Cisco IOS image was produced, the release name, and whether it is an interim build, a maintenance build, or a rebuild. The fields that make up the IOS banner are identified in bold in the following example. They are further identified in Table 3-3.

```
Cisco Internetwork Operating System Software IOS (tm)
<platform_series> Software (<image_name>), Version <version>[, <release_type>]
Copyright (c) 1986-<year> by Cisco Systems, Inc.
Compiled <day> <date> <time> by <user>
```

Table 3-3 *IOS Banner Field Definitions*

Image Banner	Definition
Platform_series	Series number of the platform
Image_name	Formal image name, as defined by Cisco IOS image naming conventions
Version	Release version number
Release_type	Type of build and release vehicle

The Cisco IOS banner is self-explanatory except for the "release_type" and the "fc" build information (defined later in this section). The remainder of the section will focus on the "release_type" field and its companion "fc" build information.

Release Type Definitions and Examples

The various types and examples of the release type fields are defined in Table 3-4:

Table 3-4 *Cisco IOS Release Type Definitions*

Release Type	Definitions
Release Software	Maintenance build images on major and Consolidated Cisco IOS Technology.
Early Deployment Release Software	Maintenance build images on a Specific Technology and X releases.

Table 3-4 *Cisco IOS Release Type Definitions (Continued)*

Release Type	Definitions
Maintenance Interim Software	Interim builds on a major and Consolidated Cisco IOS Technology release.
Early Deployment Maintenance Interim Software	Interim build of a Specific Technology release (there are no interim builds on X releases).
Cisco Development Test Version	Shadow releases on major and CTED releases and pre-integration branch images (not for customer use).
Early Deployment Cisco Development Test Version	Shadow releases on a BU-Specific Technology releases. (To date, there are and have been no BU-specific release shadow builds.)
Beta Test Software	Pre-FCS builds on major releases (main plus CTED) for the purpose of alpha, beta, and system testing.
Early Deployment Beta Test Software	Pre-FCS builds on STED releases for the purpose of alpha, beta, and system testing.
'fc1' build vs. 'fc2' build	'fc2' is an internal rebuild of the 'fc1' build. 'fc2' is usually created to fix a specific defect found in the 'fc1' build. An 'fc2' build cannot be created if the first build was already released to a public directory.
Maintenance Rebuild	12.0(2)T1 is a maintenance rebuild of 12.0(2)T, 12.0(3a) is a maintenance rebuild of 12.0(3), and 11.3(6)AA2 is a maintenance rebuild of 11.3(6)AA1, which is a rebuild of 11.3(6)AA. If a catastrophic defect is found in a maintenance version of software after it was released to the public, Cisco might decide to fix the defect and re-release a new version with the fix as a rebuild image. The defective image is usually deferred and made inaccessible to customers.
Experimental	Cisco IOS special images. Image built by individual engineers to incorporate engineering changes.

Example of Show Version Banner Output

The following are examples of the **show version** command output on various Cisco IOS release types. The examples are organized by "release_types".

Major Release Software

Cisco IOS maintenance images on major releases (main release and CTED):

```
Cisco Internetwork Operating System Software IOS (tm)
GS Software (RSP-P-MZ), Version 11.0(16), RELEASE SOFTWARE (fc1)
Copyright (c) 1986-1997 by Cisco Systems, Inc.
Compiled Tue 24-Jun-97 12:07 by mcouliba

Cisco Internetwork Operating System Software IOS (tm)
C2600 Software (C2600-JS-MZ), Version 12.0(2a)T1, RELEASE SOFTWARE (fc1)
Copyright (c) 1986-1999 by Cisco Systems, Inc.
Compiled Wed 06-Jan-99 08:15 by dschwart
```

Early Deployment Release Software

Cisco IOS maintenance images on a Specific Technology (STED) or X releases (XED):

```
Cisco Internetwork Operating System Software IOS (tm)
RSP Software (RSP-AJSV-MZ), Version 11.2 (17)BC, EARLY DEVELOPMENT RELEASE
SOFTWARE (fc1)
Copyright (c) 1986-1999 by Cisco Systems, Inc.
Compiled Thr 21-Jan-99 16:23 by preetha

Cisco Internetwork Operating Systems Software IOS (tm)
GS Software (GSR-P-MZ), Version 11.2(9)GS7, EARLY DEPLOYMENT, RELEASE SOFTWARE
(fc1)
Copyright (c) 1986-1998 by Cisco Systems, Inc.
Compiled Wed 04-Mar-98 11:47 by tamb

Cisco Internetwork Operating Systems Software IOS (tm)
C2600 Software (C2600-AJS-MZ, Version 12.0(2)XD1, EARLY DEPLOYMENT, RELEASE
SOFTWARE (fc1)
TAC:Home:SW:IOS:Specials for into
Copyright (c) 1986-1999 by Cisco Systems, Inc.
Compiled Mon 18-Jan-99 20:44 by ayeh
```

NOTE This example is a rebuild of an XED—12.0(2)XD.

Software Interim Builds

Cisco IOS interim builds on major releases:

```
Cisco Internetwork Operating System Software IOS (tm)
GS Software (RSP-P-MZ), Version 11.0(15.1), MAINTENANCE INTERIM SOFTWARE
Copyright (c) 1986-1997 by Cisco Systems, Inc.
Compiled Mon 16-Jun-97 18:28 by jaturner

Cisco Internetwork Operating System Software IOS (tm)
RSP Software (RSP-P-MZ), Version 11.2(16.1)P, MAINTENANCE INTERIM SOFTWARE
Copyright (c) 1986-1998 by Cisco Systems, Inc.
Compiled Thu 22-Oct-98 20:08 by pwade
```

NOTE Interim builds have no ’fc1’ string.

Cisco IOS Early Deployment Interim Software Builds

Cisco IOS interim builds on an STED release (there is no interim for X releases):

```
Cisco Internetwork Operating System Software IOS (tm)
7200 Software (UBR7200-P-MZ), Version 11.3(6.5)NA, EARLY DEPLOYMENT MAINTENANCE
INTERIM SOFTWARE
Copyright (c) 1986-1998 by Cisco Systems, Inc.
Compiled Fri 20-Nov-98 07:11 by rnapier
```

Cisco Development Test Images

Shadow builds on major releases and pre-integration branch images (not for customer usage—Cisco internal use only):

```
Cisco Internetwork Operating System Software IOS (tm)
5200 Software (C5200-D-L), Version 12.0(1.0.6), CISCO DEVELOPMENT TEST VERSION
Copyright (c) 1986-1998 by Cisco Systems, Inc.
Compiled Tue 13-Oct-98 16:48 by phanguye
```

```
Cisco Internetwork Operating System Software IOS (tm)
6400 Software (C6400-D-L), Version 12.0(6.6)PI, CISCO DEVELOPMENT TEST VERSION
Copyright (c) 1986-1999 by Cisco Systems, Inc.
Compiled Tue 5-Apr-99 10:24 by phanguye
```

Beta Test Software Images

Pre-released builds of major releases. Note that version number has a leading zero:

```
Cisco Internetwork Operating System Software IOS (tm)
RSP Software (RSP-P-MZ), Version 11.3(0.10), BETA TEST SOFTWARE
Copyright (c) 1986-1997 by Cisco Systems, Inc.
Compiled Mon 20-Oct-97 13:22 by tej
```

Early Deployment Beta Test Software

Pre-released software builds of Specific Technology releases:

```
Cisco Internetwork Operating System Software IOS (tm)
4500 Software (C4500-J-MZ), Version 11.3(0.8)MA, EARLY DEPLOYMENT, BETA TEST
SOFTWARE
Copyright (c) 1986-1997 by Cisco Systems, Inc.
Compiled Tue 14-Oct-97 20:54 by susingh
```

Software 'fc1' Versus 'fc2' Build Information

Cisco IOS image banners usually contain an 'fc1' or 'fc2' designator following the "release_type" field. When the software has not been released to the public and internal testing of a throttle build or shadow build reveals a major defect, an 'fc2' rebuild occurs. The maintenance version number (for example, Cisco IOS 12.0(3)) for the rebuilt images remains exactly the same as the defective 'fc1' build. The only visible difference is the 'fc2' designator in the image banner, which can only be viewed when the user issues the IOS **show version** command.

The two examples that follow show the banner for an 'fc1' and 'fc2' build of the same image.

```
Cisco Internetwork Operating System Software IOS (tm)
2500 Software (C2500-IS-L), Version 12.0(3), RELEASE SOFTWARE (fc1)

Cisco Internetwork Operating System Software IOS (tm)
2500 Software (C2500-IS-L), Version 12.0(3), RELEASE SOFTWARE (fc2)
```

When an 'fc2' build occurs, all necessary precautions are taken to avoid distribution of the sister 'fc1' build. All binary images are locked and made unreachable to both employees and customers.

Specific IOS Banner for Cisco IOS X Releases

All X releases contain "EARLY DEPLOYMENT" as part of the banner line. As such, the banner for an X release will always state "RELEASE SOFTWARE."

```
Cisco Internetwork Operating System Software IOS (tm)
C2600 Software (C2600-AJS-MZ), Version 12.0(2)XD1,
EARLY DEPLOYMENT RELEASE SOFTWARE (fc1)
TAC:Home:SW:IOS:Specials for info
Copyright (c) 1986-1999 by Cisco Systems, Inc.
Compiled Mon 18-Jan-99 20:44 by ayeh
```

NOTE Because of the transient nature of IOS X releases, most IOS XED now include the location of information pertaining to a particular X Release. This information is used only by the Cisco Technical Assistance Center (TAC).

Cisco IOS Special Images or Engineering-Built Image Banner

Cisco IOS images built by individual development engineers in an effort to address technical issues experienced by customers have the following banner string:

```
Cisco Internetwork Operating System Software IOS (tm)
2500 Software (C2500-P-M), Experimental Version 12.0(19981031:235224) [mcouliba-
conn_isp 203]
Copyright (c) 1986-1998 by Cisco Systems, Inc.
Compiled Mon 02-July-99 05:41 by mcouliba
```

The engineer who compiled the image and the branch from which the image was built is indicated in brackets. In the preceding example, [mcouliba-conn_isp 203] means that "mcouliba" is the engineer and "conn_isp" is the Cisco IOS branch. Because "conn_isp" is the Cisco IOS 12.0S branch, this "special" image (or individual engineering-built IOS image) is based on a 12.0S image. It is very important to distinguish a special image from regular IOS images as the changes introduced by the individual engineer, albeit useful, are not necessarily documented. If the changes are successful in fixing customer network issues, the engineer may later use proper internal procedures (peer review, documentation, and so forth) to make the same change on a regular IOS branch.

Software Synchronization Level Banners

To indicate the synchronization branches of the same STED releases (11.1CA, 11.1CC, and 11.1CT), an additional "Synced to" line appears in the banners. This line indicates what version of the parent branch the STED or SMED is synchronized to. This also indicates the parent-child relationship between the affected ED releases. The "Synced to" line appears in the maintenance and interim images of 11.1CA, 11.1CC, and 11.1CT releases as shown in the following banner outputs:

```
Cisco Internetwork Operating System Software IOS (tm)
GS Software (RSP-J-MZ), Version 11.1(17)CA, EARLY DEPLOYMENT RELEASE SOFTWARE (fc1)
Synced to mainline version: 11.1(17)
Copyright (c) 1986-1998 by Cisco Systems, Inc.
Compiled Tue 03-Feb-98 05:14 by richardd

Cisco Internetwork Operating System Software IOS (tm)
GS Software (RSP-J-MZ), Version 11.1(17)CC, EARLY DEPLOYMENT RELEASE SOFTWARE (fc1)
V111_17_CC_THROTTLE_BRANCH Synced to mainline version: 11.1(17)CA
Copyright (c) 1986-1998 by Cisco Systems, Inc.
Compiled Mon 23-Mar-98 21:08 by richardd

Cisco Internetwork Operating System Software IOS (tm)
GS Software (RSP-P-MZ), Version 11.1(17)CT, EARLY DEPLOYMENT RELEASE SOFTWARE (fc1)
V111_17_CT_THROTTLE_BRANCH Synced to mainline version: 11.1(17)CC
Copyright (c) 1986-1998 by Cisco Systems, Inc.
Compiled Fri 01-May-98 17:46 by tlane
```

Cisco IOS Software Product Numbering System

The Cisco IOS software maintenance revisions are packaged to enable customers to order particular IOS images of their choice. The product numbers contain information that helps the customer identify the platform, the feature set (refer to feature identifiers in Appendix B, "Cisco IOS Software Product Numbering System"), the maintenance revision number, and the IOS release train. The product number is formatted as shown in Figure 3-26.

Figure 3-26 *Cisco IOS Software Product Numbering System*

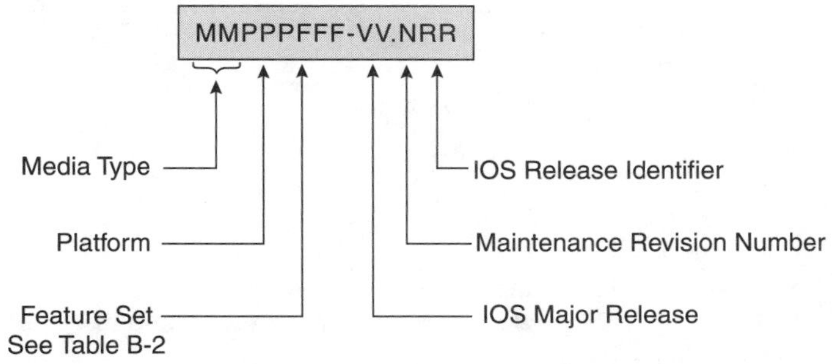

NOTE Cisco IOS software product numbers (SKU) have changed with the new IOS 12.1 and 12.1T releases. The new format and the complete list of Cisco IOS 12.1 product numbers is included in Appendix B.

A sample of this syntax is:

S72CL-12.0.4XE

MM = S = Software in Flash memory
PPP = 72 = 7200 platform
FFF = CL where C is IP only feature set and L is 56 bit IPSEC encryption
VV.N = 12.0.4
RR = XE

The complete list of IOS feature designators used to produce IOS product numbers is tabulated in Appendix B.

Cisco IOS Software Life Cycle Milestones

Two characteristics describe the stages during the life cycle of a Cisco IOS software release:

- The deployment and support status from initial deployment (also referred to as First Customer Ship or FCS) through end of life (EOL).
- The method in which maintenance revisions are provided for the release. These range from regular maintenance to mature or restricted maintenance.

Figure 3-27 shows an illustration of these two aspects and their relationships.

Figure 3-27 *Cisco IOS Release Life Cycle*

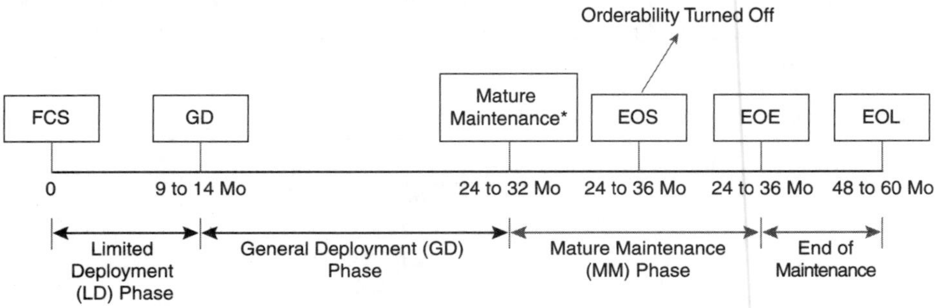

NOTE The duration of the cycle varies and changes substantially from release to release.

The type of IOS release also affects the various stages of the life cycle. For example, only main releases achieve GD certification, and XEDs do not provide maintenance or interim revisions. (The exception is 11.1CA, which achieved GD at 11.1(22)CA in December

1998.) In fact, the typical milestones for XED releases are FCS and EOE with occasional software rebuilds in between. The reference to IOS XED as "short-lived" or "one-time" releases emphasizes the fact that they do not follow the typical Cisco IOS engineering life cycle.

All other Cisco IOS releases are supported through TAC or CCO until end of life, which can occur two to five years after it goes into end of sale (EOS). The time frame varies substantially from release to release.

First Customer Shipment

First Customer Shipment (FCS) is the initial deployment date of a Cisco IOS release. It is usually marked by the first maintenance of the release.

Limited Deployment

Limited deployment phase is the timeframe between FCS and GD for main releases. Cisco IOS early deployment releases live only in limited deployment phase because they are never intended to attain GD certification.

General Deployment

General deployment (GD) applies only to main releases. It is the point at which Cisco declares a main release stable on all platforms, in all network environments. GD status applies only to main line releases. GD status applies to every maintenance release deployed after GD declaration.

Regular Maintenance

Cisco IOS maintenance revisions, deployed every 7 to 8 weeks, are identified as regular maintenance.

End of Sale

End of sale (EOS) is the next logical progression for a Cisco IOS main release. It is the last date when the software can be ordered through customer service or manufacturing. The software is, however, still available through Field Support Offices (FSO) and the Cisco Connection Online (CCO) software center at http://www.cisco.com.

After this point, a main release moves to one of two life cycle stages: end of engineering (EOE), with no further maintenance releases, or mature maintenance.

End of Engineering

End of engineering (EOE) marks the last regular maintenance revision. Engineering will no longer actively apply any defect repairs to the release, regardless of origin or severity (except for security and Y2K defects). Software images will continue to be available on CCO.

Mature Maintenance

Under normal circumstances, the release would have reached end of engineering at this point. However, customer insistence on keeping the release alive is addressed by transitioning the cycle into the mature maintenance phase. While in this phase, the IOS release will only receive defect repairs for customer-found severity 1 and severity 2 defects. Internally found problems will be addressed on a case-by-case basis.

Restricted Maintenance

Restricted maintenance can occur at several points. A release that has reached GD certification automatically enters into restricted maintenance mode. When a release reaches the end of the mature maintenance phase, it also enters the restricted maintenance mode. During this phase the IOS release source code is locked to avoid major application of fixes that might adversely affect the quality of the code.

End of Life

End of life (EOL) is the final stage for support and engineering of the release. It indicates that the software is no longer supported by Cisco personnel and is removed from CCO.

By tracking these milestones and the migration paths of your releases, you can better plan upgrades to maintain the features your system requires during the period of time the release is actively supported. The next part of the book lists these milestones as well as other characteristics of Cisco IOS software by release train.

Cisco IOS Software and the Millennium Considerations

Cisco IOS is based on UNIX whose internal time information is stored as a 32-bit unsigned integer of the number of seconds. This UNIX standard uses midnight Jan 1, 1970 Greenwich Mean Time (GMT), also referred to as universal time reference (Zulu Hours).

Cisco Systems has performed extensive year 2000 testing on its IOS software releases. As a result, Cisco has certified IOS release version 11.0 or higher to be fully Y2K compliant. Although IOS versions 11.0 or higher are certified, Y2K-compliant major releases, specific router platforms can be qualified at a different revision level of the particular release (that is, 11.0(4), 11.1(3), 12.0(5)T, and so forth). Therefore, it is important to visit Cisco's official Y2K Compliance Tables available at:

- http://cisco.com/warp/public/cc/cisco/mkt/gen/2000/prodlit/cptbl_ov.htm
- http://www.cisco.com/warp/public/cc/cisco/mkt/gen/2000/prodlit/cptbl_ov.htm#7
- http://www.cisco.com/warp/public/752/2000/
- The Cisco Y2K Test Plan is also available on line at http://www.cisco.com/warp/public/cc/cisco/mkt/gen/2000/prodlit/2test_ov.htm

Source of Cisco Router's Calendar

Cisco routers running Cisco IOS software have two main sources of time and calendar information.

1. Network time protocol (NTP) server (not covered in this book).
2. Default date and time from the IOS software or date and time obtained from the battery backup clock.

Cisco routers running IOS version 11.0 or higher can be configured to obtain clock and calendar information from NTP servers. This is the preferred method used by most companies. It enables company-wide routers to log configuration changes and other system information with the same time reference, regardless of the local time zone where the routers are physically located.

Cisco Routers with Battery Backed-up Clock

Unlike most Cisco routers, Cisco 4x00 series and Cisco 7x00 series routers have an on-board battery backed-up clock. These units have two sources where they obtain time information—either at boot time from the on-board, battery backed-up clock or from the NTP server, if configured.

Regardless of where initial time information was obtained, Cisco routers with battery backed-up clocks will maintain time and calendar accuracy even after a power failure or software reload.

Cisco Routers Without Battery Backed-up Clock

Most Cisco routers running IOS software do not have an on-board clock. They obtain their calendar information at boot time from either default time and calendar information configured in the IOS software or from the NTP server if configured and operational.

Most IOS software versions 11.0 or higher have a default date of March or February 1993. However, the default date and time might vary per platform and revision level. Assuming that NTP is not configured, the date and time can be changed manually on routers running IOS software by using the **clock set** command. Routers with an on-board, battery backed-up clock also accept the **calendar set** command and the **show calendar** command.

Cisco IOS and Application Software

Cisco routers running IOS do not use date and time information for the actual routing of network packets. Cisco designs its routers to use time information mostly for logging of system events and certain accounting and audit functions. Although not critical for the operation of the network, these functions are nonetheless important, as they constitute an integral part of the network operation. Indeed, most large companies and service providers use system events, and accounting and system logs to set up traffic routing policies. That being said, it is important to note that in order to leverage the router's system events to manage a network that spans several time-zones, NTP needs to be properly configured and operational. In this case, the Cisco router running Cisco IOS software will use the time information supplied by the NTP server and will not rely on its internal clock information.

Furthermore, third party network management applications might be used to read time stamp information gleaned from the system MIB variables or syslog outputs. In this case, it is very important to properly test the application software for year 2000 compliance.

Cisco Router Chip Sets

Many Cisco routers contain chipsets that have an embedded clock. However, data provided by the chipset is only used to compute the "uptime" date/time of the chip. The chip's embedded clock data is used by the IOS software to calculate the correct date/time, with reference to the date/time provided by either an NTP server or the default internal reference clock. Therefore, year 2000 compliance of the embedded clock of the chipset is not an issue.

Some Important Dates for Verifying Y2K Compliance

Year 2000 program glitches are not limited to January 1, 2000. The glitch can potentially happen anytime between April 9, 1999 and December 31, 2001. Here are some dates that need to be incorporated in any Y2K test plan:

Some software programs could translate April 9, 1999 as the 99th day of 1999, thereby storing the date as "9999". September 9, 1999 may also be expressed as 9/9/99 and would be stored as "9999" by some computer software. Incidentally, "9999" is also used by a number of computer programs to indicate the "end of file". Although the number of programs using this scheme is fairly limited, it might affect many low-budget applications' software.

January 1, 2000: The "19" of 1900 cannot longer be assumed. Therefore, a minimum of 4 digits in the space holder of the year is required to correctly handle the date.

January 10, 2000 will require a minimum space of seven digits to write the date.

October 10, 2000 will require a minimum space of eight digits to correctly write the date. However, most desktop computer programs reserved limited space for the dates because they assumed 19 in the writing of "1900". Until now, if the computer displayed 01/04/98, 19 was assumed in front of 98 to make up the 1998.

February 2000 contains a leap year date. The leap year was a decree from the Pope in 1582, which states that end-of-century years are not leap years except for those evenly divisible by 400. Since this would happen only every 400 years, most software programs did not bother to incorporate the exception. Hence February 29, 2000 might not exist in some computer software programs.

Cisco Y2K Summary—The Bottom Line

Cisco IOS is based on UNIX, whose internal time information is stored as a 32-bit signed integer of the number of seconds, which should not cause any problems for software such as Cisco IOS until the year 2036 (2^{32} seconds = 136.1 years. The year 1900 plus 136.1 years = year 2036). At that time, the computer industry at large should be using 32-bit unsigned values, which will push the IOS operational timeframe out to 2106.

PART II

Specification of Cisco IOS Releases

CHAPTER 4

Early Cisco IOS Software Releases: The Classic Phase of the Cisco IOS Release Process

The Singular Major Release Model

In the early days of Cisco Systems, Inc., when the company had only a handful of hardware, it needed relatively simple software to provide protocol translation and routing functions. Cisco IOS software grew into a singular, monolithic system that was fundamentally router-centric. It was arranged as a set of procedures, enabling any of the procedure(s) to call any other. This monolithic structure did not enforce data hiding and most of its operating code had structural and operational interdependencies. As the company grew, the IOS software expanded to cover more and more features. During that first phase, known as the classic release model, there existed only one IOS release vehicle. This vehicle provided new features, new platforms, and bug fixes. This process continued until approximately IOS software release version 11.0.

In an effort to address the rapid growth of the Internet and corporate networks, Cisco IOS releases 9.21 to 11.1 represented incremental engineering efforts to redesign Cisco IOS software into modular components or subsystems. Organized as a set of layers, each subsystem began providing an independent point into the system code. This enabled the base code to remain the same, yet allowed for new features to be added more independently. The subsystems themselves are defined as discreet modules that support functions within the embedded Kernel system. This layered subsystem design enabled engineering to partition Cisco IOS software into more manageable and easily upgradeable feature sets.

How Features and Hardware Platform Drivers Were Integrated into IOS during the Classic Phase

As mentioned in the preceding section, the classic release phase was characterized by one IOS release train that delivered new features, new hardware, and bug fixes. The diagram in Figure 4-1 illustrates how features, hardware drivers, and bug fixes were integrated into successive IOS maintenance revisions during this early phase of the release process.

Figure 4-1 *Cisco IOS Singular Release Model (Version 8.3 to Version 11.1)*

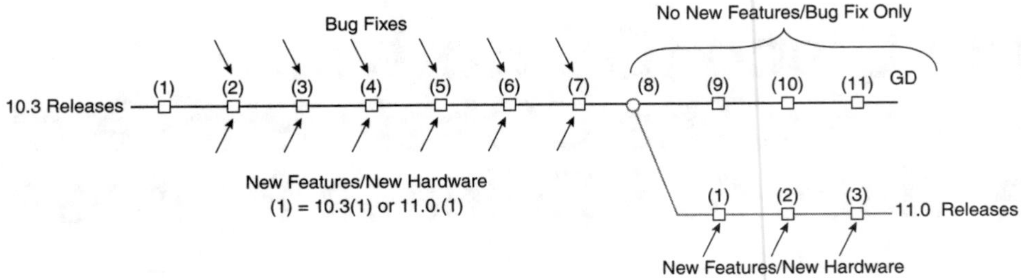

As illustrated in this figure, after the preceding main line release (shown as 10.3) reached restricted maintenance around the seventh maintenance revision, a new main line branch (shown as 11.0) was pulled from it. The newly created branch was open for new features while the former branch turned into a "bug-fix only" release train seeking higher stability, sanctioned by general deployment (GD) certification.

The following tables list the specifications of Cisco IOS software releases deployed during the classic release model. The tables cover Cisco IOS 9.x to 11.1 and associated early deployment releases.

Cisco IOS Version 9.x

<table>
<tr><td rowspan="3">Description</td><td colspan="2">Cisco IOS Software 9.x releases were introduced in December 1992 and have all reached EOS and EOL. Prior to Cisco Software 9.x, there was Cisco Software Release 8.x. Among these releases, Cisco Software Release 8.3 was particularly important in terms of innovation and features. Cisco Software Release 8.3 migrated to Cisco Software Release 9.1, which reached FCS in December 1992.</td></tr>
<tr><td colspan="2">• Cisco IOS 9.1 is a main line release that supported all existing Cisco platforms.
• Cisco IOS 9.14 is based on Cisco IOS 9.1 and introduced support for Access Servers (4000, 3000, and other low range access routers).
• Cisco IOS 9.17 is based on Cisco IOS 9.1 and ran parallel with Cisco IOS 9.14, but supported only the high-end routers (Cisco 7000, AGS/AGS+).</td></tr>
<tr><td colspan="2">Cisco IOS 9.21 unified Cisco IOS 9.14 and 9.17 to create a main line with support for all existing Cisco platforms.</td></tr>
<tr><td rowspan="3">Product Support</td><td colspan="2">Cisco IOS main releases are general-purpose IOS software developed and deployed on all current and active Cisco hardware platforms.</td></tr>
<tr><td>Main Features</td><td>Platforms</td></tr>
<tr><td>Routing enhancements
IGRP
Frame Relay
Access Servers</td><td>All active hardware at FCS</td></tr>
<tr><td>Feature Integration</td><td colspan="2">In addition to defect fixes, successive maintenance releases from Cisco IOS 8.3 to Cisco IOS 10.3(x) delivered support for new functionality and new hardware.</td></tr>
<tr><td rowspan="2">Synchronization Points with Major Releases</td><td>Based On</td><td>Ported Into</td></tr>
<tr><td>Previous release</td><td>Version 10.x releases</td></tr>
<tr><td>Release Type</td><td colspan="2">Main release</td></tr>
<tr><td>Target Market</td><td colspan="2">General purpose</td></tr>
<tr><td>Maintenance Releases</td><td colspan="2">Not applicable/EOL</td></tr>
<tr><td>Interim Builds</td><td colspan="2">Not applicable/EOL</td></tr>
<tr><td rowspan="4">Recommended Migration</td><td>From</td><td>To</td></tr>
<tr><td>9.x</td><td>10.3(x)</td></tr>
<tr><td>Before version 9.21</td><td>9.21</td></tr>
<tr><td colspan="2">The recommended migration path is the logical superceding release, which provides additional features and hardware support to the network without loss of previously configured functionality.</td></tr>
</table>

Life Cycle	**Milestones**	**Y2K Compliance**	**Certification**	**Other Dates**
	EOL	Not certified as Y2K compliant	IOS 9.x was not certified for GD	—
Internet Addresses	For more information, consult the following web pages: • Cisco IOS Software Feature Matrices: Releases 8.3 through 11.2 Product Bulletin at http://www.cisco.com/warp/public/cc/cisco/mkt/ios/rel/prodlit/511_pp.htm • Migration path information on release 9.21 appears on the IOS 9.21 Release Notes page at http://www.cisco.com/warp/customer/732/921/ • Migration path information on release 10.3x appears on the Cisco IOS Software Release 10.3 page at http://www.cisco.com/warp/public/732/103/			
Comments	EOL marks the end of Cisco's support for all 9.x releases. Network administrators should consider upgrading to an active and current Cisco IOS software release.			

Cisco IOS Version 10.x

Description	The Cisco IOS 10.x releases were introduced in 1993 and have all reached EOS and EOL. Cisco IOS 10.0, also known as the *A train*, provided very important internetworking capabilities to Cisco routers. Advanced features such as HSRP, BGP4, NLSP, E1 PRI signaling, PPP compression, new DDR protocols, fast call rerouting, and LAPB were introduced with this release. The following Cisco IOS 10.x versions were released: • Cisco IOS 10.0(x) to 10.3(x). • Cisco IOS 10.0(1) to 10.0(14) reached EOS in May 1996. • Cisco IOS 10.1(1) to 10.1(3). • Cisco IOS 10.2(1) was FCS on October 4, 1994, and delivered maintenance releases until 10.2(15). It reached EOE on December 30, 1996. • Cisco IOS 10.2(9) was the first Cisco IOS to achieve GD status. • Cisco IOS 10.3(1) was released on April 13, 1995, and delivered maintenance releases to 10.3(19). • Cisco IOS 10.3(3) introduced TACACS+ and ISDN features. • Cisco IOS 10.3(15) achieved GD status on October 7, 1996. • Cisco IOS 10.3(19) was the last regularly scheduled release of Cisco IOS 10.3, and was posted on CCO on July 28, 1997. Cisco IOS 10.3(19) was produced as spares only, could not be ordered, and was migrated to Cisco IOS 11.0. Cisco IOS 10.3 reached EOE on August 4, 1997.	
Product Support	**Main Features**	**Platforms**
	HSRP, PRI BGP4 NLSP PPP	All active hardware at FCS

<table>
<tr><td>Feature Integration</td><td colspan="2">New products and features were integrated into each maintenance release:
• AGS+/AGS/MGS/CGS/ASM with a CSC/4 processor board, not with a CSC/3 processor board.
• Cisco 7505 support was added to Cisco IOS 10.3(3).
• Cisco 7513 support was added to Cisco IOS 10.3(6).
• Cisco 7000/7010 support was added to all Cisco IOS 10.x releases.
• Cisco 4700 support was added to Cisco IOS 10.3(5).
• Cisco 4000/4000M/4500 support was added to all Cisco IOS 10.x releases.
• Cisco 310x and Cisco 3x04 (not Cisco 3202) support was added to all Cisco IOS 10.x releases.
• Cisco 2501 to 2504, Cisco 2505, and Cisco 2507 support was added to all Cisco IOS 10.x releases.
• Cisco 2509 to 2512 and Cisco 2513 to 2515 was added to all Cisco IOS 10.x releases.
• Cisco 2516 support was added to Cisco IOS 10.3(2).
• Cisco 2517 support was added to Cisco IOS 10.3(4).
• Cisco 1003 support was added to Cisco IOS 10.3(3).
• Cisco 1004 support was added to Cisco IOS 10.3(5).
• Cisco 1005 support was added to Cisco IOS 10.3(6).
• Cisco CS-500 (Access Server) support was added to all Cisco IOS 10.x releases.
• Cisco AP-EC (AccessPro Server Ethernet/Serial Router Card) support was added to all Cisco IOS 10.x releases.
Cisco AP-RC (AccessPro Server Token Ring/Serial Router Card) support was added to all Cisco IOS 10.x releases.</td></tr>
<tr><td rowspan="2">Synchronization Points with Major Releases</td><td>Based On</td><td>Ported Into</td></tr>
<tr><td>Version 9.21</td><td>Version 11.0</td></tr>
<tr><td>Release Type</td><td colspan="2">Main release</td></tr>
<tr><td>Target Market</td><td colspan="2">General purpose</td></tr>
<tr><td>Maintenance Releases</td><td colspan="2">Cisco IOS 10.x is now EOL</td></tr>
<tr><td>Interim Builds</td><td colspan="2">Provided weekly interim</td></tr>
</table>

<table>
<tr><th rowspan="4">Recommended Migration</th><th colspan="2">From</th><th colspan="2">To</th></tr>
<tr><td colspan="2">10.x</td><td colspan="2">11.1(x)</td></tr>
<tr><td colspan="2">10.3</td><td colspan="2">11.2(x)</td></tr>
<tr><td colspan="4">The recommended migration path is the logical superceding release, which provides additional features and hardware support to the network without loss of previously configured functionality.</td></tr>
<tr><th rowspan="2">Life Cycle</th><th>Milestones</th><th>Y2K Compliance</th><th>Certification</th><th>Other Dates</th></tr>
<tr><td>EOL</td><td>These releases are not Y2K compliant.</td><td>GD at 10.3(15)</td><td>GD declaration date: 10/07/96</td></tr>
<tr><th>Internet Addresses</th><td colspan="4">For more information, consult the following web pages:
• Cisco IOS 10.0 Release Notes at http://www.cisco.com/warp/customer/681/index.shtml
• Cisco IOS Software Release 10.3 Milestones at http://www.cisco.com/warp/public/732/103/583_pp.htm
• General information on Cisco IOS Software Release 10.1 at http://www.cisco.com/warp/public/732/101/
• General information on Cisco IOS Software Release 10.2 at http://www.cisco.com/warp/public/732/102/
• Cisco IOS 10.3 Release Notes at http://www.cisco.com/warp/public/732/103/
• GD Announcement for Cisco IOS Software Version 10.3 Product Bulletin at http://www.cisco.com/warp/public/417/529_pb.htm
• Because migration to versions 11.1(x) and 11.2(x) are recommended, see the Release Notes at http://www.cisco.com/univercd/cc/td/doc/product/software/ios111/rnrt111.htm or http://www.cisco.com/univercd/cc/td/doc/product/software/ios111/rnrt112.htm</td></tr>
<tr><th>Comments</th><td colspan="4">EOL marked the end of Cisco's support for the 10.x version releases. Network administrators should consider upgrading to an active IOS release.</td></tr>
</table>

Cisco IOS Version 11.0

Description	Cisco IOS 11.0 is a direct superset of Cisco IOS 10.3(x) and was released on September 18, 1995. Cisco IOS Software 11.0 reached the GD milestone on September 23, 1996 at maintenance revision 11.0(11). All subsequent maintenance releases thereafter are also GD certified.			
Product Support	**Main Features**		**Platforms**	
	New software and hardware features were introduced in successive maintenance revisions until 11.0(15).		All active platforms at FCS	
Feature Integration	New products and features were added to subsequent maintenance releases until Cisco 11.0(15). Information on new features of every maintenance revision can be found at http://www.cisco.com/warp/public/732/110/			
Synchronization Points with Major Releases	**Based On**		**Ported Into**	
	10.3		11.1	
Release Type	Main release			
Target Market	General purpose			
Maintenance Releases	Cisco IOS 11.0 reached mature maintenance phase after maintenance revision 11.0(15). Thereafter, maintenance revision builds transitioned to a 14-week cycle.			
Interim Builds	After mature maintenance, an interim build is executed once every three weeks.			
Recommended Migration	**From**		**To**	
	11.0(x)		11.2 or 12.0(x)	
	11.0BT		11.2, 11.2BC, or 12.0	
	The recommended migration path is the logical superceding release, which provides additional features and hardware support to the network without loss of previously configured functionality			
Life Cycle	**Milestones**	**Y2K Compliance**	**Certification**	**Other Dates**
	EOE has been extended until July 2000 or Cisco IOS 11.0(28)	Yes	GD at 11.0(11)	FCS: 9/18/95 GD: 9/23/96 EOS: 9/14/98 EOE: 07/10/00

Internet Addresses	For more information, consult the following web pages: • Cisco IOS Software Release 11.0 release notes at http://www.cisco.com/warp/public/732/110/ • The Feature Set Product Bulletin at http://www.cisco.com/warp/public/417/118.html • Router Products Release Notes for 11.0 at http://www.cisco.com/univercd/cc/td/doc/product/software/ios11/rnrt110/rnrt110.htm • Cisco IOS Software Release 11.0 Milestones at http://www.cisco.com/warp/public/cc/cisco/mkt/ios/rel/110/prodlit/608_pp.htm
Comments	Cisco IOS 11.0 reached end of sale as of September 14, 1998. The following GD releases are currently available either through CCO and/or manufacturing (MFG): • Cisco IOS 11.0(17) • Cisco IOS 11.0(18) • Cisco IOS 11.0(19) APPN images • Cisco IOS 11.0(20) and later The Cisco IOS 11.0 repository is currently "locked." The branch is in a restricted maintenance phase, indicating that only defects found by customers with a severity level of S1 or S2 and/or P1 or P2 will be considered for approval to be fixed in this release. Customers are strongly encouraged to migrate to newer IOS software releases.

Cisco IOS Early Deployment Releases Based on 11.0

Although the concept of targeted early deployment releases existed since Cisco IOS version 9.21, it was not until 11.0 that formalized IOS software targeting specific technology theatres flourished. Cisco IOS 11.0NA and 11.0BT are specific technology early deployment releases (STED) based on release 11.0.

Cisco IOS Version 11.0NA

Description	Cisco IOS 11.0NA is an STED that introduced support for the IPeXchange Internet Gateway on the Cisco 1000 series. IPeXchange Internet Gateway connects Novell NetWare users using IPX protocol to the Internet or other TCP/IP-based network services. IPeXchange enables NetWare client workstations to use TCP/IP-based applications such as Telnet, FTP, and Netscape Navigator without requiring a TCP/IP protocol stack on each workstation. Cisco IOS 11.0(6)NA is the first version in a series of IPeXchange releases and is based on Cisco IOS 11.0(6). This STED release provided maintenance revisions up to Cisco IOS 11.0(14)NA. The functionality of Cisco IOS 11.0NA releases was ported to main line Cisco IOS 11.0 at 11.0(15) and later.	
Product Support	**Main Features**	**Platforms**
	IPeXchange Internet Gateway Remote shell daemon (RSHD)	Cisco 1000 series Gateway routers: 1003, 1004, 1005
Feature Integration	Cisco IOS STED releases regularly synchronize with the parent IOS major release to inherit bug fixes. Additionally, successive maintenance revisions of the ED introduce new functionality.	
Synchronization Points with Major Releases	**Based On**	**Ported Into**
	11.0(6)	11.0(15) and later
Release Type	STED	
Target Market	Small and medium businesses/home offices	
Maintenance Releases	Seven-week Scheduled Regular Maintenance revisions during the life cycle. Maintenance revisions were bug synced to 11.0 main release. Cisco IOS release 11.0NA is now EOL.	
Interim Builds	Irregular interim builds	
Recommended Migration	**From**	**To**
	11.0(x)NA	11.1(1) and later
	The recommended migration path is the logical superceding release, which provides additional features and hardware support to the network without loss of previously configured functionality.	

Life Cycle	Milestones	Y2K Compliance	Certification	Other Dates
	EOE at 11.0(14)	Yes	STED	EOE: April, 1997
Internet Addresses	For more information, consult the following web page: • IPeXchange Internet Gateway Release Notes at http://www.cisco.com/univercd/cc/td/doc/product/iaabu/ipx/rnipex.htm#xtocid77450			
Comments	Functionality of Cisco IOS 11.0NA is now part of IOS software versions 11.1(15) and beyond.			

Cisco IOS Version 11.0BT

Description	The Cisco IOS 11.0BT release train was introduced in October, 1997, to deliver functionality for IBM Internetworking on the Cisco 7000 and the Cisco 7500 series routers. Cisco IOS 11.0BT includes all Cisco IOS features found in Cisco IOS 11.0 releases up to Cisco IOS 11.0(10) plus newly introduced IBM features including support for the Channel Interface Processor (CIP), CIP2, and TN3270 features.	
Product Support	**Main Features**	**Platforms**
	Includes Cisco IOS features to 11.0(10) IBM features, CIP and CIP2, and TN3270 Dynamic definition of dependent logical units (LU) SNA session switching Dynamic allocation of LUs End-to-end session visibility	Cisco 7500 Cisco 7000 with RSP7000
Feature Integration	Cisco IOS release 11.0BT maintains the core IOS features of 11.0 up to 11.0(10). In addition, it includes IBM Internetworking features such as SNA and RSRB and support for CIP, CIP2, and TN3270	
Synchronization Points with Major Releases	**Based On**	**Ported Into**
	11.0	11.1 and 11.2BC
Release Type	STED	
Target Market	Enterprise SNA	
Maintenance Releases	Seven-week Scheduled Regular Maintenance revisions	
Interim Builds	As needed for critical defect fixes	

Recommended Migration	**From**		**To**	
	11.0BT		11.2B, 12.0, or 12.0T	
	The recommended migration path is the logical superceding release, which provides additional features and hardware support to the network without loss of previously configured functionality.			
Life Cycle	**Milestones**	**Y2K Compliance**	**Certification**	**Other Dates**
	EOE in December, 1998 at 11.0(22)BT	Yes	LD	CCO FCS in October, 1997
Internet Addresses	For more information, consult the following web page: • Cisco IOS Release 11.0 BT Release Note and Update to Configuration Guides and Command References at http://www.cisco.com/univercd/cc/td/doc/product/software/ios11/rn110bte.htm			

Cisco IOS Version 11.1

Description	Cisco IOS 11.1 is a non-GD main release train released in March, 1996. Since 1998 and starting with 11.1(16) maintenance revision, the Cisco IOS 11.1 software has transitioned from the standard eight-week maintenance revision cycle to a 14-week maintenance cycle, indicating that the code has reached a higher maturity level characterized by its quality, stability, and defect trend. It reached EOE in January, 1999, at maintenance revision 11.1(24). Cisco IOS 11.1 has spawned several ED releases including Cisco IOS 11.1CA and 11.1IA. These STED depended on 11.1 for bug fixes. Since the STED outlived the parent, Cisco IOS technology division will manually attend to extremely critical customer impacting bugs affecting 11.1CA and 11.1IA.			
Product Support	**Main Features**		**Platforms**	
	Cisco IOS main releases support all active Cisco shipping routers.			
Feature Integration	New software and hardware features have been introduced to successive maintenance revisions.			
Synchronization Points with Major Releases	**Based On**		**Ported Into**	
	11.0		11.2	
Release Type	Main release			
Target Market	General purpose			
Maintenance Releases	Cisco IOS 11.1 software provided Scheduled Regular Maintenance revisions. The release reached EOE at 11.1(24). This release used an eight-week cycle prior to Cisco IOS 11.1(16) and began a 14-week maintenance cycle after 11.1(17).			
Interim Builds	Weekly interim builds prior to mature maintenance and every three weeks during mature maintenance.			
Recommended Migration	**From**		**To**	
	11.1(x)		11.2 or 12.0(x)	
	The recommended migration path is the logical superceding release, which provides additional features and hardware support to the network without loss of previously configured functionality.			
Life Cycle	**Milestones**	**Y2K Compliance**	**Certification**	**Other Dates**
	EOS: 10/12/98 EOE in January, 1999	Yes	LD	EOS: 10/12/98

Internet Addresses	For more information, consult the following web pages: • Cisco IOS Software Release 11.1 New Features at http://www.cisco.com/warp/customer/cc/cisco/mkt/ios/rel/111/prodlit/402_pp.htm • Cisco IOS 11.1 Release Notes at http://www.cisco.com/warp/customer/757/index.shtml • Additional Release Notes for Cisco IOS release 11.1 at http://www.cisco.com/univercd/cc/td/doc/product/software/ios111/rnrt111.htm

Early Deployment Releases Based on IOS 11.1

By 1995, the growth of the Internet coupled with explosive Cisco product growth in Enterprise networks put a very high demand on Cisco Systems, Inc. to deliver more features and incorporate newly adopted standards into IOS software.

It was clear that the experimental nature of some of these protocols could introduce risks in the more conservative networks such as those of financial institutions. Hence, IOS early deployment releases were adopted. During this first phase of the IOS release process, early deployment releases were specifically targeted. For example, 11.1CC was the general purpose Internet service provider (ISP) IOS release while 11.1AA targeted the dial and access market space of the ISP. Figure 4-2 illustrates the parent-child relationship of IOS ED releases during the classic phase.

Figure 4-2 *Example of Cisco IOS 11.1 and STED Relationships*

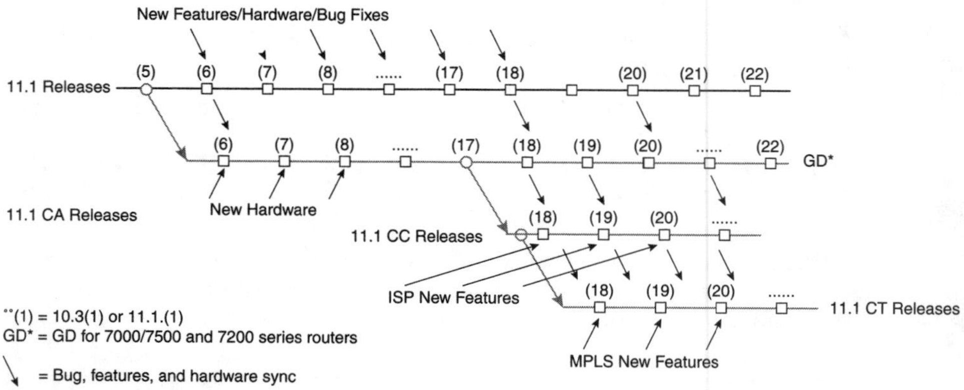

Cisco IOS Version 11.1AA

<table>
<tr><td rowspan="4">Description</td><td colspan="4">Cisco IOS 11.1AA is a platform-specific release consisting of a limited number of feature-set images that provide new features or functionality. Cisco IOS 11.1AA delivers access features and functionality for access platforms such as Cisco 1600, Cisco 3600, and Cisco 5200 series routers. Cisco IOS 11.1AA is parented by Cisco IOS 11.1(6); thus, it has all the functionality supported up to the Cisco IOS 11.1(6) major release.</td></tr>
<tr><td colspan="4">Cisco IOS 11.1AA is now EOE. The last scheduled maintenance revision was 11.1(20)AA, which reached FCS on July 6, 1998.</td></tr>
<tr><td colspan="4">Cisco IOS 11.1(6)AA was the first AA release and only supported the EIPRI and Cisco 5200.</td></tr>
<tr><td colspan="4">Cisco IOS 11.1(7)AA added support for the Cisco 1600, Cisco 5200, and Cisco 3600 series platforms.</td></tr>
<tr><td rowspan="3">Product Support</td><td colspan="2">Main Features</td><td colspan="2">Platforms</td></tr>
<tr><td colspan="2">Dial and access server features including ISDN BRI and PRI</td><td colspan="2">Cisco 1600</td></tr>
<tr><td colspan="2">Support for asynchronous and synchronous serial, synchronous serial with integrated 56-kbps CSU/DSU, ISDN BRI S/T, and ISDN BRI on various platforms</td><td colspan="2">Cisco 3600
Cisco 5200</td></tr>
<tr><td>Feature Integration</td><td colspan="4">EOE</td></tr>
<tr><td rowspan="2">Synchronization Points with Major Releases</td><td colspan="2">Based On</td><td colspan="2">Ported Into</td></tr>
<tr><td colspan="2">11.1</td><td colspan="2">11.2P</td></tr>
<tr><td>Target Market</td><td colspan="4">Internet service providers and dial access Enterprise customers</td></tr>
<tr><td rowspan="2">Maintenance Releases</td><td colspan="4">Significant maintenance revisions include 11.1(6)AA, 11.1(7)AA, and 11.1(20) which was the last maintenance revision.</td></tr>
<tr><td colspan="4">Cisco IOS 11.1AA is now EOE.</td></tr>
<tr><td>Interim Builds</td><td colspan="4">Cisco IOS 11.1AA provided a weekly interim build until EOE.</td></tr>
<tr><td rowspan="3">Recommended Migration</td><td colspan="2">From</td><td colspan="2">To</td></tr>
<tr><td colspan="2">11.1AA</td><td colspan="2">11.3AA or 12.0T. Also 12.0XA or 12.0XJ</td></tr>
<tr><td colspan="4">The recommended migration path is the logical superceding release, which provides additional features and hardware support to the network without loss of previously configured functionality.</td></tr>
<tr><td rowspan="2">Life Cycle</td><td>Milestones</td><td>Y2K Compliance</td><td>Certification</td><td>Other Dates</td></tr>
<tr><td>EOE in July, 1998</td><td>Yes</td><td>LD</td><td>EOS: 4/6/98</td></tr>
</table>

Internet Addresses	For more information, consult the following web pages: • Cisco IOS 11.1AA Release Notes at http://www.cisco.com/univercd/cc/td/doc/product/software/ios111/rn111aa.htm • Cisco IOS 11.1 Release Software at http://www.cisco.com/warp/customer/732/111/

Cisco IOS Version 11.1CA

Description	Cisco IOS software 11.1CA is a platform-specific STED release that supports virtually all hardware modules developed for the Cisco 7500, Cisco 7200, and Cisco 7000 series. In fact, port adapters not supported on the newer 11.2 releases are frequently supported on this release. Cisco IOS 11.1CA has been the de facto release for Enterprise networks and has gained the admiration of network administrators as a very stable IOS release. These quality attributes made it a good candidate for the first ever Cisco IOS STED to be qualified as a platform-specific GD release. Until Cisco IOS 12.0 reaches GD status, 11.1CA remains the preferred GD release for the Cisco 7200 and 7500 series router. It offers significant maturity and field exposure with substantially more hardware support. However, 11.1CA has significantly fewer software features than 11.2P or 12.0. Cisco IOS 11.1CA supports high-end Cisco router interfaces including: • VIP2-50, VIP2-40, VIP2-15 • RSP4 (Cisco 7500) and NPE-200 (Cisco 7200) processors • Fast Ethernet interface processor with distributed switching and services (FEIP2-DSW) • More than 20 port adapters including ATM, HSSI, high-performance serial, as well as compression service adapters The Cisco IOS 11.1CA is slated to reach EOE in September, 2000.	
Product Support	**Main Features**	**Platforms**
	The following hardware features were committed in 11.1CA and sync to 11.1CC and 11.1CT: • Channelized T3 interface processor (CT3IP) • Full duplex FDDI port adapters (PA-F/FD-MM, PA-F/FD-SM) • Compression Service Adapters (SA-COMP/1, SA-COMP/4) • High Speed Serial Interface port adapter (PA-H, PA-2H) • 8 port synchronous serial port adapters (PA-8-V35, PA-8T-X21, PA-8T-232) • Enhanced 4 port synchronous serial port adapter (PA-4T+) • ISDN BRI port adapters on Cisco 7200 (PA-8B-ST, PA-4B-U) • RSP4 Route Switch Processor for the Cisco 7500 • Packet-Over-Sonet interface processor for the Cisco 7500 (POSIP-40) • Full-duplex Token Ring port adapter (PA-4R-FDX) • 100VG-Any LAN port adapter (PA-100VG) • ATM OC3 port adapter (PA-A1-OC3MM, PA-A1-OC3SM) • Channelized / PRI T1 and E1 port adapters (PA-2CT1, PA-2E1) • Network Processing Engine 200 for the Cisco 7200 (NPE-200)	

	Support for advanced hardware modules	Cisco 7500
	See Hardware Compatibility Matrix: http://www.cisco.com/cgi-bin/front.x/Support/HWSWmatrix/hwswmatrix.cgi	Cisco 7200
	RSP7000 and RSP7000CI	Cisco 7000
Feature Integration	Successive maintenance revision of 11.1CA introduced new software and hardware features until 11.1(18)CA when it reached mature maintenance.	
Synchronization Points with Major Releases	In addition to regular sync with the 11.1 major release for bug fix inheritance, features of 11.1CA IOS software release were also ported to other IOS releases as indicated by the table below.	
	Based On	**Ported Into**
	Cisco IOS 11.1(5)CA to 11.1(7)CA	Cisco IOS 11.2(5)P
	Cisco IOS 11.1(8)CA to 11.1(9)CA	Cisco IOS 11.2(7)P
	Cisco IOS 11.1(1)CA to 11.1(20)CA	Cisco IOS 12.0(1)
	Cisco IOS 11.1(17)CA	Cisco IOS 11.1(17)CC
Release Type	SMED/STED	
Target Market	Enterprise and Internet service providers	
Maintenance Releases	Unique Scheduled Regular Maintenance follows these points: • Cisco IOS 11.1CA followed the Cisco IOS 11.1 maintenance release cycle until 11.1 reached EOE. • Originally an eight-week maintenance cycle, it has now transitioned as of Cisco IOS 11.1(18) to a 14-week mature maintenance cycle. • Only even-numbered releases beyond IOS 11.1(18) are on the 14-week cycle. • Maintenance revision 11.1(18)CA is the last revision to integrate additional new features.	
Interim Builds	This release followed a unique interim build pattern: • During the eight-week cycle, the release built three interim builds on alternating weeks between maintenance every two maintenance revisions. • In the 14-week cycle, interim software were built on odd weeks and their names/numbers are so indicated: 11.1(15.1)CA, 11.1(15.3)CA, 11.1(15.5)CA	

<table>
<tr><th rowspan="5">Recommended Migration</th><th colspan="2">From</th><th colspan="2">To</th></tr>
<tr><td colspan="2">ISP on 11.1CA</td><td colspan="2">Cisco IOS 11.1CC, 12.0S</td></tr>
<tr><td colspan="2">Large Enterprise on 11.1CA</td><td colspan="2">Cisco IOS 11.1CC, 12.0, 12.0S</td></tr>
<tr><td colspan="2">Enterprise</td><td colspan="2">Cisco IOS 12.0, 12.0T</td></tr>
<tr><td colspan="4">The recommended migration path is the logical superceding release, which provides additional features and hardware support to the network without loss of previously configured functionality.</td></tr>
<tr><th rowspan="3">Life Cycle</th><th>Milestones</th><th>Y2K Compliance</th><th>Certification</th><th>Other Dates</th></tr>
<tr><td>11.1(22)CA reached GD on 12/3/98</td><td>Yes</td><td>GD</td><td>EOE is slated for September, 2000</td></tr>
<tr><td colspan="4">This release is currently in restricted mode.</td></tr>
<tr><th>Internet Addresses</th><td colspan="4">For more information, consult the following web pages:
• Hardware Compatibility Matrix at http://www.cisco.com/cgi-bin/front.x/Support/HWSWmatrix/hwswmatrix.cgi
• Release Notes for Cisco IOS Release 11.1 CA and Feature Modules at http://www.cisco.com/univercd/cc/td/doc/product/software/ios111/ca111/index.htm
• Cisco IOS 11.1 Release Notes at http://www.cisco.com/univercd/cc/td/doc/product/software/ios111/ca111/index.htm
• Release Notes for Cisco 7000 Family for Cisco IOS Release 11.1 CA at http://www.cisco.com/univercd/cc/td/doc/product/software/ios111/ca111/rn111ca.htm</td></tr>
<tr><th>Comments</th><td colspan="4">Cisco IOS 11.1(472) and 11.1(5)CA are the first special and maintenance releases of Cisco IOS 11.1CA.
Cisco 11.1(18)CA achieved mature maintenance at 11.1(18)CA.</td></tr>
</table>

Cisco IOS Version 11.1CC

Description	Cisco IOS 11.1CC is a feature-specific software release based on 11.1CA. Cisco IOS 11.1CC inherits platforms committed to 11.1CA via regular synch. Therefore, the two releases support virtually the same platforms. Cisco IOS 11.1CC distinguishes itself from 11.1CA by being very focused on advanced routing and scalability features for the Internet. In fact, Cisco IOS 11.1CC, also known as "ISP Geek release," introduced several innovated advanced networking features and performance improvement features for highly loaded Internet backbone routers. Functionality such as Differentiated Services and Managed Congestion Control comprised of advanced QoS features like CAR, WFQ and WRED make Cisco IOS 11.1CC the preferred Internet Service Provider release. Together, these features allow for traffic to be placed in different classes with varying levels of bandwidth and priority. WFQ and WRED ensure that higher priority traffic is delivered first in case of network congestion. Cisco IOS 11.1CC is expected to reach EOE in December 1999 or early 2000.	
Product Support	**Main Features**	**Platforms**
	Multicast, Advanced BGP, OSPF, and IS-IS features	Cisco 7500 routers
	CEF, NetFlow, Advanced Compression algorithms	Cisco 7200 routers
	Policy routing QoS CAR Queuing RSVP WRED/RED See 11.1CA Main Features	Cisco 7000 routers
	Supports all features from the parent 11.1CA releases	
Feature Integration	New features were incrementally integrated into successive maintenance revisions until 11.1(22)CC. In addition to regular sync with the 11.1CA for bug fixes and platform feature inheritance, software features directly committed to 11.1CC were also ported to other IOS releases as indicated in the following rows.	
Synchronization Points with Major Releases	**Based On**	**Ported Into**
	Cisco IOS 11.1(17)CC to 11.1(19)CC (except CE3)	Cisco IOS 12.0(1)
	Cisco IOS 11.1(20)CC to 11.1(22)CC (including CE3 and NPE-300)	Cisco IOS 12.0(3)T
	Cisco IOS 11.1(20)CC to 11.1(22)CC (including CE3, excluding project Paris)	Cisco IOS 12.0(2)S

Release Type	SMED
Target Market	Internet service providers and network service providers
Maintenance Releases	Unique Scheduled Regular Maintenance with the following points: • For the most part Cisco IOS 11.1CC followed its parent IOS release (11.1CA) maintenance revision cycle with some variation. • Cisco IOS 11.1 and 11.1CA were originally on an eight-week release cycle up until maintenance revision 11.1(18). They switched to a 14-week maintenance cycle thereafter. However, IOS release 11.1CC continued to use the eight-week maintenance cycle until IOS 11.1(24)CC. Thereafter, it switched to the mature maintenance 14-week cycle.
Interim Builds	The interim builds for IOS 11.1CC also follow a unique pattern: • During the eight-week cycle, there were two interim builds according to the following timing structure: — CCO post date + 1 week = first interim build First interim build + 2 weeks = second interim build For example: Maintenance revision 11.1(17)CC was posted on CCO on November 30, 1998. The first interim build, 11.1(18.1)CC was performed on December 14, 1998 (2 week delta). The second interim build, 11.1(18.2)CC was performed on January 4, 1999 (3 week delta). The next maintenance revision, 11.1(24)CC was posted on CCO on January 25, 1999 (3 week delta). During the 14-week cycle, two interim builds are performed between maintenance revisions. The odd-numbered releases are not tested and not released to the public. For example: Maintenance revision 11.1(24)CC was posted on CCO on January 18, 1999. The first interim, 11.1(24.1)CC, was built on January 25, 1999 (1 week delta). The second interim, 11.1(24.2), was built on February 15, 1999 (3 week delta). Maintenance revision 11.1(25)CC was built on March 1, 1999 (2 week delta). The Business Unit release team has discretion to test and release, which might or might not happen. The next interim, 11.1(25.1)CC, was built on March 15, 1999 (2 week delta). The following interim, 11.1(25.2)CC, was built on April 5, 1999 (3 week delta). Finally, maintenance revision 11.1(26)CC was posted on CCO on April 26, 1999 (3 week delta).

<table>
<tr><th rowspan="5">Recommended Migration</th><th colspan="2">From</th><th colspan="2">To</th></tr>
<tr><td colspan="2">ISP on 11.1CC</td><td colspan="2">12.0S</td></tr>
<tr><td colspan="2">Large Enterprise on 11.1CC</td><td colspan="2">12.0T, 12.0S</td></tr>
<tr><td colspan="2">Enterprise on 11.1CC</td><td colspan="2">12.0, 12.0XE</td></tr>
<tr><td colspan="4">The recommended migration path is the logical superceding release, which provides additional features and hardware support to the network without loss of previously configured functionality.</td></tr>
<tr><th rowspan="2">Life Cycle</th><th>Milestones</th><th>Y2K Compliance</th><th>Certification</th><th>Other Dates</th></tr>
<tr><td>EOE in December, 1999</td><td>Yes</td><td>LD</td><td>CCO FCS: 11/30/98
MM: 2/1/99</td></tr>
<tr><th>Internet Addresses</th><td colspan="4">For more information, consult the following web pages:
• Release Notes for Cisco IOS Release 11.1CC and Feature Modules at http://www.cisco.com/univercd/cc/td/doc/product/software/ios111/cc111/index.htm
• Cisco IOS Software Release Process for Release 11.1 CC at http://www.cisco.com/warp/customer/cc/cisco/mkt/ios/rel/111/prodlit/754_pp.htm
• Cisco IOS Software Release 11.1CC New Features at http://www.cisco.com/warp/public/cc/cisco/mkt/ios/rel/111/prodlit/727_pb.htm</td></tr>
<tr><th>Comments</th><td colspan="4">While 11.1CC contains all the hardware and functionality committed to 11.1CA, it does not include the features added to the later 11.2 and 11.3 IOS releases. Indeed features such as Network Address Translation (NAT), Encryption, Named Access Control Lists, Hot Standby Router Protocol (HSRP) for ATM LANE are not supported in 11.1CA or 11.1CC. (See Importance of Unification)
The following is the not-so-complete list of features that are available in 11.2 and 12.0 but NOT in 11.1CC:
• On demand routing
• OSPF On-Demand Circuit
• OSPF Not-So-Stubby-Areas
• Network Address Translation
• Named IP Access Control List
• Resource Reservation Protocol
• Random Early Detection (*)
• Generic Traffic Shaping
• Enhanced IGRP Optimizations</td></tr>
</table>

	• AppleTalk Load Balancing • Novell Display SAP by Name • IPX Access Control List Violation Logging • Plain English IPX Access Lists • IPeXchange Internet Gateway • IPX Routing over ISL • DECnet, Banyan Vines and XNS support on LANE interfaces • Integrated Routing and Bridging • Multichassis Multilink PPP • Layer 2 forwarding • Virtual Private Dial-Up Network • Dialer Profiles • Combinet Packet Protocol Support • Half Bridge/Half Router for Combinet Packet Protocol and PPP • Frame Relay SVC support • Simple Server Redundancy for LANE • Hot Standby Router Protocol for LANE • UNI 3.1 signaling • Rate Queues for ATM SVCs • AToM MIB • Native Client Interface Architecture Server • TN3270 Server • Fast-switching of SR/TLB • Response Time Reporter • APPN Central Resource Registration • APPN SLUR MIB • LAN Network Manager (LNM) over DLSW+ • Native Service Point (NSP) over DLSW+ • Down Stream Physical Unit (DSPU) over DLSW+ • APPN over DLSW+ • Source-Route Bridging over FDDI to DLSW+ • Router Authentication and Network-Layer Encryption • Double Authentication • Tacacs+ Enhancements • HTTP server on Cisco 7200 • HTTP security • (*) Later implementation of RED is slightly different than WRED in 11.1CC

Cisco IOS Version 11.1CT

Description	Cisco IOS 11.1CT is based on 11.1(17)CC. It is an STED specializing in Tag Switching (EITF standard multiprotocol label switching or MPLS) functionality on the Cisco 7500, Cisco 7200, and RSP7000 routers. Tag Switching functionality and connectivity with IOS software on the BPX 8600 and 8800 were introduced after Cisco IOS 11.1(19)CT as part of the tag switch controller (TSC) played by a 7500 or 7200 series router. In this scenario, the TSC can be a tag switch router (TSR) that controls the operation of a separate ATM switch. Together, the router and ATM switch function as a single ATM Tag Switching router (ATM-TSR). With the 7200 or 7500 series router acting as a TSC, and a Cisco BPX 8600 Service Node (8620 wide area switch or 8650 IP+ATM switch) acting as the VSI-controlled ATM switch, the TSC can control the ATM switch using the Cisco Virtual Switch Interface (VSI), which runs over an ATM link connecting the two. Based on Cisco IOS 11.1CC, Cisco IOS 11.1CT consolidates advanced routing features such as CEF, differentiated IP quality of services (QoS) for the Enterprise networks, and Internet service provider environments. Cisco IOS 11.1CT regularly synch to 11.1CC for bug fixes and new hardware/software support. The features of 11.1CC were ported to Cisco IOS 12.0T at Cisco IOS 11.1(19)CT. Newer MPLS feature developments are concentrated on 12.0ST and 12.0S releases. Cisco IOS 11.1CT software stopped introducing new features after 11.1(19)CT.	
Product Support	**Main Features**	**Platforms**
	Tag Switching (MPLS) Tag Distribution Protocol (TDP) Dynamic Tag Switching Tag Switch Path Tunnels (TSP Tunnels) Traffic Engineering Static Tag Switching VPN RSVP Class of service MPLS LSC (6400 support) Ships in the Night Label Switch Controller (LSC) Consolidation of advanced IP routing features and new port adapters See 11.1CA Main Features	Cisco RSP7000, 7200, and 7500 series; the BPX8600 at Cisco IOS 11.1(19)CT

<table>
<tr><th>Feature Integration</th><td colspan="4">New MPLS features and enhancements continued to be integrated to successive maintenance revisions of Cisco IOS 11.1CT until 11.1(19)CT. Thereafter, development efforts went into 12.0S and 12.0ST.</td></tr>
<tr><th rowspan="3">Synchronization Points with Major Releases</th><th colspan="2">Based On</th><th colspan="2">Ported Into</th></tr>
<tr><td colspan="2">Cisco IOS 11.1CC</td><td colspan="2">Cisco IOS 12.0 at 11.1(19)CT</td></tr>
<tr><td colspan="4">Regularly syncs with parent release 11.1CC for all base code fixes.</td></tr>
<tr><th>Release Type</th><td colspan="4">Specific technology early deployment (STED)</td></tr>
<tr><th>Target Market</th><td colspan="4">Internet service provider/Telecommunications</td></tr>
<tr><th>Maintenance Releases</th><td colspan="4">Provides regularly scheduled maintenance revision using eight-week release cycle. The release cycle switched to 14-weeks after MM.</td></tr>
<tr><th>Interim Builds</th><td colspan="4">Interims were irregularly built two or three times between maintenance revisions. They followed this pattern:
11.1(X)CT—Maintenance revision
11.1(X.0)CT1—as needed weekly interim not synced to 11.1CC
11.1(X.1)CT—synced interim build
11.1(X.1)CT1—as needed weekly interim not synced
11.1(X.1)CT2—as needed weekly interim
11.1(X.2)CT—synced interim build
11.1(X.2)CT1—as needed weekly interim not synced
11.1(Z)CT—next maintenance revision</td></tr>
<tr><th rowspan="3">Recommended Migration</th><th colspan="2">From</th><th colspan="2">To</th></tr>
<tr><td colspan="2">11.1CT</td><td colspan="2">12.0T, 12.0ST, 12.0S</td></tr>
<tr><td colspan="4">The recommended migration path is the logical superceding release, which provides additional features and hardware support to the network without loss of previously configured functionality.
MPLS VPN, which was developed in 12.0ST, was also ported to 12.0T starting with 12.0(5)T. It is available on the following platforms: 12000, 7500, 7200, 4700, 4500, and 3600.</td></tr>
<tr><th rowspan="2">Life Cycle</th><th>Milestones</th><th>Y2K Compliance</th><th>Certification</th><th>Other Dates</th></tr>
<tr><td>EOE: 10/2/00</td><td>Yes</td><td>LD</td><td>—</td></tr>
</table>

Internet Addresses	For more information, consult the following web pages: • Cisco IOS Software Release Process for Release 11.1CT Product Bulletin at http://www.cisco.com/warp/customer/cc/cisco/mkt/ios/rel/111/prodlit/758_pp.htm • Cisco IOS Software Release 11.1CT New Features at http://www.cisco.com/warp/public/cc/cisco/mkt/ios/rel/111/prodlit/757_pp.htm • Release Notes for Tag Switching for Cisco IOS Release 11.1 CT at: http://www.cisco.com/univercd/cc/td/doc/product/software/ios111/ct111/rn111ct.htm
Comments	Cisco IOS 11.1CT is in mature maintenance mode. The Label Switch Controller (LSC) within the Cisco BPX 8620 wide area switch and BPX 8650 IP and ATM switch delivers scalable integration of IP services over an ATM network. The LSC enables BPX 8600 to participate in an MPLS network, to be a direct peer with IP edge routers, and support the full suite of IP features available in Cisco IOS software.

Cisco IOS Version 11.1IA

Description	Cisco IOS 11.1IA was released specifically to deliver functionality for the DistributedDirector platforms. Cisco DistributedDirector provides dynamic, transparent, and scalable Internet traffic load distribution between multiple topologically-dispersed servers. DistributedDirector is a global Internet service scaling solution that uses Cisco IOS software and leverages routing table information in the network infrastructure to make "intelligent network" load distribution decisions. It transparently redirects end-user service (HTTP URL, FTP, DNS, etc.) requests to the topologically closest Internet server, resulting in increased access performance and reduced transmission costs. Cisco IOS 11.1IA is not a router software image and does not provide full routing functionality. The IA software release is based on 11.1(9) main Cisco IOS software and was optimized for the DistributedDirector and its Internet scaling functionality. Because DistributedDirector is a dedicated platform, Cisco IOS 11.1IA software is only available bundled with DistributedDirector platforms	
Product Support	**Main Features**	**Platforms**
	DistributedDirector Internet scaling features Web server and DNS load balancing Director Response Protocol (DRP) server agent support HTTP and DNS Redirection	Only as bundled with DistributedDirector platforms: DistributedDirector 2501 DistributedDirector 2502 DistributedDirector 4700-M
Feature Integration	Successive maintenance revisions introduced incremental feature enhancements.	
Synchronization Points with Major Releases	**Based On**	**Ported Into**
	11.1	12.0(3)T

<table>
<tr><th>Release Type</th><td colspan="4">Specific technology early deployment (STED)</td></tr>
<tr><th>Target Market</th><td colspan="4">Internet scalability/Internet and Network service providers/Internet portals/Enterprise Internet services</td></tr>
<tr><th>Maintenance Releases</th><td colspan="4">Cisco IOS 11.1IA did provide successive releases during its regular life cycle, but is now in restricted mode with most enhancements going into maintenance revisions of 12.0(3)T and later.</td></tr>
<tr><th>Interim Builds</th><td colspan="4">Cisco IOS 11.1IA is now on a 14-week mature maintenance cycle.</td></tr>
<tr><th rowspan="3">Recommended Migration</th><th colspan="2">From</th><th colspan="2">To</th></tr>
<tr><td colspan="2">Cisco IOS 11.1IA</td><td colspan="2">Cisco IOS 12.0(3)T or later</td></tr>
<tr><td colspan="4">The recommended migration path is the logical superceding release, which provides additional features and hardware support to the network without loss of previously configured functionality.</td></tr>
<tr><th rowspan="2">Life Cycle</th><th>Milestones</th><th>Y2K Compliant</th><th>Certification</th><th>Other Dates</th></tr>
<tr><td>EOE is slated for April 24, 2000</td><td>Yes</td><td>LD</td><td>—</td></tr>
<tr><th>Internet Addresses</th><td colspan="4">For more information, consult the following web pages:
• Distributed Director Home Page on CCO at http://www.cisco.com/warp/public/cc/cisco/mkt/scale/distr/index.shtml
• Cisco IOS Software Release 11.1IA Content and Platform Support at http://www.cisco.com/warp/public/751/distdir/586_pp.htm</td></tr>
<tr><th>Comments</th><td colspan="4">Cisco IOS 11.1(9)IA was the first maintenance of 11.1IA release.
Maintenance revision 11.1(18)IA introduced supports for DRP-MED option, the DRP-RTT metric, the “portion” metric, and the DRP-RTT Tolerance parameter.
Cisco IOS 11.1IA is not available as a stand-alone software product.</td></tr>
</table>

CHAPTER 5

Cisco IOS Releases During the NGRP Phase

Necessity of a Another Cisco IOS Release Process

It was clear by 1995 that another Cisco IOS release process was needed. The existing classic release model no longer reflected the diverging networking market. Additionally, the classic release process, consisting of one release train for all feature commits, could not efficiently accommodate the sheer number of hardware offerings and software features. Furthermore, rapid growth of the Internet created an Internet service provider market that demanded increasingly faster development and new internetworking technologies.

Analysis of the internetworking market of the early 1990s reveals two emerging market theatres for Cisco and its IOS software:

- **The corporate network**—This network provides office desktop connections with client server and e-mail distribution. This includes emerging partners distribution networks, remote office connections, financial institution networks, and so forth. This market is also described in general terms as the enterprise market segment, and it wants to implement only proven and reliable technology.
- **The new Internet service providers**—This segment pushes the barriers of internetworking technology. They are generally referred to as early adopters of new technologies and, for the most part, they eagerly try new technology to gain a competitive advantage in their marketplace. The earlier the adopters, the better the chance of capturing a larger market share.

The proposed Cisco IOS release model, also called the next generation of release process (NGRP), was created to address the market segments as previously defined. Cisco IOS 11.2 main release provided only bug fixes and was aimed toward higher stability. It targeted the enterprise market. The IOS 11.2P platform was a superset of 11.2M but enabled new platforms and was attractive to those enterprise customers who sought the benefits of the price/performance of new platforms. Finally, IOS 11.2F became the release for early adopters. It provided new platforms, new features and bugs fixes. Figure 5-1 shows the difference between the NGRP and the classic release model, 11.1.

Figure 5-1 *The NGRP Model As It Evolved from the End of the Classic Release Model*

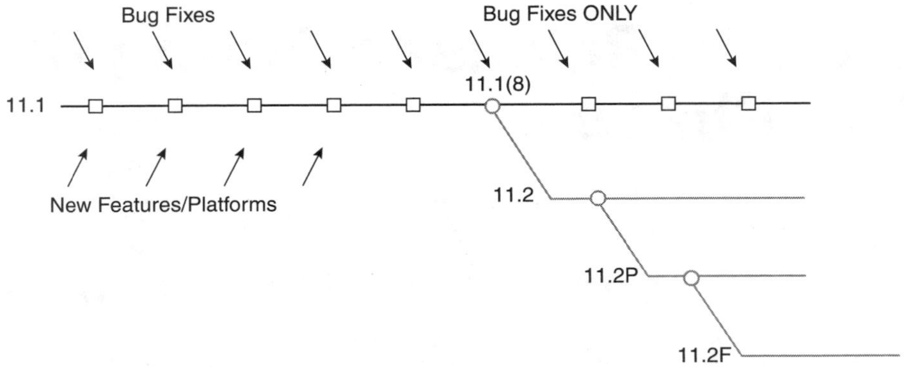

Description of the NGRP Release Process

The advent of the three concurrent major releases, 11.2, 11.2P, and 11.2F, characterizes the NGRP release process. Under this new process, no new features or platforms were added to the main software, 11.2, after its FCS milestone. Only bug fixes were integrated with each subsequent maintenance revision. As a result, the main Cisco IOS release progressively attained a higher code stability.

Cisco IOS 11.2P (the platform release) maintains a close relationship with 11.2M by regularly synchronizing with it. This process enables all bug fixes committed into 11.2M to trickle down to 11.2P. Moreover, 11.2P introduces new hardware and hardware-specific features in successive maintenance revisions.

Cisco IOS 11.2F (the feature release) was the combination of Cisco IOS 11.2M and Cisco IOS 11.2P. It picked up bug fixes and platform-specific features committed to both the main line and the platform release. It also directly introduced new software features to maintenance revisions of 11.2F. Upon close examination, we may notice that the IOS 11.2F release is in fact equivalent to the classic release train. It combined new features, new platforms, and bug fixes into one release. Figure 5-2 illustrates the integration of new features, platforms, and bug fixes in the NGRP model.

Figure 5-2 *The NGRP Model*

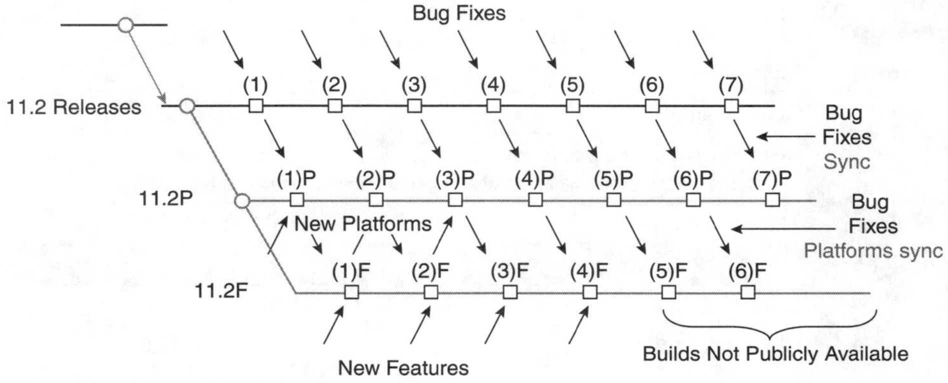

Cisco IOS 11.2 Main Release

Description	Cisco IOS 11.2 was deployed in October, 1996, as the first major release of the next generation of release process. 11.2P and 11.2F immediately followed it. Cisco IOS 11.2(1), as the first maintenance of 11.2, introduced features such as Network Address Translation (NAT), Named IP Access Control List, multimedia support, Quality of Service, multiprotocol routing, and advanced switching. Cisco IOS 11.2 reached GD status in April 1998 at maintenance revision 11.2(13a) and has since transitioned to mature maintenance mode.	
Product Support	**Main Features**	**Platforms**
	ODR enhancements	Cisco 7500, 7200, and 7000 series
	OSPF enhancements Multicast Routing	Cisco 4000 series (Cisco 4000, 4000-M, 4500, 4500-M, 4700, 4700-M, 2500, and 1000 series
	BGP4 enhancements DHCP NAT, named IP ACL features RSVP and RED features See the new features section of the release notes for the complete list of features.	AccessPro PC Card, Cisco AS5100, and AS5200
Feature Integration	The Cisco IOS Software Release 11.2 main line did not provide any additional new features other than the ones introduced in the first maintenance revision.	

Synchronization Points with Major Releases	**Based On**		**Ported Into**	
	11.1		11.3	
Release Type	Main release			
Target Market	General purpose			
Maintenance Releases	Regularly scheduled maintenance revisions, currently on a 14-week cycle; The maintenance revisions were on a seven-week cycle prior to 11.2(12).			
Interim Builds	Three-week cycle			
Recommended Migration	**From**		**To**	
	Cisco IOS 11.1(x)		Cisco IOS 11.2 or 12.0	
	Cisco IOS 11.2		Cisco IOS 11.3 or 12.0	
	Cisco IOS 11.2P		Cisco IOS 11.3T, 12.0, or 12.0T	
	Cisco IOS 11.2F		Cisco IOS 11.3T, 12.0, or 12.0T	
	The recommended migration path is the logical superceding release, which provides additional features and hardware support to the network without loss of previously configured functionality			
Life Cycle	**Milestones**	**Y2K Compliance**	**Certification**	**Other Dates**
	EOE tentatively scheduled for July, 2000, with Cisco IOS 11.2(23)	Yes	GD at 11.2(13a)	CCO FCS in April, 1996 GD in April, 1998 Restricted maintenance schedule for January, 2000
Internet Addresses	For more information, consult the following web pages: • Cisco IOS 11.2 Feature Matrix at http://www.cisco.com/warp/public/cc/cisco/mkt/ios/rel/prodlit/511_pp.htm • Release Notes for Cisco IOS Release 11.2 at http://www.cisco.com/univercd/cc/td/doc/product/software/ios112/rn112.htm • Cisco IOS Software Release 11.2 Product Bulletin at http://www.cisco.com/warp/public/732/112/487_pp.htm			
Comments	Cisco IOS 11.2 is one of the most stable releases available to date.			

Cisco IOS 11.2P (Platform Specific Major Release)

Description	Cisco IOS 11.2P is based on the main base code at 11.2(2) and was released in December, 1996. Cisco IOS 11.2, 11.2F, and 11.2P characterized the next generation of release process (NGRP) model. This model allows for no new additional features to be introduced to revisions of the main line, incremental integration of hardware features into 12.2P, and incremental integration of software features into 11.2F. Maintenance revisions of 11.2P periodically sync to 11.2. This enabled software fixes committed to 11.2 to trickle down into the maintenance revisions of 11.2P. Cisco IOS 11.2P reached mature maintenance in July, 1998. End of engineering is slated for July, 2000.	
Product Support	**Main Features**	**Platforms**
	Channelized T3 interface processor	Cisco 1600
	RSP Optimum or Flow Switched Fragmented IP packets	Cisco 3600
	The Cisco IOS Firewall Feature Set and Context-Based access control	Cisco AS5200
	NPE-200 Network Processing Engine for Cisco 7200 series router	Cisco 4000 and 4700 series
	100VG-AnyLAN port adapter	Cisco 7200 and 7000 series
	PA-4R-FDX Token Ring Full-Duplex port adapter	Cisco 2500
	PA-A1-OC3MM and PA-A1-OC3SM ATM port adapters	Cisco 2600
	PA-2CE1/PRI-75, PA-2CE1/PRI-120, and PA-2CT1/PRI Channelized E1 and T1 port adapters	Cisco AS5300
	FDDI Full-Duplex Single-Mode and Multimode port adapters	Cisco 3800 series
	High-Speed Serial interface port adapters	Cisco 1600 series
	SA-Comp/1 and SA-Comp/4 Data Compression Service adapters	CSRSM
	Synchronous serial port adapters	
	Data Encryption Service adapter	
	Clock Rate Command enhancements	

	Web Cache Control protocol 16-Port and 32-Port Asynchronous Network modules for Cisco 3600 series routers 56K 12-Port Modem modules for the Cisco AS5200 Access Server Compression Network module for Cisco 3600 series routers Packet OC-3 interface processor PA-8B-ST and PA-4B-U basic rate interface port adapters Half-Duplex and Bisync for Synchronous serial port adapters on Cisco 7200 series routers Particle-Based Transparent Bridging on Cisco 7200 series routers Fast-switched fragmented IP packets on Cisco 7200 series routers Fast-switched SMRP packets on Cisco 7200 series routers Turbo flooding of UDP datagrams on Cisco 7200 series routers Various new hardware, new port adapters, and new WIC were added with each maintenance revision. Refer to Cisco IOS 11.2 Feature Matrix for complete list at http://www.cisco.com/warp/public/cc/cisco/mkt/ios/rel/prodlit/511_pp.htm	
Feature Integration	Cisco IOS 11.2P was the platform release. During the NGRP, all Cisco hardware development was done on this release. Except for 11.2(7)P and 11.2(8)P, new hardware support was introduced into maintenance releases of 11.2P until 11.2(12)P.	
Synchronization Points with Major Releases	**Based On**	**Ported Into**
	Cisco IOS 11.2(2)	11.2F , 11.3, and 12.0
	Regularly sync to 11.2	
Release Type	NGRP major release	
Target Market	General purpose	
Maintenance Releases	Scheduled Regular Maintenance revisions, using a 14-week cycle	

<table>
<tr><td>Interim Builds</td><td colspan="4">Three-week build cycle</td></tr>
<tr><td rowspan="3">Recommended Migration</td><td colspan="2">From</td><td colspan="2">To</td></tr>
<tr><td colspan="2">11.2P</td><td colspan="2">11.3T, 12.0, or 12.0T</td></tr>
<tr><td colspan="4">The recommended migration path is the logical superceding release, which provides additional features and hardware support to the network without loss of previously configured functionality.</td></tr>
<tr><td rowspan="2">Life Cycle</td><td>Milestones</td><td>Y2K Compliance</td><td>Certification</td><td>Other Dates</td></tr>
<tr><td>EOE tentatively scheduled for July, 2000, with Cisco IOS 11.2(23)P</td><td>Yes</td><td>LD</td><td>CCO FCS in December, 1996</td></tr>
<tr><td>Internet Addresses</td><td colspan="4">For more information, consult the following web pages:
• Cisco IOS Hardware Matrix at http://www.cisco.com/cgi-bin/front.x/support/hwswmatrix/hwswmatrix.cgi
• Cisco IOS Release 11.2(2)P Features at http://www.cisco.com/univercd/cc/td/doc/product/software/ios112/fgtocp.htm
• Release Notes for Cisco IOS Release 11.2P at http://www.cisco.com/univercd/cc/td/doc/product/software/ios112/ios112p/xprn112/141503.htm
• Cisco IOS Software Release 11.2P Content and Platform Support at http://www.cisco.com/warp/public/cc/cisco/mkt/ios/rel/112/prodlit/553_pp.htm
• Cisco IOS Feature Guide for 11.2P at http://www.cisco.com/univercd/cc/td/doc/product/software/ios112/fgtocp.htm
• Cisco IOS 11.2 Feature Matrix for complete list at http://www.cisco.com/warp/public/cc/cisco/mkt/ios/rel/prodlit/511_pp.htm</td></tr>
<tr><td>Comments</td><td colspan="4">When 11.2F stopped shipping at 11.2(5)F, software features were directly committed to maintenance revisions of 11.2P.</td></tr>
</table>

Cisco IOS 11.2F Release (Feature Specific Major Release)

Description	Cisco IOS 11.2F is the third major release of the NGRP model. It was deployed as the software specific release. In addition to software fixes and hardware features that it acquires as the result of regular sync to 11.2P, software features newly developed by Cisco engineers were also directly committed to this release. Consequently, Cisco IOS 11.2F contained the highest concentration of new features and platforms of the three major releases of the NGRP phase. This constant addition and modification of its code base contributed to its demise. Cisco Systems decided to stop public release of 11.2F at 11.2(5)F	
Product Support	**Main Features**	**Platforms**
	AppleTalk access list enhancements Encrypted Kerberized Telnet Frame Relay MIB extensions Layer 2 Forwarding—Fast Switching Leased-Line ISDN at 128 kbps Socket Interface for TCP TCP Selective Acknowledgment TCP Timestamp Tunneling of asynchronous security protocols Double authentication DRP server agent IP enhanced IGRP route authentication IPeXchange Internet gateway IPX named access lists IPX SAP-after-RIP Per-User configuration PPP over ATM TCP Intercept Virtual Interface Template service Virtual Profiles Virtual Templates for protocol translation X.25 on ISDN X.28 emulation	Most platforms that run Cisco IOS software at the time were supported on 11.2F. Please consult the 11.2 feature matrix for a complete list of platforms and features. This release is end of life. Cisco 1000 series Cisco 2500 series Cisco 3800 series Cisco 4000/4500 series Cisco 7000/7200/7500 series Cisco 3600 series Cisco AS5200

<table>
<tr><td>Feature Integration</td><td colspan="4">Software features were incrementally introduced in successive maintenance revisions of 11.2F up to 11.2(5)F.</td></tr>
<tr><td rowspan="3">Synchronization Points with Major Releases</td><td colspan="2">Based On</td><td colspan="2">Ported Into</td></tr>
<tr><td colspan="2">Cisco IOS 11.2(2)</td><td colspan="2">11.3</td></tr>
<tr><td colspan="4">Successive maintenance revisions introduced additional new software features until 12.0(5)F</td></tr>
<tr><td>Release Type</td><td colspan="4">NGRP major release</td></tr>
<tr><td>Target Market</td><td colspan="4">General purpose</td></tr>
<tr><td>Maintenance Releases</td><td colspan="4">Scheduled Regular Maintenance revisions, using a six-week cycle prior to EOE</td></tr>
<tr><td>Interim Builds</td><td colspan="4">EOE</td></tr>
<tr><td rowspan="3">Recommended Migration</td><td colspan="2">From</td><td colspan="2">To</td></tr>
<tr><td colspan="2">11.2F</td><td colspan="2">11.3T or 12.0</td></tr>
<tr><td colspan="4">The recommended migration path is the logical superceding release, which provides additional features and hardware support to the network without loss of previously configured functionality.</td></tr>
<tr><td rowspan="2">Life Cycle</td><td>Milestones</td><td>Y2K Compliance</td><td>Certification</td><td>Other Dates</td></tr>
<tr><td>EOS at Cisco IOS 11.2(5)F; EOE in December, 1997</td><td>Yes</td><td>LD</td><td>CCO FCS in December, 1996</td></tr>
<tr><td>Internet Addresses</td><td colspan="4">For more information, consult the following web pages:
• Features of Cisco IOS 11.3 at http://www.cisco.com/warp/customer/cc/cisco/mkt/gen/bulletin/soft/ios_113/index.shtml
• Cisco IOS 11.2 Feature Matrix at http://www.cisco.com/warp/public/cc/cisco/mkt/ios/rel/113/prodlit/705_pp.htm
• Feature Guide for Cisco IOS Release 11.2 at http://www.cisco.com/univercd/cc/td/doc/product/software/ios112/fglistf.htm
• Release Notes for Cisco IOS Release 11.2F at http://www.cisco.com/univercd/cc/td/doc/product/software/ios112/rn112f.htm</td></tr>
<tr><td>Comments</td><td colspan="4">Cisco IOS 11.2F stopped shipping to customers at Cisco IOS 11.2(4)F. Internal rework and builds continued until Cisco IOS 11.2(7)F. In December 1997, Cisco IOS 11.3 was created, based on Cisco IOS 11.2(8)F.</td></tr>
</table>

Cisco IOS Early Deployment Software Based on 11.2 Releases

Cisco IOS 11.2BC

<table>
<tr><th>Description</th><td colspan="2">Cisco IOS 11.2BC is a specific technology early deployment release based on 11.2(12)P. In addition to features of 11.2(12)P, it introduced additional IBM Internetworking features including support of Channel Interface Processor (CIP) and TN3270-related features.</td></tr>
<tr><th rowspan="2">Product Support</th><th>Main Features</th><th>Platforms</th></tr>
<tr><td>CIP support
TN3270-related functionality
IBM networking solutions (SDLC, SNA, RSRB, DLSW)
LU address mapping (nailing)
LU model matching
Limiting LU sessions
1646 printer support
Function Management Header (FMH) support
Unformatted System Services Table (USSTAB) conversion
IP type of service and precedence setting
LU pooling and Response Time MIB
IP host backup
CLAW packing</td><td>Cisco 7500 series
Cisco 7000 with RSP</td></tr>
<tr><th>Feature Integration</th><td colspan="2">Maintenance revisions introduced incremental additional new features until 11.2(16)BC.</td></tr>
<tr><th rowspan="3">Synchronization Points with Major Releases</th><th>Based On</th><th>Ported Into</th></tr>
<tr><td>Cisco IOS 11.2(12)P</td><td>12.0 and 12.0 based ED</td></tr>
<tr><td colspan="2">Cisco IOS 11.2BC regularly sync to 11.2P.</td></tr>
<tr><th>Release Type</th><td colspan="2">STED</td></tr>
<tr><th>Target Market</th><td colspan="2">Enterprise, IBM networks</td></tr>
<tr><th>Maintenance Releases</th><td colspan="2">Scheduled Regular Maintenance following the Cisco IOS 11.2 cycle. Currently in mature maintenance mode.</td></tr>
<tr><th>Interim Builds</th><td colspan="2">Three-week cycle</td></tr>
</table>

Recommended Migration	From		To	
	11.2BC		12.0/12.0T	
	The recommended migration path is the logical superceding release, which provides additional features and hardware support to the network without loss of previously configured functionality.			
Life Cycle	Milestones	Y2K Compliance	Certification	Other Dates
	EOE tentatively scheduled for July, 2000 with Cisco IOS 11.2(23)BC	Yes	LD	—
Internet Addresses	For more information, consult the following web pages: • Feature Guide for Cisco Release 11.2BC at http://www.cisco.com/univercd/cc/td/doc/product/software/ios112/bclist.htm • Release Notes for Cisco IOS Release 11.2BC at http://www.cisco.com/univercd/cc/td/doc/product/software/ios112/rn112bc.htm			
Comments				

Cisco IOS 11.2GS

Description	Cisco IOS 11.2GS is a specific technology early deployment release based on 11.2(8)P. It introduced the Cisco 12000 gigabit switch routers (GSR) series with support for high-end port adapters and bandwidth aggregation software features. Cisco IOS 11.2GS has been customized to address the unique environment and requirements of Internet service providers and large corporate networks. The Cisco IOS 11.2GS also uses a slightly different numbering convention. For example, 11.2(14)GS1 has two parts: 11.2(14) and GS1. The first part, 11.2(14) shows the sync point level to 11.2(14)P while the "1" in "GS1" refers to the GSR specific maintenance revision level. Chapter 3, "Characteristics of Cisco IOS: Definitions, Naming Convention, Versioning, Numbering, and Feature Packaging," provides detailed instructions on Cisco IOS numbering conventions.	
Product Support	Main Features	Platforms
	11.2(14)GS: • New buffer header (internal SW feature) • CAR/ACL on OC48	Cisco 12000 Series (including the Cisco 12008 and 12012)

	• RP redundancy • SDH MPS (SDH equivalent of APS) • ChSTM4-STM1 (Raptor) 11.2(15)GS1 (Sync to 11.2(15)P): • WRED (w/out DRR) • Gigabit Ethernet (inc. ISL, HSRP) • 1483 bridged VC encapsulation • Frame Relay switching • 4xOC3-ATM features (SVC's, IP) • Multicast, PVC OAM mgmt) • APS on OC48 11.2(15)GS2: • GSR alarm board • Eight-port Fast Ethernet linecard • Spatial Reuse Protocol (SRP) linecard • Bandwidth aggregation • Refer to release notes HSRP, SDH MPS CAR/ACL on OC48 for RP redundancy WRED, Gigabit, Ethernet, 4xOC3-ATM features	GRS Alarm Board
Feature Integration	Maintenance revisions introduce additional features.	
Synchronization Points with Major Releases	**Based On**	**Ported Into**
	11.2(8)P	12.0T, 12.0S, and 12.0XE
	Cisco IOS 11.2GS syncs periodically to 11.2P. The major number of the maintenance revision indicates the sync level. For example, Cisco IOS 11.2(9)GS includes all software fixes of 11.2P up to 11.2(9)P.	
Release Type	STED	
Target Market	Internet service providers and large corporations.	
Maintenance Releases	As needed (refer to the "Synchronization Points with Major Releases" section).	

Interim Builds	As needed. Cisco IOS 11.2GS specific interim builds follow the naming convention such as 11.2(17)GS(4.3), where the numbers in parentheses following the "GS" identifier indicate the interim level. In this example, it indicates the third interim build of the maintenance revision 11.2(17)GS(4).			
Recommended Migration	**From**		**To**	
	11.2GS		12.0S/12.0XE	
	The recommended migration path is the logical superceding release, which brings additional features and hardware support to the network without loss of previously configured functionality.			
Life Cycle	**Milestones**	**Y2K Compliance**	**Certification**	**Other Dates**
	—	Yes	LD	CCO FCS in October, 1997, with 11.2(9)GS
Internet Addresses	For more information, consult the following web pages: • Cisco IOS Software Release 11.2GS Product Bulleting at http://www.cisco.com/warp/public/cc/cisco/mkt/ios/rel/112/ed/prodlit/717_pp.htm • Release Notes for Cisco 12000 Series • Gigabit switch routers for Cisco IOS • Release 11.2 GS at http://www.cisco.com/univercd/cc/td/doc/product/software/ios112/ios112p/gsr/rn12000.htm			
Comments	Only the most recent maintenance release of Cisco IOS 11.2GS (11.2(18)GS(x) or above) is available through manufacturing. All maintenance releases are available electronically through CCO.			

Cisco IOS 11.2SA

Description	Cisco IOS 11.2SA specific technology release was based on Cisco IOS 11.2(8)P and optimized for ATM switching. It was introduced to provide support for the Catalyst 2900XL ATM Module with later support for the Catalyst 3500XL.	
Product Support	**Main Features**	**Platforms**
	ATM modules VLANs TACACS+ STP UplinkFast Network Time protocol	Catalyst 2900XL Catalyst 3500XL

	Catalyst 3500 Series XL switch support at 11.2(8.1)SA6 Multiple virtual LANs Each ATM trunk supports a maximum of 64 active virtual LANs (VLANs) The ATM module supports multiple emulated LANs (ELANs). You can logically group users on Ethernet and ATM networks by mapping VLANs on the Ethernet network to ELANs on the ATM network. RFC-1483 PVC support. The ATM modules support multiple VLAN mappings for RFC-1483 logical link control (LLC) encapsulation for bridged Ethernet. (IEEE 802.3). With RFC 1483, you can transport Ethernet frames over PVCs.	
Feature Integration		
Synchronization Points with Major Releases	**Based On**	**Ported Into**
	Cisco IOS 11.2(8)SA	12.0WX, 12.1E
	Cisco IOS 11.2(8)SA is a one-time sync release. It only synced to 11.2(8)P (and some 11.2(8)P interim). Therefore, successive maintenance releases continue to show the sync level by following the naming structure 11.2(8)SA2, 11.2(8)SA3, or 11.2(8.1)SA6 and so on.	
Release Type	STED	
Target Market	LAN switching	
Maintenance Releases	Because Cisco IOS 11.2SA is a one-time sync release, subsequent revisions will follow the naming convention of Cisco IOS 11.2(8)SA2, 11.2(8)SA3, and so on.	
Interim Builds	Catalyst 2900 series XL switches are supported by a special release of Cisco IOS software that is not released on the same regular maintenance cycle used for traditional router platforms.	
Recommended Migration	**From**	**To**
	11.2(8)SAx	11.2(8)SAx=1, 12.0(2)XF, 12.0XP
	The recommended migration path is the logical superceding release, which provides additional features and hardware support to the network without loss of previously configured functionality.	

Life Cycle	Milestones	Y2K Compliance	Certification	Other Dates
	—	Yes	LD	CCO FCS in December, 1997
Internet Addresses	For more information, consult the following web pages: • Release Notes for the Catalyst 2900 Series XL Cisco IOS Release 11.2(8)SA2 at http://www.cisco.com/univercd/cc/td/doc/product/lan/c2900xl/c29xl/78492304.htm • Catalyst 2900 and 3500 Release Notes at http://www.cisco.com/univercd/cc/td/doc/product/lan/c2900xl/index.htm			
Comments				

Cisco IOS 11.2WA3

Description	Cisco IOS 11.2WA3 is a specific technology early deployment release based on Cisco 11.2(2)P. It introduces functionality of the LightStream 1010 ATM switch. The Cisco IOS 11.2WA3(x) releases are another example of the expanded Cisco IOS number convention. The numbers before the STED identifier indicate the sync level with 11.2P and the numbers following the ED identifier WA (that is, 3(x)) show the STED-specific major release number and maintenance revision level. The Cisco IOS numbering convention of Chapter 3 provides more detail on this subject.	
Product Support	**Main Features**	**Platforms**
	ATM switching functionality	LightStream 1010
	E.164 enhancement	
	ATM accounting	
	ATM remote monitoring (RMON)	
	25-Mbps port adapter module (PAM)	
	OC-12 Long Reach PAM	
	OC-3 Long Reach PAM	
	Configurable well-known VCs for Signaling/ILMI/PNNI	
	Soft-VC route optimization	
	E.164 address translation	

	UNI 4.0 features (ABR Signaling, PCR negotiation, Frame Discard, Anycast, and incremental QoS parameters) Access List based on Time of Day and Access List MIB PNNI MIBs IISP Auto configuration LANE services (LES/BUS/LECS) on ASP Enable/disable of Signaling/PNNI/SSCOP on a per-port basis			
Feature Integration	Successive maintenance revisions of Cisco IOS 11.2WA introduced new features.			
Synchronization Points with Major Releases	**Based On**		**Ported Into**	
	11.2(2)P		11.3WA4 and 12.0W5	
	This release is synced to 11.2P on an as needed basis.			
Release Type	STED			
Target Market	Enterprises, ISP, Network service providers			
Maintenance Releases	Regular maintenance revisions until EOE			
Interim Builds	As needed			
Recommended Migration	**From**		**To**	
	11.2WA3		11.3WA4 or 12.0W5(x) or 12.1E	
	The recommended migration path is the logical superceding release, which provides additional features and hardware support to the network without loss of previously configured functionality.			
Life Cycle	**Milestones**	**Y2K Compliance**	**Certification**	**Other Dates**
	EOE in early 2000	Yes	LD	—
Internet Addresses	For more information, consult the following web page: • Cisco IOS 11.2 Release Notes for LightStream 1010 ATM Switch Software at http://www.cisco.com/univercd/cc/td/doc/product/atm/ls1010s/wa3/11_2_10/4012_04.htm			
Comments	The LightStream 1010 supports the routing of ATM signaling requests across a network of switches using ATM routing protocols. Two standard routing protocols have been developed by the ATM Forum: Interim InterSwitch Signaling Protocol (IISP) and the Private Network-to-Network Interface (PNNI) Protocol version 1.0. Both protocols are supported by the Cisco IOS software for LightStream 1010.			

Cisco IOS 11.2(4)XA

Description	Cisco IOS 11.2(4)XA is an XED based on 11.2(4)P. In addition to software features of 11.2(4)P, it introduced added support for newly developed network modules for the Cisco 1600 series and 3600 series routers. Cisco IOS 11.2(4)XA received no maintenance revisions and all functionality were ported into 11.2(6)P and later revisions.	
Product Support	**Main Features**	**Platforms**
	Platform-specific features One-port serial One-port ISDN BRI with S/T interface One-port ISDN BRI with NT1 and U interface	Cisco 1600 series
	Platform-specific features One Ethernet and two WAN interface card slots Two Ethernet and two WAN interface card slots One Ethernet, one Token Ring, and two WAN interface card slots One-port serial WAN interface card One-port ISDN BRI WAN interface card One-port ISDN BRI with NT1 WAN interface card One-port ISDN BRI with NT1 and U interface card slots One-port channelized T1/ISDN PRI network module One-port channelized T1/ISDN PRI with CSU network module One-port channelized T1/ISDN PRI network module Two-port channelized T1/ISDN PRI with CSU network module One-port channelized E1/ISDN PRI balanced network module One-port channelized E1/ISDN PRI unbalanced network module	Cisco 3600 series

	Two-port channelized E1/ISDN PRI balanced network module Two-port channelized E1/ISDN PRI unbalanced network module Blank network module panel Four-port ISDN BRI network module with an S/T interface Four-port ISDN BRI with NT1 network module Eight-port ISDN BRI network module with an S/T interface Eight-port ISDN BRI with NT1 network module Four-port asynchronous/synchronous serial network module Eight-port asynchronous/synchronous serial network module One-port Ethernet network module			
Feature Integration	Refer to software features of 11.2(4)P.			
Synchronization Points with Major Releases	**Based On**		**Ported Into**	
	Cisco 11.2(4)P		Cisco 11.2(6)P	
Release Type	XED			
Target Market	SOHO, SMB, ISP, Enterprise			
Maintenance Releases				
Interim Builds				
Recommended Migration	**From**		**To**	
	11.2(4)XA		11.2(5)P	
			12.0/12.0T	
	The recommended migration path is the logical superceding release, which provides additional features and hardware support to the network without loss of previously configured functionality.			
Life Cycle	**Milestones**	**Y2K Compliance**	**Certification**	**Other Dates**
	EOE	Yes	LD	—
	Short-lived release			

Internet Addresses	For more information, consult the following web pages: • Cisco IOS Release 11.2(4)XA Features at http://www.cisco.com/univercd/cc/td/doc/product/software/ios112/fgtocpxa.htm • Release Notes for Cisco IOS Release 11.2(4)XA at http://www.cisco.com/univercd/cc/td/doc/product/software/ios112/rn112xa.htm	
Comments		

Cisco IOS 11.2(9)XA

Description	Cisco IOS 11.2(9)XA is an XED based on Cisco IOS 11.2(9)P. It contains the features of 11.2P up to 11.2(9)P maintenance revision. Cisco IOS 11.2(9)XA introduced support for the AS5300 platform and support for integrated digital modems for the 3600 platforms. Cisco IOS 11.2(9)XA received no maintenance revisions and all functionality were ported into Cisco 11.2(10)P and subsequent releases.			
Product Support	**Main Features**		**Platforms**	
	New Platform support		Cisco 5300	
	Integrated Digital Modems		Cisco 3600	
	Refer to Release Notes for complete list of features.			
Feature Integration				
Synchronization Points with Major Releases	**Based On**		**Ported Into**	
	11.2(9)P		11.2(10)P	
Release Type	XED			
Target Market	Dial market, ISP, Enterprise, Branch Office			
Maintenance Releases				
Interim Builds				
Recommended Migration	**From**		**To**	
	11.2(9)XA		11.2(10)P, 11.3AA	
	The recommended migration path is the logical superceding release, which provides additional features and hardware support to the network without loss of previously configured functionality.			
Life Cycle	**Milestones**	**Y2K Compliance**	**Certification**	**Other Dates**
	EOE	Yes	LD	CCO FCS in November, 1997

	Short-lived release
Internet Addresses	For more information, consult the following web pages: • Cisco IOS Software Release 11.2(9)XA Product Bulletin at http://www.cisco.com/warp/public/732/112/683_pp.htm • Cisco IOS Release 11.2(2)P Features at http://www.cisco.com/univercd/cc/td/doc/product/software/ios112/fgtocp.htm
Comments	

CHAPTER 6

Cisco IOS Releases 11.3/11.3T and Related STED: The Beginning of the Technology Release Model

Starting with Cisco IOS 11.3 and 11.3T in late 1997, Cisco Systems adopted another IOS software release model, which is characterized by two simultaneous major releases: the main line release, 11.3, and the closely-related 11.3T CTED release.

The technology release process is still used today, although some changes are expected in the 12.1 and 12.1T timeframe. The dual-track structure of this model enables Cisco engineers to develop numerous features and platform enhancements in one train, while consistently maintaining stable revisions in the main line release. In order to achieve this goal, the main line (11.3) only provides incremental bug fixes to the base code with no additional new features, thereby achieving higher stability and availability at the expense of newer features. The accompanying CTED releases, 11.3T, and their parented STED, SMED, and XED releases serve as vehicles for delivering new software and hardware features.

The Plan for Deploying 11.3 and 11.3T

During the life cycle of the NGRP release model, Cisco Systems, Inc., quickly realized that it was not very efficient to concurrently maintain three Cisco IOS major releases. Furthermore, the NGRP release model exhibited some redundancy that did not add any value to the usage and implementation of IOS releases. A decision was made to stop 11.2F and transition it to 11.3 main release. Cisco IOS release 11.3 is based on all the features contained in 11.2F and is accompanied by 11.3T (initially called 11.3P), which serves as the combined platform and feature release vehicle.

The Transitional Nature of 11.3/11.3T

Although the 11.3/11.3T pair came about because of the shortcomings of the NGRP release model, the transition to the dual-track technology model was a gradual evolution marked by intermediary solutions. For example, although 11.2F was taken off the market, the 11.2 main release and the 11.2P platform release continued to provide regular maintenance revisions. In order to prevent the complete deficit of the software feature release vehicle, 11.3/11.3T was created as the transitional release to bridge the gap between 11.2 releases and the next major release, 12.0. In order to expedite this transition, the plan was that 11.3T would only accept new features and platforms for the first three maintenance revisions (up to 1.3(3)T). Thereafter, only bug fixes would be allowed and a private branch of 11.3T would be created to start the development process for 12.0 and 12.0T. Albeit a good plan, it undoubtedly contributed to the creation of new STED releases and the extension of the life cycle of existing STED such 11.1CA and 11.1CC.

Indeed, you might have noticed that although 11.3 is a newer IOS release, it is not the migration path for 11.1CA, 11.1CC, or 11.1CT. It is not even the migration path for IOS STED based on 11.2. This non-linear upgrade migration path shows that the 11.3/11.3T pair is a strategic Cisco IOS release which enables Cisco IOS software to consolidate the features of 11.2/11.2P/11.2F into one major release and move toward a unified release. For those reasons, 11.3/11.3T needed to reach EOE as soon as possible to avoid further divergence in IOS software releases. An IOS release train that unified previously deployed IOS ED was badly needed and the 12.0/12.0T pair was the ultimate goal. Figure 6-1 and Figure 6-2 show the evolution of maintenance revisions and the path for integration of new features between Cisco IOS 11.2(7)F and the 12.0/12.0T pair.

Starting with the technology release process, the introduction of features and platforms were done through the use of a software pre-integration branch. This enabled the various development groups to resolve conflicts before merging to the release branch, thereby reducing software conflicts.

Figure 6-1 *The Release Model Transitions from the 11.2F NGRP Line to the 11.3/11.3T Pair*

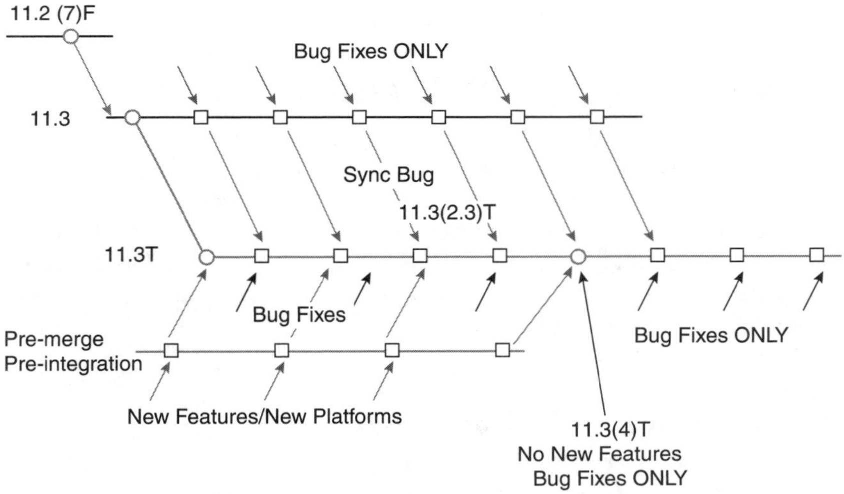

Figure 6-2 *The Transition of the 11.3/11.3T Pair into the 12.0/12.0T Pair*

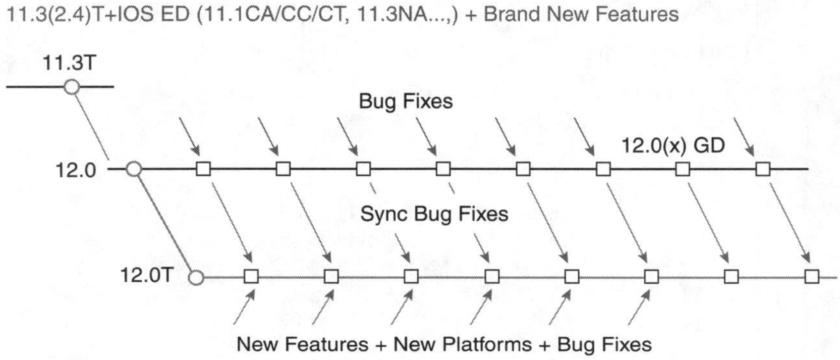

Cisco IOS 11.3 Main Release

Description	Cisco IOS 11.3 is based on Cisco IOS 11.2(7)F maintenance revision. Cisco IOS 11.3(1) was released on December 22, 1997, as a short-term transitional main release, which will not be considered for GD certification. Cisco IOS 11.3 is a stable software release that provides the market place with the features of 11.2F combined with the platforms committed up to 11.2(4)P. As a main release, Cisco IOS 11.3 (also referred to as 11.3M) is now closed to new additional features. Successive maintenance revisions provided incremental bug fixes only.	
Product Support	**Main Features**	**Platforms**
	As with other Cisco IOS main releases, release 11.3 is a main release that supports all active shipping products. For a full list of features and platforms, see the Release Notes and product bulletin 706.	
	Reflexive Access List	Cisco AS5200
	TCP Intercept	Cisco AS5100
	HTTP Security	Cisco 1000 series
	Fast Switch Policy routing	Cisco 1600 series
	VLAN routing	Cisco 3600
	ISL	Cisco 2500
	Easy IP features (NAT, PAP, DHCP)	

<table>
<tr><td></td><td colspan="2">ISDN Caller ID Callback
PPP over ATM
L2F load sharing
Vendor-Proprietary RADIUS Attributes
Encrypted Kerberized Telnet</td><td colspan="2">MC 3800
Cisco 4500–4700
RSM
LS 1010
Cisco 7200
Cisco 7500</td></tr>
<tr><td>Feature Integration</td><td colspan="4">The maintenance releases for Cisco IOS 11.3 regularly fix core code issues; however, the main line does not receive feature or product enhancements.</td></tr>
<tr><td rowspan="2">Synchronization Points with Major Releases</td><td colspan="2">Based On</td><td colspan="2">Ported Into</td></tr>
<tr><td colspan="2">Cisco IOS 11.2(7)F</td><td colspan="2">12.0/12.0T</td></tr>
<tr><td>Release Type</td><td colspan="4">Main release</td></tr>
<tr><td>Target Market</td><td colspan="4">General purpose</td></tr>
<tr><td>Maintenance Releases</td><td colspan="4">Starting with 11.3 and 11.3T, the regularly scheduled maintenance revision cycle was increased from six weeks to an eight-week cycle.</td></tr>
<tr><td>Interim Builds</td><td colspan="4">Weekly builds</td></tr>
<tr><td rowspan="4">Recommended Migration</td><td colspan="2">From</td><td colspan="2">To</td></tr>
<tr><td colspan="2">11.3</td><td colspan="2">12.0</td></tr>
<tr><td colspan="2">11.3T</td><td colspan="2">12.0/12.0T</td></tr>
<tr><td colspan="4">The recommended migration path is the logical superceding release, which provides additional features and hardware support to the network without loss of previously configured functionality.</td></tr>
<tr><td rowspan="2">Life Cycle</td><td>Milestones</td><td>Y2K Compliance</td><td>Certification</td><td>Other Dates</td></tr>
<tr><td>EOE in August, 1999 at 11.3(11)</td><td>Yes</td><td>LD</td><td>FCS in December, 1997</td></tr>
<tr><td>Internet Addresses</td><td colspan="4">For more information, consult the following web pages:
• Product Specific Release Notes for Cisco IOS Release 11.3 at http://www.cisco.com/univercd/cc/td/doc/product/software/ios113ed/ios113p/index.htm
• Cisco IOS Software Release 11.3 Product Bulletins at http://www.cisco.com/warp/public/732/113/</td></tr>
<tr><td>Comments</td><td colspan="4">Cisco IOS 11.3/11.3T saw the introduction of the "Plus" feature sets identified by a lowercase "s" in the feature set definition. They provide value-added features to existing IOS packages. However, it is important to note that the content "Plus" features sets varies from platform to platform. The following is an example of Plus Feature Sets:</td></tr>
</table>

	Platforms	Value-added "Plus" Feature Set Content
	1003/4	OSPF, PIM, SMRP, NLSP, ATIP, ATAURP, RSVP, and NAT
	1005	OSPF, PIM, SMRP, NLSP, ATIP, ATAURP, RSVP, NAT, FRSVC, full WAN, X.25
	1600	OSPF, IPMULTICAST, NHRP, NTP, NAT, RSVP, FRAM-RELAY-SVC AT images also include SMRP, ATIP, AURP. IPX IMAGES ALSO INCLUDE NLSP, NHRP
	2500	NAT, RMON, IBM, MMP, and VPDN/L2F
	3600	NAT, IBM, MMP, and VPDN/L2F
	4000	NAT, IBM, and MMP
	4500/4700	NAT, ISL, LANE, IBM, and MMP
	AS5200	NAT, PROTOCOL TRANSLATION, V120, RMON, MANAGED MODEMS, IBM, V110 MMP, and VPDN/L2F

Cisco IOS 11.3T Consolidated Technology Release

Description	Cisco IOS 11.3T is a CTED, which was released in December, 1997. In addition to bug fixes, each subsequent maintenance releases of Cisco IOS 11.3T introduced new Cisco IOS functionality and/or support for newer Cisco hardware. Refer to the Release Notes for a full listing of features. In order to provide migration and transition of features and hardware to the next major release (Cisco IOS 12.0), new code additions stopped at Cisco IOS 11.3(4)T. Maintenance releases thereafter only integrated bug fixes, allowing this technology release train to change its focus towards higher stability and a quality level similar to that of its parent, Cisco IOS 11.3M.	
Product Support	**Main Features**	**Platforms**
	IPSec, Cisco IOS Firewall Feature Set (including CBAC and Java blocking) IP Security (IPSec) Cisco IOS Firewall Feature Set Always On/Dynamic ISDN (AO/DI) Multiple ISDN switch types Cisco VPDN enhancements Voice over IP Protocol-Independent Multicast (PIM) version 2 MS Callback Named method lists for AAA authorization and accounting Digital Subscriber Line Bridge Support PPP over Frame Relay GRE VPN QoS RSM/TR-VLAN GRE precedence, VoIP, and IBM enhancements See Release Notes for complete list of features	Cisco AS5200 Cisco AS5100 Cisco 1000 series Cisco 1600 series Cisco 3600 series Cisco 2600 series Cisco 4000/4500/4700 Cisco 2500 Cisco 7200 Cisco 7000/7500 RSM CS-RSP LS1010
Feature Integration	Cisco IOS 11.3T focuses on delivering new features and platform enhancements. All features and platforms up to release 11.3(3)T have been ported to the 12.0 and 12.0T major releases. After maintenance release 11.3(3)T, no new features or platforms were introduced in this release.	

<table>
<tr><th rowspan="3">Synchronization Points with Major Releases</th><th colspan="2">Based On</th><th colspan="2">Ported Into</th></tr>
<tr><td colspan="2">11.2(7)F</td><td colspan="2">12.0/12.0T</td></tr>
<tr><td colspan="4">Cisco IOS 11.3T regularly inherits core code fixes from the maintenance releases of 11.3 main line.</td></tr>
<tr><th>Release Type</th><td colspan="4">CTED</td></tr>
<tr><th>Target Market</th><td colspan="4">General purpose—multi-technology support</td></tr>
<tr><th>Maintenance Releases</th><td colspan="4">Scheduled Regular Maintenance revisions using an eight-week cycle</td></tr>
<tr><th>Interim Builds</th><td colspan="4">Weekly builds</td></tr>
<tr><th rowspan="4">Recommended Migration</th><th colspan="2">From</th><th colspan="2">To</th></tr>
<tr><td colspan="2">11.3</td><td colspan="2">12.0/12.0T</td></tr>
<tr><td colspan="2">11.3T</td><td colspan="2">12.0/12.0T</td></tr>
<tr><td colspan="4">The recommended migration path is the logical superceding release, which provides additional features and hardware support to the network without loss of previously configured functionality.</td></tr>
<tr><th rowspan="2">Life Cycle</th><th>Milestones</th><th>Y2K Compliance</th><th>Certification</th><th>Other Dates</th></tr>
<tr><td>EOE in August, 1999, at Cisco IOS 11.3(11)T</td><td>Yes</td><td>LD</td><td>CCO FCS in December, 1997</td></tr>
<tr><th>Internet Addresses</th><td colspan="4">For more information, consult the following web pages:
• Cisco IOS Software Release 11.3T New Features at http://www.cisco.com/warp/public/cc/cisco/mkt/ios/rel/113/prodlit/712_pp.htm
• Cisco IOS 11.3T New Features (Documentation) at http://www.cisco.com/univercd/cc/td/doc/product/software/ios113ed/113t/index.htm</td></tr>
<tr><th>Comments</th><td colspan="4">Migration to 12.0 or 12.0T is recommended. Although no new features were added after 11.3(3)T, support for some network modules of the 3600 and 2600 series routers were introduced after 11.3(4)T. Additionally, the TR-RSM was introduced in 11.3(6)T.</td></tr>
</table>

Specific Technology Early Deployment Release Based on 11.3 Major Releases

Cisco IOS 11.3AA

Description	Cisco IOS 11.3AA is an STED based on the 11.3T CTED. It delivers access server and dial solution technologies. It introduced the AS5800 and provided several enhancements to the AS5300, AS5200 and the 7200 series routers. The Cisco IOS 11.3AA release also contributed to IOS software in general by introducing some very important scalability features which became part of the infrastructure changes implemented in 12.0 base code. As maintenance revisions are performed on the 11.3T releases, the software fixes are synced to maintenance releases of 11.3AA. For every maintenance release of 11.3, there is a maintenance release of 11.3AA, which contains all defect corrections on 11.3/11.3T, in addition to new functionality unique to 11.3AA.	
Product Support	**Main Features**	**Platforms**
	Access Servers and dial-in features including L2F, L2TP, and Nitro redundancy	5800 Series
	Cisco AS5800 Universal Access Server feature module	5200 and 5300 Series
	System error messages for Cisco AS5800 Universal Access Server	Cisco 3640
	Cisco IOS file system	c7200 Series
	Conditionally triggered debugging	
	Shelf Discovery and Auto-configuration	
	Health Monitor	
	Virtual Console	
	FTP server	
	Syslog disk logging	
	AAA scalability feature	
	OSPF LSA group pacing	
	OSPF Point-to-Multipoint Networks with Neighbors	
	Cisco AS5800	
	Multiple ISDN switch types	
	National ISDN switch types	
	7200 scalability	
	See Release Notes for full list of features	

<table>
<tr><td>Feature Integration</td><td colspan="4">New features and functionality have been added to subsequent maintenance releases.</td></tr>
<tr><td rowspan="3">Synchronization Points with Major Releases</td><td colspan="2">Based On</td><td colspan="2">Ported Into</td></tr>
<tr><td colspan="2">11.3T</td><td colspan="2">12.0T and 12.0 based ED</td></tr>
<tr><td colspan="4">As with other ED releases, this release regularly synchronizes bug fixes to the base code of its parent main line release, Cisco IOS 11.3.</td></tr>
<tr><td>Release Type</td><td colspan="4">STED/SMED</td></tr>
<tr><td>Target Market</td><td colspan="4">Internet service providers, Network access providers, and large enterprises</td></tr>
<tr><td>Maintenance Releases</td><td colspan="4">Scheduled Regular Maintenance, on an eight-week cycle</td></tr>
<tr><td>Interim Builds</td><td colspan="4">Bi-weekly builds</td></tr>
<tr><td rowspan="4">Recommended Migration</td><td colspan="2">From</td><td colspan="2">To</td></tr>
<tr><td colspan="2">11.3(3)AA[1]</td><td colspan="2">12.0 /12.0T</td></tr>
<tr><td colspan="2">11.3AA</td><td colspan="2">12.0T or 12.0 based ED</td></tr>
<tr><td colspan="4">The recommended migration path is the logical superceding release, which provides additional features and hardware support to the network without loss of previously configured functionality.</td></tr>
<tr><td rowspan="2">Life Cycle</td><td>Milestones</td><td>Y2K Compliance</td><td>Certification</td><td>Other Dates</td></tr>
<tr><td>EOE at 11.3(11)AA in August, 1999
EOE of 7200 images at 11.3(9)AA in October, 1999</td><td>Yes</td><td>LD</td><td>CCO FCS in March, 1998 with 11.3(2)AA.
11.3(1)AA was not officially released to the public.</td></tr>
<tr><td>Internet Addresses</td><td colspan="4">For more information, consult the following web pages:
• Cisco IOS Software Release 11.3AA Product Bulletin at http://www.cisco.com/warp/public/cc/cisco/mkt/ios/rel/113/prodlit/738_pp.htm
• Cisco IOS Software Release 11.3T New Features at http://www.cisco.com/warp/public/cc/cisco/mkt/ios/rel/113/prodlit/712_pp.htm
• Cisco IOS 11.3T New Features (Documentation) at http://www.cisco.com/univercd/cc/td/doc/product/software/ios113ed/113t/index.htm</td></tr>
<tr><td>Comments</td><td colspan="4">11.3AA is now EOE. No further maintenance revisions will be provided after 11.3(11)AA.</td></tr>
</table>

1. Cisco IOS 11.3AA merged with Cisco IOS 12.0 at Cisco IOS 11.3(3)AA. The migration path for Cisco IOS 11.3(4)AA or later should be to Cisco IOS 12.0T.

Cisco IOS 11.3DA

Description	Cisco IOS 11.3(1)DA was released on July 28, 1998, as an STED to deliver functionality for the digital subscriber line access multiplexer (DSLAM), the Cisco 6200. Cisco IOS 11.3(1)DA*x* is directly based on 11.3(1) main maintenance release. The "x" increases sequentially with each maintenance revision, the first of which was 11.3(1)DA1. Cisco IOS 11.3(x)DA is not a full-fledged Cisco IOS routing software release. It leverages Cisco IOS integrated applications such as Telnet, FTP, SNMP, and Command Line Interface (CLI) to provide xDSL and DSLAM specific features. The Cisco 6200 DSLAM is a layer 2 ATM multiplexer which does not support layer 3 routing despite the fact that it runs Cisco IOS software. Because of this dissociation from IOS features, 11.3(1)DAx maintenance revisions will not sync with 11.3 maintenance revisions.	
Product Support	**Main Features**	**Platforms**
	DSLAM functionality Eight-Port CAP Subscriber Line card One-Port OC-3 Network Trunk cards Management Processor card In-Band management Eight-Port DMT Subscriber Line card	Cisco 6200 xDSL
Feature Integration	Maintenance releases of this release provided continued enhancements	
Synchronization Points with Major Releases	**Based On**	**Ported Into**
	11.3	12.0T or 12.0(5)DA
	No regular sync to 11.3	
Release Type	STED	
Target Market	Telco and Internet service providers	
Maintenance Releases	Restricted maintenance with irregular maintenance revisions	
Interim Builds	As needed	
Recommended Migration	**From**	**To**
	11.3DA	12.0T or 12.0DA
	The recommended migration path is the logical superceding release, which provides additional features and hardware support to the network without loss of previously configured functionality.	

Life Cycle	Milestones	Y2K Compliance	Certification	Other Dates
	FCS: 7/28/98	Yes	LD	EOE date not set
Internet Addresses	For more information, consult the following web pages: • Product Specific Release Notes for Cisco IOS Release 11.3 at http://www.cisco.com/univercd/cc/td/doc/product/software/ios113ed/ios113p/index.htm • Cisco IOS 11.3DA Release Notes at http://www.cisco.com/univercd/cc/td/doc/product/dsl_prod/6200/rnda3.htm • Cisco IOS Software Release 11.3 Product Bulletins at http://www.cisco.com/warp/public/732/113/			
Comments				

Cisco IOS 11.3DB

Description	Cisco IOS 11.3(5)DB1 was released in December, 1998 to introduce the node route processor (NRP) on the Cisco 6400 Universal Access Concentrator (UAC) platform. The NRP is a router blade, which resides in the Cisco 6400 platform. It is a custom hardware design derived from a Cisco 7200 router to offer Digital Subscriber Loop (xDSL) technology features. The Cisco 6400 is a broadband Concentrator enabling Network Operators, PTTs, and ISPs to deliver aggregate xDSL services. Cisco IOS 11.3DB is an STED based on 11.3AA and directly parented to 11.3(5)AA.	
Product Support	**Main Features**	**Platforms**
	NEBS/ETSI-compliant xDSL technology via NRP ATM switching and routing capabilities NEBS level 3-certified and ETSI-compliant Ethernet Cable Consolidation OC12/STM4 VPI/VCI Indexing to service profile L2TP per User PPP Session Aggregation (L2TP tunneling and bridging) or Session Termination (routing) IPCP Subnet SSG with CEF SSG IOS NAT	Cisco 6400
Feature Integration	New features are added through the maintenance releases.	

<table>
<tr><th rowspan="3">Synchronization Points with Major Releases</th><th colspan="2">Based On</th><th colspan="2">Ported Into</th></tr>
<tr><td colspan="2">11.3(5)AA</td><td colspan="2">12.0DA</td></tr>
<tr><td colspan="4">The Cisco IOS 11.3DB ED release train is directly synchronized to Cisco IOS 11.3(5)AA. Cisco IOS 11.3(5)AA is pulled from Cisco IOS 11.3T. For that reason, Cisco IOS 11.3DB will inherit all bug fixes from Cisco IOS 11.3AA on scheduled maintenance releases and will reach end of engineering (EOE) the same time as Cisco IOS 11.3AA.</td></tr>
<tr><th>Release Type</th><td colspan="4">STED</td></tr>
<tr><th>Target Market</th><td colspan="4">Internet service providers, Network Operators, and PTTs</td></tr>
<tr><th>Maintenance Releases</th><td colspan="4">Cisco IOS 11.3DB irregularly sync to 11.3AA. The sync level is indicated in the maintenance revision number. For example, 11.3(8)BD is sync to 11.3(8)AA. Additionally, 11.3(8)DB1 is a maintenance rebuild of 11.3(8)DB which is sync to 11.3(8)AA.</td></tr>
<tr><th>Interim Builds</th><td colspan="4">As needed</td></tr>
<tr><th rowspan="3">Recommended Migration</th><th colspan="2">From</th><th colspan="2">To</th></tr>
<tr><td colspan="2">11.3DB</td><td colspan="2">12.0DC</td></tr>
<tr><td colspan="4">The recommended migration path is the logical superceding release, which provides additional features and hardware support to the network without loss of previously configured functionality.</td></tr>
<tr><th rowspan="2">Life Cycle</th><th>Milestones</th><th>Y2K Compliance</th><th>Certification</th><th>Other Dates</th></tr>
<tr><td>Milestones follow the Cisco IOS 11.3AA life cycle</td><td>Yes</td><td>LD</td><td>CCO FCS in December, 1998</td></tr>
<tr><th>Internet Addresses</th><td colspan="4">For more information, consult the following web pages:
• Cisco IOS 11.3DB Product Bulletin at http://www.cisco.com/warp/customer/cc/cisco/mkt/ios/rel/113/prodlit/870_pp.htm
• Cisco IOS Software Release 11.3AA Product Bulletin at http://www.cisco.com/warp/public/cc/cisco/mkt/ios/rel/113/prodlit/738_pp.htm
• Cisco IOS Software Release 11.3T New Features at http://www.cisco.com/warp/public/cc/cisco/mkt/ios/rel/113/prodlit/712_pp.htm</td></tr>
<tr><th>Comments</th><td colspan="4">Cisco IOS 11.3(5)DBx refers to a DB release that is parented to Cisco IOS 11.3(5)AA. The “x” suffix, which can be 1, 2, 3, and so on, represents the successive maintenance rebuild numbers.</td></tr>
</table>

Cisco IOS 11.3HA

Description	Cisco IOS 11.3HA is an STED release train that delivers functionality for the Integrated Synchronous Optical Network/Synchronous Digital Hierarchy (SONET/SDH) Router 3300 series platform. The Cisco Integrated SONET/SDH Router (ISR) 3303 is an access platform with full SONET interoperability that enables service providers to deliver time-division multiplexing (TDM) -based voice and IP provision IP services in a single, integrated solution. Cisco IOS 11.3(4)HA1 was the first HA release. This release is unique in that it inherits only ISR 3300-related bug fixes from the 11.3 mainline. Cisco IOS 11.3(4)HA will eventually merge into 12.1T. Cisco IOS 11.3(4)HA delivers functionality for the following features:	
Product Support	**Main Features**	**Platforms**
	OC-3 interface support; section, line, STS path and VT path (near-end and far-end) PM SONET UPSR support for VTs; SONET APS support; revertive and non-revertive switching STS-1 pass-through; UPSR auto-provisioning; VT PM on dropped circuits OC, STS-1, and VT loopbacks; Remote defect identification (RDI); redundant synchronization via OC-3s Synchronous status messaging (rx/tx); OSI DCC via TL 1 tunneling; OSI CLNP interoperability Section Trace support DSX-1 signal level with LBO; Near-end and far-end PM; Extended Superframe (ESF) Superframe (SF); Unframed (UNF); Alternate mark inversion (AMI) B8ZS; DS1 equipment and facility loopbacks; Integrated CSU functionality for serial DS1	ISR 3300 series

	Integrated BER testing and pattern generation; DS1 retiming for external DS1 lines; Single timing input through external DS1			
	DS1 Retiming			
	Static routing; policy routing; ARP			
	Cisco Discovery Protocol (CDP); Comprehensive Access Lists; Custom & Priority Queuing MIB			
	Custom Queuing Addresses and Protocols; Fast Switched Policy Routing; ICMP services			
	ICMP Path Discovery; In-bound Access Lists; Integrated IS-IS			
Feature Integration	Most routing functions of 11.3(4) were removed and replaced by ISR 3300 specific features. The list of IOS commands not supported by this release can be found at http://www.cisco.com/univercd/cc/td/doc/product/access/acs_mod/3300/comdhand/33chbapp.htm			
Synchronization Points with Major Releases	**Based On**		**Ported Into**	
	11.3(4)		12.1T	
	Cisco IOS 11.3HA does not regularly sync to 11.3, hence the numbers 11.3(4)HAx where x increments with every build. The last sync point of 11.3(4) is always indicated.			
Release Type	STED			
Target Market	Local exchange carriers and other telecommunication companies			
Maintenance Releases	Maintenance revisions are selective and follow an eight-week cycle; the naming convention reflects this pattern: 11.3(4)HA1, 11.3(4)HA2, 11.3(4)HA3, and so on. (See Chapter 2, " An Overview of the Evolution of Cisco IOS Release Models," for more information on the naming convention.)			
Interim Builds	No interim builds			
Recommended Migration	**From**		**To**	
	11.3(4)HAx		12.1(x)T	
	The recommended migration path is the logical superceding release, which provides additional features and hardware support to the network without loss of previously configured functionality.			
Life Cycle	**Milestones**	**Y2K Compliance**	**Certification**	**Other Dates**
	—	Yes	LD	FCS in April, 1999
	EOE date was not announced as of this writing.			

Internet Addresses	For more information, consult the following web page: • The Cisco IOS 11.3(4)HA Product Bulletin at http://www.cisco.com/warp/customer/cc/cisco/mkt/ios/rel/113/prodlit/952_pp.htm
Comments	

Cisco IOS 11.3MA

Description	Cisco IOS 11.3(1)MA is an STED release focused on delivering functionality for the Cisco MC3800 multiservice concentrators series. This STED Cisco IOS release applies only to the Cisco MC3810 which delivers several Voice over IP, digital, and analog modem features. The Cisco IOS 11.3(1)MA train is fully synchronized with Cisco IOS 11.3(1)T at 11.3(1)T. In order to provide successive non-sync maintenance revisions, the MA release train adopted a slightly different numbering scheme. The difference between maintenance releases is tracked via a number designation after the ED identifier "MA". For example, Cisco IOS 11.3(1)MA1, 11.3(1)MA2, and 11.3(1)MA3 are the first three maintenance releases of the MA release train. The 11.3(1) prefix indicates the synchronization point to Cisco 11.3(1)T, while the trailing MA1, MA2, and MA3 designate the maintenance releases. Similarly, interim builds are denoted as Cisco IOS 11.3(1)MA2.1, 11.3(1)MA2.2, and 11.3(1)MA3.1.	
Product Support	**Main Features**	**Platforms**
	Voice, Analog Async ports	Cisco MC3810
	Dual Tone Multiple Frequency (DTMF)	
	Voice Quality	
	Packetized Voice	
	Pass-Through Voice	
	Fax support	
	Call management	
	Video support	
	Voice	
	Video	
	Multiflex Trunk support	
	Frame Relay and ATM	
	Multiflex Trunk module	
	Digital voice module	
	Analog voice module	
	Voice compression module	

<table>
<tr><th>Feature Integration</th><td colspan="4">New features have been added to subsequent maintenance releases.</td></tr>
<tr><th rowspan="3">Synchronization Points with Major Releases</th><th colspan="2">Based On</th><th colspan="2">Ported Into</th></tr>
<tr><td colspan="2">11.3T</td><td colspan="2">12.0(3)T or later</td></tr>
<tr><td colspan="4">This STED release is synchronized with 11.3(1)T.</td></tr>
<tr><th>Release Type</th><td colspan="4">SMED/STED</td></tr>
<tr><th>Target Market</th><td colspan="4">Network Operators, ISP, SOHO</td></tr>
<tr><th>Maintenance Releases</th><td colspan="4">Scheduled Regular Maintenance, based on an eight-week cycle</td></tr>
<tr><th>Interim Builds</th><td colspan="4">Weekly builds</td></tr>
<tr><th rowspan="5">Recommended Migration</th><th colspan="2">From</th><th colspan="2">To</th></tr>
<tr><td colspan="2">11.3(1)MA1 through 11.3(1)MA5</td><td colspan="2">Cisco IOS 12.0(1)XA</td></tr>
<tr><td colspan="2">11.3(1)MA5 or later</td><td colspan="2">Cisco IOS 12.0(3)T or later</td></tr>
<tr><td colspan="2">Cisco IOS 11.3(1)MAx</td><td colspan="2">Cisco 12.0(3)XG* (new features) or 12.0(5)T</td></tr>
<tr><td colspan="4">The recommended migration path is the logical superceding release, which provides additional features and hardware support to the network without loss of previously configured functionality.</td></tr>
<tr><th rowspan="3">Life Cycle</th><th>Milestones</th><th>Y2K Compliance</th><th>Certification</th><th>Other Dates</th></tr>
<tr><td>EOE in December, 1998 at Cisco IOS 11.3(1)MA7</td><td>Yes</td><td>LD</td><td>CCO FCS in February, 1998</td></tr>
<tr><td colspan="4">Ported to Cisco IOS 12.0(3)T</td></tr>
<tr><th>Internet Addresses</th><td colspan="4">For further or related information, consult the following page:
• Cisco IOS 11.3MA Release Notes at http://lbj.cisco.com/push_targets1/ucdit/cc/td/doc/product/software/ios113ed/ios113p/rn3810.htm</td></tr>
<tr><th>Comments</th><td colspan="4">The Cisco 3801 and 3803 are EOL.</td></tr>
</table>

Cisco IOS 11.3NA

Description	Cisco IOS 11.3NA is an STED release train that was introduced to deliver functionality for a variety of voice, video, and multimedia features including Cisco Voice over IP (VoIP), H.323 Multimedia Conference Manager, Voice-to-Fax, and other voice/video compression techniques. It also introduced capabilities for new hardware such as the Cable modem or Universal broadband router (UBR). Cisco IOS 11.3(2)NA, directly parented by Cisco IOS 11.3(2)T, was the first maintenance of the NA release which was created to bridge the gap between Cisco IOS 11.3(3)T and 12.0(3)T releases.	
Product Support	**Main Features**	**Platforms**
	Cisco VoIP and multimedia features H.323 Multimedia Conference Manager Voice-to-Fax and other voice/video features • IVR • Rotary call pattern RSVP • IP telephony VoIP GateKeeper • E.164 address support VoIP Gateway • Telephone prefix E1 R2 Signaling Upstream traffic Shaping QoS Profile enforcement The complete list of features is available at http://www.cisco.com/univercd/cc/td/doc/product/software/ios113ed/113na/113naall/index.htm.	Cisco 2500 and 3600 Cisco 5300
Feature Integration	Cisco IOS 11.3NA provided incremental new features with each maintenance revision.	
Synchronization Points with Major Releases	**Based On**	**Ported Into**
	11.3T	12.0T
	As with other ED releases, this release regularly synchronizes bug fixes to the base code of its parent main line release, Cisco IOS 11.3T	
Release Type	STED	

Target Market	Early adapters using advanced voice over IP, Video Conferencing, and other multimedia technologies. SOHO Cable modem market and ISP.			
Maintenance Releases	Scheduled Regular Maintenance, eight-week cycle			
Interim Builds	Weekly builds			
Recommended Migration	**From**		**To**	
	11.3NA		12.0T or 12.0 based ED	
	The recommended migration path is the logical superceding release, which provides additional features and hardware support to the network without loss of previously configured functionality.			
Life Cycle	**Milestones**	**Y2K Compliance**	**Certification**	**Other Dates**
	EOE in August, 1999 at 11.3(11)NA	Yes	LD	CCO FCS in May, 1998
Internet Addresses	For more information, consult the following web pages: • Cisco IOS Software Release 11.3NA Product Bulletin at http://www.cisco.com/warp/public/cc/cisco/mkt/ios/rel/113/prodlit/762_pp.htm • Cisco IOS 11.3 NA New Features (Documentation) at http://www.cisco.com/univercd/cc/td/doc/product/software/ios113ed/113na/index.htm			
Comments	Only 11.3(2)NA through 11.3(5)NA introduce major new features. 11.3(6)NA2 was not a rebuild but in fact an XED based on 11.3(6)NA branch.			

Cisco IOS 11.3(x)WA4(x)

Description	The Cisco IOS 11.3(x)WA4(x) is an STED deployed to deliver a variety of advanced layer 2 and layer 3 switching features including the Multilayer Switching (MLS) and Multiprotocol over ATM (MPOA). This release began with 11.3(2)WA4(x) and added feature and platform enhancements as well as bug fixes with subsequent maintenance revisions. As described in Chapter 3,"Characteristics of Cisco IOS: Definitions, Naming Convention, Versioning, Numbering, and Feature Packaging," this release uses a slightly modified version of the Cisco IOS software numbering conventions. The first part of the version number indicates the major release number followed in parentheses by the sync maintenance revision number. For example, 11.3(6) of 11.3(6)WA4(9) shows that this maintenance is sync to 11.3(6) main release. The second part of the name is made of the STED identifier, WA4, which is followed in parentheses by the STED specific revision number, (that is, WA4(9) of 11.3(6)WA4(9)).

<table>
<tr><th rowspan="2">Product Support</th><th colspan="2">Main Features</th><th>Platforms</th></tr>
<tr><td colspan="2">MLS, Layer 3 switching features, and ATM features
MPOA
Catalyst 5000 series multilayer LAN switches.
Catalyst 5000 series RSMs providing Cisco IOS-based multiprotocol routing and network services.
The NetFlow Feature Card (NFFC) in the Cisco 4500, Cisco 4700, Cisco 7200, and Cisco 7500 series routers provides a modular feature card upgrade for the Catalyst 5000 series Supervisor Engine III to provide Layer 3 switching.</td><td>Cisco Catalyst 5000 RSM, LightStream 1010 family of switches
Cisco 4500 and 4700 routers
Cisco 7200
Cisco 8500 series</td></tr>
<tr><th>Feature Integration</th><td colspan="3">Features and enhancements were integrated into subsequent maintenance revisions.</td></tr>
<tr><th rowspan="3">Synchronization Points with Major Releases</th><th colspan="2">Based On</th><th>Ported Into</th></tr>
<tr><td colspan="2">11.3(2)</td><td>12.0W5/12.1E</td></tr>
<tr><td colspan="3">11.3WA4 IOS release software is directly sync to 11.3 maintenance revisions. For example, 11.3(6)WA4(x) is bug to bug sync to 11.3(6) main release.</td></tr>
<tr><th>Release Type</th><td colspan="3">STED</td></tr>
<tr><th>Target Market</th><td colspan="3">Workgroups, ATM LANE, VLAN, Layer 3 Switching</td></tr>
<tr><th rowspan="6">Maintenance Releases</th><td colspan="3">Cisco IOS 11.3(x)WA4(x) uses an eight-week maintenance cycle.
Please note the IOS numbering scheme used by the Wx releases is slightly different. Refer to Chapter 3 for a detailed description of the numbering convention.</td></tr>
<tr><th>Maintenance Release</th><th>Enhancement</th><th>CCO FCS Date</th></tr>
<tr><td>Cisco IOS 11.3(2a)WA4(4)</td><td>LightStream 1010 and RSP images</td><td>June 11, 1998</td></tr>
<tr><td>Cisco IOS 11.3(2.5) WA4(4m)</td><td>Digital modem card carrier NM, LAN emulation (LANE), permanent virtual circuit (PVC) shaping</td><td>June 15, 1998</td></tr>
<tr><td>Cisco IOS 11.3(2a)WA4(4a)</td><td>See Release Notes</td><td>July 7, 1998</td></tr>
<tr><td>Cisco IOS 11.3(3)WA4(5)</td><td>EARL2 and MPOA</td><td>July 24, 1998</td></tr>
</table>

	Cisco IOS 11.2(15)WA3(6)	See Release Notes		August 15, 1998
	Cisco IOS 11.3(3a)WA4(6)	See Release Notes		August 15, 1998
	Cisco IOS 11.3(4)WA4(7)	See Release Notes		September, 1998
Interim Builds	Weekly builds			
Recommended Migration	Due to the variation of platforms and feature support within this release, Cisco IOS 11.3(x)WA4(x) has the following multiple migration paths.			
	Platforms/ Images	**Last Maintenance Support on Cisco IOS 11.3WA**		**Migration Path**
	c5rsm, c4500, c7200, rsp	11.3(11)WA4(14)		12.0(3c)W5(8)
	c5atm-wblane, c5atm-wtall	11.3(11)WA4(14)		12.0(4a)W5(10)
	c5atm-wbpvc	11.3(6)WA4(9d)		12.1(x)E*
	c5atm-wtoken	11.3(11)WA4(14)		12.0(6)T
	ls1010	11.3(5)WA4(8d)		12.0(2a)
	Others	11.3WA or 12.0W5		12.1(1)E
	The recommended migration path is the logical superceding release, which provides additional features and hardware support to the network without loss of previously configured functionality.			
Life Cycle	**Milestones**	**Y2K Compliance**	**Certification**	**Other Dates**
	EOE: 11/22/99	Yes	LD	—
Internet Addresses	For more information, consult the following web pages: • Release Notes for Cisco IOS Release 11.3WA4 at http://www.cisco.com/univercd/cc/td/doc/product/lan/cat5000/c5krn/rsm_rns/5990_01.htm • Cisco IOS Software Release 11.3T New Features at http://www.cisco.com/warp/public/cc/cisco/mkt/ios/rel/113/prodlit/712_pp.htm • Cisco IOS 11.3T New Features (Documentation) at http://www.cisco.com/univercd/cc/td/doc/product/software/ios113ed/113t/index.htm			

Comments	MLS features support the following: • Catalyst 5000 series multilayer LAN switches. • Catalyst 5000 series RSMs providing Cisco IOS-based multiprotocol routing and network services. • The NFFC in the Cisco 4500, Cisco 4700, Cisco 7200, and Cisco 7500 series routers is a modular feature card upgrade for the Catalyst 5000 series Supervisor Engine III to provide Layer 3 switching. Some milestones: • Cisco IOS 11.3(2a)WA4(4) was released on June 11, 1998, for LightStream 1010 and Route/Switch Processor (RSP) images. • Cisco IOS 11.3(2.5) WA4(4m) for the digital modem card carrier NM (LAN emulation (LANE), permanent virtual circuit (PVC) shaping) was released on June 15, 1998. • Cisco IOS 11.3(2a)WA4(4a) was released on July 7, 1998. • Cisco IOS 11.3(3)WA4(5), with support for Enhanced Address Recognition Logic 2 (EARL2) and MPOA, was released on July 24, 1998. • Cisco IOS 11.2(15)WA3(6) was released on August 15, 1998. • Cisco IOS 11.3(3a)WA4(6) was released on August 15, 1998. • Cisco IOS 11.3(4)WA4(7) was released on September 11, 1998. Cisco IOS 11.3WA4 releases have reached EOE.

Cisco IOS Release 11.3(2)XA

Description	Cisco IOS 11.3(2)XA is a one-time, technology-specific, "X" release or XED. It is based on Cisco IOS 11.3(2)T and was created to introduce new IOS features for the uBR7246 Universal Broadband routers and the Cisco 2600 series routers. In addition to the uBRE7246, this release also supports the features of 11.3(2)T.	
Product Support	**Main Features**	**Platforms**
	All features of its parent 11.3(2)T	uBR7246
	Cable modem capabilities	Cisco 2600 series
Feature Integration	One-time release	
Synchronization Points with Major Releases	**Based On**	**Ported Into**
	Cisco IOS 11.3(2)T	Cisco 11.3(3)T and later
Release Type	XED	
Target Market	Cable modems, cable providers, ISP	

<table>
<tr><th>Maintenance Releases</th><td colspan="4">One-time release</td></tr>
<tr><th>Interim Builds</th><td colspan="4">—</td></tr>
<tr><th rowspan="3">Recommended Migration</th><th colspan="2">From</th><th colspan="2">To</th></tr>
<tr><td colspan="2">11.3(2)XA</td><td colspan="2">11.3(3)T, 12.0(1)T, or a 12.0-based X release</td></tr>
<tr><td colspan="4">The recommended migration path is the logical superceding release, which provides additional features and hardware support to the network without loss of previously configured functionality.</td></tr>
<tr><th rowspan="2">Life Cycle</th><th>Milestones</th><th>Y2K Compliance</th><th>Certification</th><th>Other Dates</th></tr>
<tr><td>One-time release/ EOE</td><td>Yes</td><td>LD</td><td>EOL</td></tr>
<tr><th>Internet Addresses</th><td colspan="4">For more information, consult the following web page:
• Cisco IOS Software Release 11.3(2)XA Product Bulletin at http://www.cisco.com/warp/customer/cc/cisco/mkt/ios/rel/113/prodlit/731_pp.htm</td></tr>
<tr><th>Comments</th><td colspan="4"></td></tr>
</table>

CHAPTER 7

Current Cisco IOS Releases: Extension of the Technology Model

As I alluded to in Chapter 6, "Cisco IOS Releases 11.3/11.3T and Related STED: The Beginning of the Technology Release Model," the Cisco IOS release 11.3/11.3T pair were released to bridge the gap between 11.2F and the next major release, 12.0. This transition accounted for a stable main line, 11.3M, and successive deployment of new features and new platforms via 11.3T. On the horizon, Cisco IOS 12.0 was launched to bring together all active Cisco IOS releases to produce a truly unified release. Figure 7-1 shows the consolidation plan for the preceding releases to the 12.0/12.0T pair, not including the XED releases.

Figure 7-1 *Timeline of Active Cisco IOS Releases*

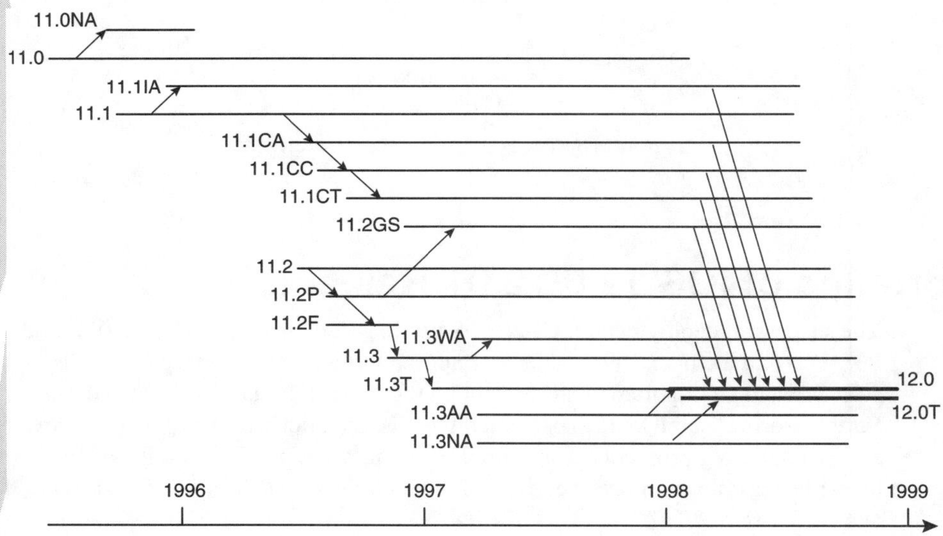

Unification of the Releases, IOS Version 12.0/12.0T

In order to be a true unifying release, Cisco IOS 12.0 needed to include features and functionality deployed in 11.1CA, 11.1CC, 11.1CT, 11.3AA, 11.3NA, 11.3WA4, 11.3M, and 11.3T. The Cisco IOS release team would meet their goal if hardware running any of the above Cisco IOS versions could be upgraded to an IOS 12.0 image without loss of functionality. Not withstanding the details, one can only imagine the challenge of continuing to provide new networking features in regular maintenance revisions of current IOS releases, while creating a new IOS release train that brings all existing Cisco IOS features together. Figure 7-2 illustrates the complex coordination that was required to make 12.0 a unified IOS software release.

Figure 7-2 *The Making of Cisco IOS 12.0*

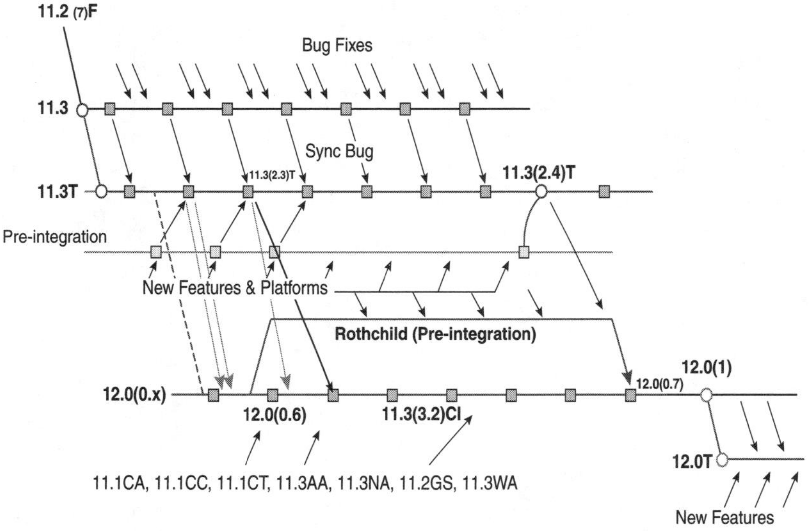

Importance of IOS 12.0/12.0T Releases

The successful deployment of Cisco IOS version 12.0 (also known as 12.0M) and its sister IOS 12.0T in October 1998 marks an important milestone in the legacy of Cisco IOS software and an important achievement by the Cisco IOS development and release team. Furthermore, Cisco IOS 12.0 permitted the consolidation of several new improvements in advanced routing protocols. These improvements were previously only available in disparate specific technology early deployment releases such as 11.1CC, 11.1CT, 11.3AA and 11.3NA.

Difference Between IOS 12.0 and 12.0T

It is important to note the difference between Cisco IOS 12.0 and the CTED IOS 12.0T. Cisco IOS 12.0 is a consolidation of previously deployed features. Examples include MPOA from 11.3WA4, CEF from 11.1CC, Tag Switching from 11.1CT, and H.323 multimedia Conference manager from 11.3NA. Although 12.0 did not itself introduce new networking functionality, there were significant Cisco IOS infrastructure changes. Furthermore, a new and improved Cisco IOS file system was introduced along with ftp, rcp, and other remote access capabilities. Cisco IOS 12.0 was also designed to achieve GD certification.

Cisco IOS 12.0T on the other hand, augmented everything that 12.0M had to offer and added new software and hardware features. Some new features of 12.0T include expression MIB, Output Modifier, CAR on GSR, IPX MLS, Timed Access List, BGP Rework, Fast Switched Compressed RTP header, H.323 Version 2, Advanced Voice Over IP features, and many more. (See Appendix C for the complete list.) In fact, more than 100 enhancements supporting new features, hardware, and protocols are expected to be introduced in 12.0T by the time it reaches mature maintenance.

Description of Current Release Process

Starting with IOS 12.0/120T pair, the technology release process enabled new features and platforms to be added to the 12.0T CTED up to the sixth maintenance revision. Figure 7-3 illustrates the current Cisco IOS release process, indicating the path to future releases. Upon successful release of the sixth maintenance revision, the 12.0T CTED source code will be relabeled as the next main IOS release train. In essence, 12.0(6)T was to become 12.1(1). [For unrelated reasons, the sixth maintenance revision of 12.0T was called 12.0(7)T. 12.(6)T was never built. Hence, 12.0(7)T became 12.1(1)] In other words, 12.0(7)T and 12.1(1) are exactly the same except for additional bug fixes in 12.1(1). Consistent with the nature of IOS mainlines, the newly created main release will provide maintenance revisions until it reaches GD and eventually EOE (about 24 months later). At the same time, a new IOS CTED will be cloned from the main line 12.1(1) to serve as the vehicle for newly developed IOS features. This process of piggy-back should theoretically continue until the next major IOS milestone.

Figure 7-3 *The Current Cisco IOS Release Process*

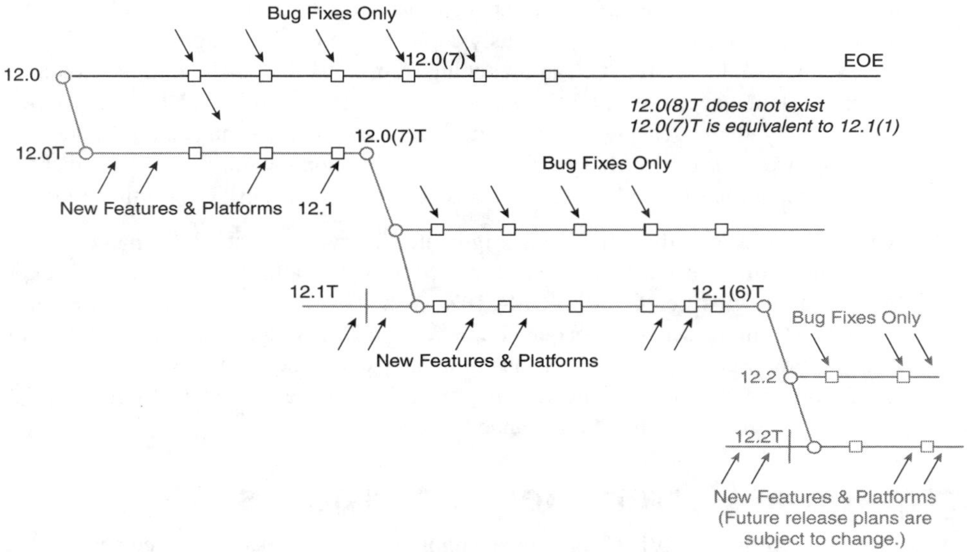

Appearance of Multiple Short-Lived Early Deployment Releases

Cisco Systems, Inc. experienced tremendous growth in the mid to late nineties. For example, in 1999 alone, Cisco shipped more products than in the preceding five years combined! It was impossible to integrate and test all these products into only one Cisco IOS software within the eight-week maintenance cycle. As a result, an extension to the release model enabled Cisco business units to successfully develop and timely market features on IOS XED while maintaining continued convergence to the CTED. The short-lived IOS early deployment or X releases (XED) became the preferred vehicle for newly developed IOS features and platforms.

Cisco IOS XED are always based on the major release CTED, such as 12.0T or 12.1T, and they merge back to the parent CTED at the earliest possible commit opportunity. Figure 7-4 is an illustration of the XED release process, including porting features back to the CTED. (See Figure 2-5 for more detail).

Figure 7-4 *The Cisco IOS XED Release Process*

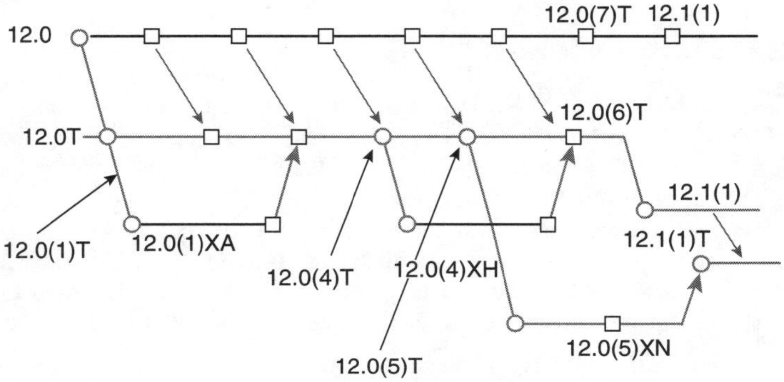

It should be noted that Cisco IOS XED releases do not provide maintenance revisions. They are one-time Cisco IOS releases that occasionally provide software rebuilds as fixes to catastrophic defects. Cisco hardware running IOS XED should be upgraded to the equivalent IOS CTED software image at or above the integration point of the XED software. For example, Cisco IOS XED version 12.0(1)XA would upgrade to 12.0(3)T or later, as shown in Figure 7-4.

Summary Specifications of Cisco IOS Releases

Cisco IOS 12.0 Main Release

Description	Cisco IOS 12.0 or 12.0M is the main line consolidation of all preceding Cisco IOS releases. Based on Cisco IOS 11.3(3.2)T, the 12.0 main line was deployed in September 1998 as a GD candidate release. Among the ED releases that were ported to Cisco IOS 12.0 are Cisco IOS 11.1CA, Cisco IOS 11.1CC, and Cisco IOS 11.1CT, up to and including features and hardware in Cisco IOS 11.1(17)C(x). As such, features added to Cisco IOS 11.1(19)CC are not available in Cisco IOS 12.0. They are ported to Cisco IOS 12.0T and/or 12.0S. Features and platforms that were once dispersed and inherent to a particular pre-12.0 train have been merged into Cisco IOS 12.0/12.0T base code. To ensure the stability and quality requirement of this main software and GD candidate release, Cisco IOS 12.0 was closed to any additional new features. Maintenance revisions of 12.0 only provide incremental software fixes to features already present in the code base at FCS.	
Product Support	**Main Features**	**Platforms**
	As with other Cisco IOS main releases, release 12.0 is a main release that supports all active shipping products. For a full list of features and platforms, see the Release Notes	
	The consolidation of previous ED releases CAR, wRED, dWFQ, MPOA over Ether LANE	All active Cisco Routers (except for AS5800)
Feature Integration	The maintenance revisions for Cisco IOS 12.0 regularly fix core code defects. However, the main line does not receive feature or product enhancements.	
Synchronization Points with Major Releases	**Based On**	**Ported Into**
	Cisco IOS 11.3(3.2)T	12.0T
Release Type	Main release	
Target Market	General purpose/Enterprise	
Maintenance Releases	Scheduled Regular Maintenance revisions using an eight-week cycle	
Interim Builds	Weekly builds	
Recommended Migration	**From**	**To**
	12.0	12.1
	The recommended migration path is the logical superceding release, which provides additional features and hardware support to the network without loss of previously configured functionality.	

Life Cycle	Milestones	Y2K Compliance	Certification	Other Dates
	GD announcment on 1/25/2000	Yes	GD candidate 12.0(8)[1] on 1/25/2000	CCO FCS in September, 1998
Internet Addresses	For more information, consult the following web pages: • Cisco IOS Software Release 12.0 New Features at http://www.cisco.com/warp/customer/cc/cisco/mkt/ios/rel/120/prodlit/816_pb.htm • Cisco IOS Software Release 12.0 New and Changed Information at http://www.cisco.com/univercd/cc/td/doc/product/software/ios120/relnote/xprn120/120newf.htm • Cisco IOS Software Release 12.0 Product Bulletins at http://www.cisco.com/warp/public/732/120/			
Comments	Major infrastructure and scalability changes were introduced with Cisco IOS 12.0.			

1. 12.0(8) is the first maintenance of 12.0 to be certified as GD. Every subsequent maintenance thereafter is also GD.

Cisco IOS Release 12.0T CTED

Description	Cisco IOS 12.0T is the CTED release that focuses on progressive deployment of new features in addition to making enhancements to existing functionality. Cisco IOS 12.0T was first shipped in November 1998. In addition to software defect fixes integrated from the 12.0M line, each subsequent maintenance revision of Cisco IOS 12.0T introduces new Cisco hardware and software functionality. As defined by the technology release process, Cisco IOS 12.0T ended in December 1999 with the sixth maintenance revisions. The release was relabeled and became the new 12.1 main line release.	
Product Support	**Main Features**	**Platforms**
	A complete list of features can be found at http://www.cisco.com/warp/customer/cc/cisco/mkt/ios/rel/120/prodlit/815_pb.htm and in Appendix C. CLI String Search Layer 2 Tunneling Protocol (L2TP) BGP Rework MBGP DHCP server FS-CRTP Voice over IP Voice over FR Voice over ATM Security features SNA switch Flow Random Early Detection Class-based Weighted Fair Queuing NetFlow policy routing Trigerred IP Response time reporter MPLS Class of Service Multicast routing monitor Time-based Access-List H.323 Version 2 Voice over IP enhancement for 5300 High Density Voice Over IP	All shipping Cisco platforms Cisco 1000 Cisco 1600 Cisco 1700 Cisco 2500 Cisco 2600 Cisco 2800 Cisco 2900 ATM Cisco 3600 Cisco 6400 Cisco 7100 Cisco 7200 Cisco 800 Cisco 805 Cat 8510 MSR Cat 8510 CSR Cat 8540 CSR MC3810 LS1010 RPM RSP UBR7200 UBR 900

	SS7 Access Controller Signaling Controller Network Director Forwarding agent ATM Lane Fast Simple Redundancy protocol			
Feature Integration	Software revision builds of Cisco IOS 12.0T inherit bug fixes from the 12.0 main line via periodic sync.			
Synchronization Points with Major Releases	**Based On**		**Ported Into**	
	12.0		12.1T	
Release Type	CTED			
Target Market	General purpose			
Maintenance Releases	Scheduled Regular Maintenance revisions using an eight-week cycle			
Interim Builds	Weekly builds			
Recommended Migration	**From**		**To**	
	12.0T		12.1T	
	The recommended migration path is the logical superceding release, which provides additional features and hardware support to the network without loss of previously configured functionality.			
Life Cycle	**Milestones**	**Y2K Compliance**	**Certification**	**Other Dates**
	12.0(7)T last of 12.0T was released in December 1999.	Yes	LD	CCO FCS in November, 1998
Internet Addresses	For more information, consult the following web pages: • 12.0T new Features at http://www.cisco.com/warp/public/cc/cisco/mkt/ios/rel/120/prodlit/809_pp.htm • Release Notes for Cisco IOS 12.0 and 12.0T at http://www.cisco.com/univercd/cc/td/doc/product/software/ios120/relnote/index.htm • Cisco IOS Software Release 12.0T Feature Matrix at http://www.cisco.com/warp/customer/cc/cisco/mkt/ios/rel/120/prodlit/815_pb.htm • New Features in Release 12.0 T at http://www.cisco.com/univercd/cc/td/doc/product/software/ios120/120newft/120t/index.htm			
Comments	Cisco IOS 12.0(6)T was never built. 12.0(7)T is the sixth maintenance revision and the last of 12.0T release.			

Specific Technology Early Deployment Releases Based on 12.0

Cisco IOS Release 12.0DA

Description	Cisco IOS 12.0DA is an STED based on 12.0T, which was deployed to deliver support for the numerous Digital Subscriber Line (DSL) technology specific platforms. Cisco IOS 12.0DA supports platforms such as the Cisco 6260. The Cisco 6260 DSL Access Multiplexer is an ATM-based DSL Access Concentrator. Cisco IOS Release 12.0(5)DA runs on the Network Interface-2 card (NI-2) of the Cisco 6260, enabling the release to be configured and managed using the Cisco IOS command-line interface (CLI) features and capabilities. Cisco IOS 12.0(5)DA has been optimized for the xDSL technology and does not support layer 3 routing or networking capabilities for user data flow. The Cisco IOS 12.0DA release also supports the Cisco 6130 and the Cisco 6100 DSL Access Concentrators, configured with the NI-2 hardware.	
Product Support	**Main Features**	**Platforms**
	Advanced Services ATM Architecture Scalability with Fair-service Subtending Standards-compliant ADSL support Switched virtual circuits (SVCs) Soft PVC provisioning Life-line POTS Splitter support Support for the Cisco IOS command line interface (CLI) SNMP agent and MIB support for managing the platform through an optional element manager software application (Cisco DSL Manager) Configuration of all 6260 interfaces (DSL, WAN, and subtend interfaces) and all system-wide parameters UNI 3.1/4.0 signaling support UNI 3.1/4.0 traffic management support Monitoring of status and traffic flow for each interface Display, investigation, and disabling of critical, major, and minor alarms Maintenance and test support for isolation and resolution of problems	Cisco 6200, 6100 Series configured with the NI-2 System Card

	Support for 6260 alarm relay contacts and environmental monitoring of key system resources Network Management Support including SNMP agent support for communicating between the 6260 and the DSL Access Manager (the EMS for the 6260)			
Feature Integration	Cisco IOS 12.0DA has planned additional new features and functionality to be introduced in subsequent maintenance revisions.			
Synchronization Points with Major Releases	**Based On**		**Ported Into**	
	12.0		12.1T	
Release Type	STED			
Target Market	Telco, PTT, LEC			
Maintenance Releases	As needed			
Interim Builds	As needed			
Recommended Migration	**From**		**To**	
	12.0(5)DA		12.0(5)DAx or 12.1T	
	The recommended migration path is the logical superceding release, which provides additional features and hardware support to the network without loss of previously configured functionality.			
Life Cycle	**Milestones**	**Y2K Compliance**	**Certification**	**Other Dates**
	—	Yes	LD	CCO FCS of 12.0(5)DA in September, 1999
Internet Addresses	For more information, consult the following web pages: • http://www.cisco.com/warp/customer/cc/cisco/mkt/ios/rel/120/prodlit/964_pp.htm • The Cisco 6260 at http://www.cisco.com/cpropart/salestools/cc/cisco/mkt/access/6000dsl/prodlit/62 60_ds.htm			
Comments				

Cisco IOS Release 12.0DB

<table>
<tr><td>Description</td><td colspan="2">Cisco IOS 12.0DB is an STED that was developed to deliver functionality for the Node Switch Processor (NSP) on the Cisco 6400 Series Serial Universal Access Concentrator platforms. The Cisco 6400 is a concentrator that is capable of aggregating inputs from several DSLAM, which get carried to another DSLAM, where they are broken up into individual xDSL lines. The NSP is an ATM switching blade based on the LightStream 1010, which resides in the Cisco 6400. A Cisco 6400 can accommodate multiple or combined NSPs and NRPs at any one time. This custom hardware design combined with the Cisco IOS software offers advanced xDSL technology features.

The first maintenance 12.0(1)DB, which is based on 12.0(1)main, was released in December 1998. In fact, maintenance revisions 12.0(1)DB to 12.0(4)DB are parented to 12.0M. Starting with 12.0(5)DB, the maintenance revisions were sync to 12.0T CTED in an effort to acquire some features of 12.0T.</td></tr>
<tr><td rowspan="2">Product Support</td><td>Main Features</td><td>Platforms</td></tr>
<tr><td>Ethernet Cable consolidation
VPI/VCI Radius accounting
ATM Half-Bridging
Feature set from EWAN
Sonet APS Switchover Compliance
PPP/L2TP Session Scaling (500 session, 25 tunnels, 50kpps)
VPI/VCI indexing to service profile
AC PEM
OC12/STM4
IPCP subnet
SSG w/CEF
SSG IOS NAT
L2TP per user PPP (1,000 Sessions)
Radius Interim Accounting Record
New feature in 12.0(7)DB: OC12 (6400 NSP)</td><td></td></tr>
<tr><td>Feature Integration</td><td colspan="2">New features and functionality have been added to subsequent maintenance revisions.</td></tr>
<tr><td rowspan="3">Synchronization Points with Major Releases</td><td>Based On</td><td>Ported Into</td></tr>
<tr><td>12.0/12.0(5)T</td><td>12.1T</td></tr>
<tr><td colspan="2">As with other ED releases, this release regularly inherits bug fixes to the base code of its parent main line release.</td></tr>
</table>

Release Type	STED			
Target Market	PTT, Telco, ISP, LEC			
Maintenance Releases	Scheduled Regular Maintenance, on an eight-week cycle.			
Interim Builds	As needed			
Recommended Migration	**From**		**To**	
	12.0(x)DB		12.0(x+1)DB or 12.1(1)T	
	The recommended migration path is the logical superceding release, which provides additional features and hardware support to the network without loss of previously configured functionality.			
Life Cycle	**Milestones**	**Y2K Compliance**	**Certification**	**Other Dates**
	—	Yes	LD	FCS in November, 1998
	Cisco IOS 12.0DB will follow the standard Cisco life cycle			
Internet Addresses	For more information, consult the following web pages: • The 6400 TSDN at http://www.cisco.com/univercd/cc/td/doc/pcat/185.htm • Release Notes for 6400 NRP at http://www.cisco.com/univercd/cc/td/doc/product/dsl_prod/6400/rn6400dc.htm			
Comments	For information on the support of NRPs, see IOS Release 12.0DC.			

Cisco IOS Release 12.0DC

Description	Cisco IOS 12.0DC is an STED based on 12.0(3)DB . It was developed to deliver the functionality of the Node Switch Router (NRP) on the Cisco 6400 Serial Universal Access Concentrator platforms. The Cisco 6400 is a concentrator that is capable of aggregating inputs from several DSLAM, which get carried to another DSLAM, where they are broken up into individual xDSL lines. The NRP is an ATM switching blade based on the 7200 series router, which resides in the Cisco 6400. A Cisco 6400 can accommodate multiple or combined NSPs and NRPs at any one time. This custom hardware design combined with the features of IOS software offers advanced xDSL technology features. This release also adds new functionality such as PPP over Ethernet and the Service Selection Gateway (NRP-SSG) feature set. Cisco IOS 12.0DC is the first Cisco IOS release to incorporate web-based service selection.

Product Support	Main Features	Platforms
	Ethernet Cable consolidation VPI/VCI Radius accounting ATM Half-Bridging Feature set from EWAN Sonet APS Switchover Compliance PPP/L2TP Session Scaling (500 session, 25 tunnels, 50kpps) VPI/VCI indexing to service profile AC PEM OC12/STM4 IPCP subnet SSG w/CEF SSG IOS NAT L2TP per user PPP (1,000 Sessions) Radius Interim Accounting Record IP multicast PPP/ATM TCP Telenet TFTP UDP Transparent bridging VLAN EIGRP IS-IS OSPF PIM RIP AAA CHAP FTP PAP RADIUS SNMP TACACS ATM	Platforms introduced with 12.0(7)DC: ubr920 c3660

<table>
<tr><td>Feature Integration</td><td colspan="4">New software features and new hardware support are planned for the next few maintenance revisions of 12.0DC.</td></tr>
<tr><td rowspan="3">Synchronization Points with Major Releases</td><td colspan="2">Based On</td><td colspan="2">Ported Into</td></tr>
<tr><td colspan="2">12.0DB</td><td colspan="2">12.1T</td></tr>
<tr><td colspan="4">As with other ED releases, this release regularly inherits bug fixes from its parent release, Cisco IOS 12.0DB.</td></tr>
<tr><td>Release Type</td><td colspan="4">STED</td></tr>
<tr><td>Target Market</td><td colspan="4">Telco, ISP, Network service providers, LEC</td></tr>
<tr><td>Maintenance Releases</td><td colspan="4">In addition to 12.0(3)DC, there will be two more scheduled maintenance revisions at approximately eight-week intervals. Subsequent maintenance revisions will be named Cisco IOS 12.0(5)DC and 12.0(6)DC or 12.0(7)DC.</td></tr>
<tr><td>Interim Builds</td><td colspan="4">No planned interim builds</td></tr>
<tr><td rowspan="3">Recommended Migration</td><td colspan="2">From</td><td colspan="2">To</td></tr>
<tr><td colspan="2">12.0DC</td><td colspan="2">12.1T</td></tr>
<tr><td colspan="4">The recommended migration path is the logical superceding release, which provides additional features and hardware support to the network without loss of previously configured functionality.</td></tr>
<tr><td rowspan="3">Life Cycle</td><td>Milestones</td><td>Y2K Compliance</td><td>Certification</td><td>Other Dates</td></tr>
<tr><td>—</td><td>Yes</td><td>LD</td><td>FCS of 12.0(3)DC in June, 1999</td></tr>
<tr><td colspan="4">Medium life cycle</td></tr>
<tr><td>Internet Addresses</td><td colspan="4">For more information, consult the following web pages:
• New Features of 12.0DC at http://www.cisco.com/univercd/cc/td/doc/product/software/ios120/120newft/120limit/120dc/120dc3/index.htm
• Cisco IOS Software Release 12.0DC Product Bulletin at http://www.cisco.com/warp/public/cc/cisco/mkt/ios/rel/120/prodlit/907_pp.htm
• Release Notes for Cisco 6400 NRP for Cisco IOS Release 12.0(3)DC at http://www.cisco.com/univercd/cc/td/doc/product/dsl_prod/6400/rn6400dc.htm#xtocid211840</td></tr>
<tr><td>Comments</td><td colspan="4">Cisco IOS 12.0(3)DC is the first release. There will be two scheduled maintenance releases at approximately eight-week intervals. They will be 12.0(5)DC and 12.0(6 or 7)DC.</td></tr>
</table>

Cisco IOS Release 12.1E

Description	Cisco IOS 12.1E software is the next Enterprise early deployment release vehicle. It initially syncs to 12.0(7)XE which is parented to 12.0(7)T. Upon 12.0T mutation to become 12.1, Cisco IOS 12.1E will re-sync to 12.1 main release and continue to inherit defect fixes off the main maintenance revisions. Furthermore, new features added to the 12.1E will also be ported to the 12.1T release at every other maintenance revision (that is, 12.1(1)T, 12.1(3)T, 12.1(5)T and so on) to maintain unification of IOS major releases. Cisco IOS 12.1E will consolidate Enterprise and Workgroup features and platforms into a single release train. The plan is to provide a unified software migration path for 11.3WA, 12.0XE and 12.0W5 releases. Hence, 12.1E will include support for the catalyst 6000, the 8500, the LS1010, the 7500, the 7200, and the 7100 series routers. Cisco IOS 12.1(1)E is slated for early 2000 and subject to change.			
Product Support	**Main Features**		**Platforms**	
	Refer to Release Notes and product bulletin.			
	CAR, wRED, dWFQ, MPOA over Ether LANE, voice features, VPN, and QoS		LS1010, RSM, 8500 series, 7100, 7200, 7500, GSR1200	
Feature Integration	Not defined at the time of this writing. Cisco IOS 12.1E will most likely follow the standard feature integration of STED releases.			
Synchronization Points with Major Releases	**Based On**		**Ported Into**	
	12.0(7)/12.0(7)XE		12.1T	
Release Type	SMED			
Target Market	Enterprise, multiservice, Network service providers			
Maintenance Releases	Standard STED/SMED maintenance cycle			
Interim Builds	Standard STED/SMED interim builds			
Recommended Migration	**From**		**To**	
	12.1E		12.1E / 12.2T (see 12.1E Product bulletin)	
	The recommended migration path is the logical superceding release, which provides additional features and hardware support to the network without loss of previously configured functionality.			
Life Cycle	**Milestones**	**Y2K Compliance**	**Certification**	**Other Dates**
	Not yet released	Yes	LD	CCO FCS slated early 2000
Internet Addresses	For more information, consult the following web pages: • Cisco IOS Software Center at http://www.cisco.com/public/sw-center/sw-ios.shtml			
Comments	The deployment plans for 12.1E are subject to change.			

Cisco IOS Future 12.1/12.1T Release

Description	Cisco IOS 12.1 is the next IOS software main release. Essentially, Cisco IOS version 12.1 main release is 12.0(7)T with additional software fixes. Starting with 12.1(1), no new additional features will be introduced to successive maintenance revisions. The software and hardware features of 12.1 releases should be identical to those of 12.0(7)T. Successive maintenance revisions will only provide incremental software fixes. Cisco IOS 12.1T will be the CTED release parented to 12.1 main line and will serve as the release vehicle for deploying multitechnology software and hardware features. The main goal of release 12.1 is to consolidate previous IOS features from 12.0T and 12.0X releases into a highly stable IOS software main release. This provides customers of early deployment IOS releases with a migration path leading to a potential GD certification. As the technology release process matures into its third major IOS software release, it is expected that the experience acquired during the past 3 years will be used to make additional enhancements to the release process. Cisco IOS 12.1(1) is slated for February 2000.	
Product Support	**Main Features**	**Platforms**
	Refer to Release Notes and product bulletin on CCO.	
Comments	Plans for future Cisco IOS releases are subject to change.	

Cisco IOS Release 12.0S

Description	Cisco IOS 12.0S is directly on the IOS 12.0 main line. In addition to Internet service provider specific features directly committed to 12.0S, it includes the features of 12.0 main line and several features ported from 12.0T. The primary objective of Cisco IOS 12.0S is to meet the requirements for running the core Internet backbone routers. As such, the first maintenance revisions of Cisco IOS 12.0S were initially released to the Internet service provider only. It was only in July, 1999, and starting with maintenance revision 12.0(5)S that the maintenance revisions were packaged and released to the general networking public. Because Cisco IOS 12.0S seeks to deliver higher quality and stability combined with advanced routing performance, it adopted a conservative feature integration approach. For example, features of Cisco 12.0(1)S to 12.0(4)S are integrated into 12.0(5)T and 12.0(7)T. Also, secured shell (SSH) and the Routing with Resource Reservation (RRR), first introduced in 12.0(5)S, will be available in 12.0(7)T and 12.1(1)T respectively. Other 12.0S features may be ported to Cisco IOS 12.1T in early 2000.

Product Support	Main Features	Platforms
	Advanced Routing protocols, Traffic Aggregation MBGP, Sonet, OC48 IS-IS OSPF IPSEC and Crypto BGP Rework MPLS Tag Switching Frame Relay Sonetization Sonet APS Parser Bookmarks & CLI string search IP Multicast support on ATM SVCs support on ATM LC CAR/ACL support on OC48 SDH MSP APS on OC48 WRED (without IR) 1483 Bridged VC Encap Multicast Routing Monitor ATM subinterfaces MIB ATM PVC traps ATM 64-bit counters MSDP Parser Bookmarks & CLI string search K2 Frame Relay scalability VP shaping on ATM Deluxe ABR for ATM Deluxe Multicast routing monitor MPLS (RRR) SSH Version 1 ATM subinterfaces MIB ATM PVC traps	Cisco 7200, 7500, and 12000 series routers

<table>
<tr><td rowspan="1">Feature Integration</td><td colspan="4">Software and hardware feature enhancements beyond the first maintenance were ported to other IOS releases as follows: Cisco IOS 12.0S to 12.0(4)S have been ported to 12.0(5)T or 12.0(7)T.
A number of features have also been ported either to 12.0(7)XE or 12.1T.</td></tr>
<tr><td rowspan="2">Synchronization Points with Major Releases</td><td colspan="2">Based On</td><td colspan="2">Ported Into</td></tr>
<tr><td colspan="2">12.0</td><td colspan="2">12.0(7)XE or 12.1T[1]</td></tr>
<tr><td>Release Type</td><td colspan="4">SMED</td></tr>
<tr><td>Target Market</td><td colspan="4">Internet service providers and Networks service providers</td></tr>
<tr><td>Maintenance Releases</td><td colspan="4">Scheduled Regular Maintenance revisions after 12.0(5)S</td></tr>
<tr><td>Interim Builds</td><td colspan="4">Bi-weekly</td></tr>
<tr><td rowspan="3">Recommended Migration</td><td colspan="2">From</td><td colspan="2">To</td></tr>
<tr><td colspan="2">12.0(x)S</td><td colspan="2">12.0(x+1)S</td></tr>
<tr><td colspan="4">The recommended migration path is the logical superceding release, which provides additional features and hardware support to the network without loss of previously configured functionality.</td></tr>
<tr><td rowspan="3">Life Cycle</td><td>Milestones</td><td>Y2K Compliance</td><td>Certification</td><td>Other Dates</td></tr>
<tr><td>12.0(5)S was the first publicly available release</td><td>Yes</td><td>LD</td><td>CCO FCS in July, 1999</td></tr>
<tr><td colspan="4">Standard two-year support plan</td></tr>
<tr><td>Internet Addresses</td><td colspan="4">For more information, consult the following web pages:
Cisco IOS 12.0S Overview at http://www.cisco.com/warp/customer/cc/cisco/mkt/ios/rel/120/prodlit/934_pb.htm
Cisco IOS 12.0S Ordering Info at http://www.cisco.com/warp/customer/cc/cisco/mkt/ios/rel/120/prodlit/935_pb.htm
New Features in 12.0-Based Limited Lifetime Releases at http://www.cisco.com/univercd/cc/td/doc/product/software/ios120/120newft/120limit/index.htm
Release Notes for Cisco IOS 12.0 and 12.0T at http://www.cisco.com/univercd/cc/td/doc/product/software/ios120/relnote/index.htm</td></tr>
<tr><td>Comments</td><td colspan="4">12.0(7)S introduced RSP8, IP Over DCC, Reflector Mode, Gigabit Ethernet, ISIS over ISL, VIP based traffic shaping, IP Precedence/ATM CLP mapping, and the GSR+ OC48 fabric.</td></tr>
</table>

1. Most features of this release will appear in 12.0(7)XE and 12.1T. However, many other features will remain on the 12.0S release train.

Cisco IOS Release 12.0SC

Description	Cisco Systems, Inc., released the Cisco IOS 12.0SC as the software support vehicle for cable routers, also known as universal broadband routers. Cisco IOS 12.0SC is directly based on the Cisco IOS 12.0(6)S software branch, and, therefore, supports similar features. Furthermore, Cisco IOS 12.0SC will maintain periodic sync with the revisions of 12.0S in an effort to capture software fixes and enhancements. Released on the uBR7200 in August, 1999, 12.0(6)SC introduced features such as multimedia cable network system (MCNS) 2-way, Baseline privacy, TelcoReturn, and Virtual Private Network (VPN).	
Product Support	**Main Features**	**Platforms**
	MCNS 2-way Downstream QoS MCNS Baseline Privacy TelcoReturn VPN Data Over Cable System Interface Specification (DOCSIS)compliant Dynamic host configuration Protocol (DHCP) relay Subscriber ID insertion	uBR7200 Universal broadband routers
Feature Integration		
Synchronization Points with Major Releases	**Based On**	**Ported Into**
	12.0(6)S	12.1T
	Sync to 12.0S	
Release Type	STED	
Target Market	ISP, Telco companies, and Broadband network providers	
Maintenance Releases	Scheduled Regular Maintenance, on an eight-week cycle	
Interim Builds	As needed	
Recommended Migration	**From**	**To**
	12.0(x)SC	12.0(x+1)SC
	The recommended migration path is the logical superceding release, which provides additional features and hardware support to the network without loss of previously configured functionality.	

Life Cycle	Milestones	Y2K Compliance	Certification	Other Dates
	Expected EOE in late 2000	Yes	LD	CCO FCS in August, 1999
Internet Addresses	For more information, consult the following web pages: • Cisco IOS 12.0SC Product Bulletin at http://www.cisco.com/warp/customer/cc/cisco/mkt/ios/rel/120/prodlit/972_pp.htm			
Comments				

Cisco IOS Release 12.0ST

Description	Cisco IOS 12.0ST STED software was developed as the support vehicle for Multi-Protocol Label Switching (MPLS) functionality. It is directly based on the Cisco IOS 12.0S software branch and, therefore, supports the advanced routing and scalability features of 12.0S. Furthermore, most advanced layer 3 MPLS services of 12.0ST are periodically ported to 12.0S. Hence, Cisco IOS 12.0ST releases, which combine Tag switching innovations of 11.1CT with advanced networking capabilities of 12.0S, offers unprecedented MPLS capabilities for the service provider market. At the time of this writing, 12.0ST was only available to selected customers. General public release is expected at 12.0(8)ST or 12.0(9)ST by March 2000[1].	
Product Support	Main Features	Platforms
	MPLS VPN MPLS Traffic Engineering [also in 12.0(5)S] Routing with Resource Reservation (RRR) Secured Shell (SSH) MPLS ATM Multicast AToM [Any Transport over MPLS] 6400 MPLS LSC/LER/VPN MBGP MDS Fast Reroute Class of Service for MPLS MPLS Label Switch Controller (6400 support) 6400 MPLS LSC/LER/VPN	Cisco 7200, 7500, and 12000 series routers

Feature Integration	Software and hardware feature enhancements beyond the first maintenance were ported to other IOS releases as follows: Cisco IOS 12.0S to 12.0(4)S have been ported to 12.0(5)T or 12.0(7)T. A number of features have also been ported either to 12.0(7)XE or 12.1T.			
Synchronization Points with Major Releases	**Based On**		**Ported Into**	
	12.0		12.0S or 12.1T[2]	
Release Type	SMED			
Target Market	Internet service providers and Networks service providers			
Maintenance Releases	Scheduled Regular Maintenance revisions after 12.0(5)S			
Interim Builds	Bi-weekly			
Recommended Migration	**From**		**To**	
	From 11.1CT to 12.0ST			
	12.0(x)S		12.0(x+1)S	
	The recommended migration path is the logical superceding release, which provides additional features and hardware support to the network without loss of previously configured functionality.			
Life Cycle	**Milestones**	**Y2K Compliance**	**Certification**	**Other Dates**
	12.0(5)S was the first publicly available release	Yes	LD	CCO FCS in July, 1999
	Standard two-year support plan			
Internet Addresses	For more information, consult the following web pages: Cisco IOS 12.0S Overview at http://www.cisco.com/warp/customer/cc/cisco/mkt/ios/rel/120/prodlit/934_pb.htm Cisco IOS 12.0S Ordering Info at http://www.cisco.com/warp/customer/cc/cisco/mkt/ios/rel/120/prodlit/935_pb.htm New Features in 12.0-Based Limited Lifetime Releases at http://www.cisco.com/univercd/cc/td/doc/product/software/ios120/120newft/120limit/index.htm Release Notes for Cisco IOS 12.0 and 12.0T at http://www.cisco.com/univercd/cc/td/doc/product/software/ios120/relnote/index.htm			
Comments	Cisco IOS 12.0ST was not generally available at the time of this writing. Future release plans are subject to change			

1. Future release plans are subject change.
2. Most features of this release will appear in 12.0(7)XE and 12.1T. However, many other features will remain on the 12.0S release train.

Cisco IOS Release 12.0(0.6)WA5

Description	Cisco IOS 12.0(0.6)WA5 was a one-time STED that supports the Jaguar ATM OC-12 line card on the 8500 multiservice switch router (MSR). The IOS software 12.0(0.6)WA5 is actually based on the pre-released version of 12.0 and was later ported to IOS 12.0W5. It delivered features such as ATM Switching with wire speed, multiprotocol routing, Gigabit Ethernet, VLAN, FEC, ISL over FEC, and quality of service.			
Product Support	**Main Features**		**Platforms**	
	QoS Layer 3 switching ATM Switching, VLAN, FEC, and ISL over FEC		ATM OC-12 card on 8500 series router	
Feature Integration				
Synchronization Points with Major Releases	**Based On**		**Ported Into**	
	Beta code of 12.0 (12.0(0.6))		Cisco 12.0W5	
	N/A			
Release Type	STED			
Target Market	Workgroup/Enterprise			
Maintenance Releases	—			
Interim Builds	—			
Recommended Migration	**From**		**To**	
	12.0(0.6)WA5		12.0W5	
	The recommended migration path is the logical superceding release, which provides additional features and hardware support to the network without loss of previously configured functionality.			
Life Cycle	**Milestones**	**Y2K Compliance**	**Certification**	**Other Dates**
	EOE	Yes	LD	CCO FCS in July, 1998
	Short-lived			
Internet Addresses	For more information, consult the following web pages: • The 8500 multiservice router at http://www.cisco.com/warp/public/cc/cisco/mkt/switch/cat/8500/index.shtml			
Comments				

Cisco IOS Release 12.0W5(x)

<table>
<tr><td>Description</td><td colspan="2">Cisco IOS 12.0W5(x) was released in January, 1999, to provide multiservice and ATM functionality to the 8500 series multiservice routers and the Cisco LS1010 ATM switches. The software branch is based on the Cisco IOS 12.0 main line and provides features such as IP Multilayer Switching (MLS), IPX MLS, Multiprotocol over ATM (MPOA), IP MLS over ATM, and Fast Simple Server Redundancy Protocol (FSSRP).

Cisco IOS Release 12.0(x)W5(x) will continue to provide new features and hardware features with successive maintenance revisions. The maintenance releases will follow a slightly different naming convention as indicated below:

Cisco IOS 12.0(1)W5(X)

Cisco IOS 12.0(1)W5(Y)

Cisco IOS 12.0(x)W5(Z)

Cisco IOS 12.0(y)W5(Zb)

The lowercase x and y preceding W5 show the sync maintenance revision level with the main line 12.0. The X, Y, or Z in the parentheses following W5 indicate this STED specific maintenance revision level. Chapter 3, "Characteristics of Cisco IOS: Definitions, Naming Convention, Versioning, Numbering, and Feature Packaging," provides more details on Cisco IOS naming conventions.</td></tr>
<tr><td>Product Support</td><td>Main Features</td><td>Platforms</td></tr>
<tr><td></td><td>IP Multicast Multilayer Switching (MLS)

IPX MLS

Multiprotocol over ATM (MPOA)

IP MLS over ATM

Fast Simple Server Redundancy Protocol (FSSRP)

MLS and other Layer 3 switching</td><td>LightStream 1010

Catalyst 8500 series</td></tr>
<tr><td>Feature Integration</td><td colspan="2">New features and functionality are expected in maintenance revisions</td></tr>
<tr><td rowspan="3">Synchronization Points with Major Releases</td><td>Based On</td><td>Ported Into</td></tr>
<tr><td>Cisco 12.0</td><td>Cisco 12.1E</td></tr>
<tr><td colspan="2">This release is slated to EOE in early- to mid-2000. Features and platforms will be ported to 12.1E.</td></tr>
<tr><td>Release Type</td><td colspan="2">STED</td></tr>
<tr><td>Target Market</td><td colspan="2">Enterprise, Workgroups, multiservice, LAN switching</td></tr>
<tr><td>Maintenance Releases</td><td colspan="2">Scheduled Regular Maintenance revisions</td></tr>
<tr><td>Interim Builds</td><td colspan="2">As needed</td></tr>
</table>

<table>
<tr><th rowspan="3">Recommended Migration</th><th colspan="2">From</th><th colspan="2">To</th></tr>
<tr><td colspan="2">12.W5(x)</td><td colspan="2">12.1E</td></tr>
<tr><td colspan="4">The recommended migration path is the logical superceding release, which provides additional features and hardware support to the network without loss of previously configured functionality.</td></tr>
<tr><th rowspan="2">Life Cycle</th><th>Milestones</th><th>Y2K Compliance</th><th>Certification</th><th>Other Dates</th></tr>
<tr><td>—</td><td>Yes</td><td>LD</td><td>CCO FCS in September, 1998</td></tr>
<tr><th>Internet Addresses</th><td colspan="4">For more information, consult the following web pages:
• Cisco IOS 12.0W5 Release Notes at http://www.cisco.com/univercd/cc/td/doc/product/lan/cat5000/c5krn/rsm_rns/rn6794.htm
• ATM Support in Cisco IOS at http://www.cisco.com/univercd/cc/td/doc/product/atm/
• LightStream 1010 ATM Switch Release 12.0 Documents at http://www.cisco.com/univercd/cc/td/doc/product/atm/ls1010s/wa5/12/index.htm
• Release Notes for the Catalyst 6000 at http://www.cisco.com/univercd/cc/td/doc/product/lan/cat6000/relnotes/index.htm</td></tr>
<tr><th>Comments</th><td colspan="4">In accordance with the Cisco IOS XED conventions, Cisco released 12.0(4a)WX5(11a) as a one-time software to introduce some new software and hardware features on the 8510CSR and the 8540CSR routers.
Cisco IOS 12.0(4a)WX5(11a) introduces the following features:
• Eight-port Gigabit Ethernet module for the Catalyst 8540
• Access List Daughter Card (ACL) for the Catalyst 8540
• Support for 64K entry line cards for the Catalyst 8540
• AppleTalk Routing Support
• EIGRP/OSPF Neighbor Optimizations
For more information on the Catalyst 8510 and 8540, please visit the following web sites:
• Catalyst 8540 at http://www.cisco.com/cgi-bin/tablebuild.pl/cat8540c
• Catalyst 8510 at http://www.cisco.com/cgi-bin/tablebuild.pl/cat8510c</td></tr>
</table>

Cisco IOS Short Lived Early Deployment Releases (XED) Based on 12.0

Cisco IOS Release 12.0(1)XA

<table>
<tr><td>Description</td><td colspan="2">Cisco IOS 12.0(1)XA is an XED based on 12.0(1)T. It introduced new software features for the Cisco 1400 and 1700 series router platforms as well the Cisco MC3810 Multiservice Access Concentrator. The features of 12.0(1)XA have been integrated into 12.0T starting with 12.0(2)T.</td></tr>
<tr><td rowspan="2">Product Support</td><td>Main Features</td><td>Platforms</td></tr>
<tr><td>Traffic Shaping
Call Detail Records
Cisco MC3810 IGX 8400 Interworking
Common Channel Signaling features
Default Routes
Facility Data Link (FDL) Capability on the Multiflex Trunk module
G.726 (ADPCM)
Multiflex Trunk Module with integrated BRI interface
Multilength Dial Patterns
OPX Ring-through
Preference-based Hunt Group</td><td>Cisco 1400
Cisco 1700 series
MC3810</td></tr>
<tr><td>Feature Integration</td><td colspan="2">—</td></tr>
<tr><td rowspan="3">Synchronization Points with Major Releases</td><td>Based On</td><td>Ported Into</td></tr>
<tr><td>Cisco IOS 12.0(1)T</td><td>Cisco IOS 12.0(2)T</td></tr>
<tr><td colspan="2">Cisco platforms currently running Cisco IOS XED software should consider upgrading to an equivalent software image of the CTED at or above the "ported into" revision level.</td></tr>
<tr><td>Release Type</td><td colspan="2">XED</td></tr>
<tr><td>Target Market</td><td colspan="2">SOHO, SMB, Enterprises, and ISP</td></tr>
<tr><td>Maintenance Releases</td><td colspan="2">Cisco IOS 12.0(1)XA is a one-time release.</td></tr>
<tr><td>Interim Builds</td><td colspan="2"></td></tr>
</table>

Recommended Migration	**From**		**To**	
	12.0(1)XA(x)		12.0(2)T	
	The recommended migration path is the logical superceding release, which provides additional features and hardware support to the network without loss of previously configured functionality.			
Life Cycle	**Milestones**	**Y2K Compliance**	**Certification**	**Other Dates**
	—	Yes	ED	FCS in November, 1998
	Short-lived			
Internet Addresses	For more information, consult the following web pages: • Release Notes for MC3810 at http://www.cisco.com/univercd/cc/td/doc/product/access/multicon/3810rn/rn3810xa.htm • Cisco IOS Software Release 12.0(1)XA Product Bulletin at http://www.cisco.com/warp/customer/cc/cisco/mkt/ios/rel/120/prodlit/813_pp.htm			
Comments	Continued maintenance software features introduced by XED is performed on the major release CTED.			

Cisco IOS Release 12.0(1)XB

Description	Cisco IOS 12.0(1)XB is an XED based on 12.0(1)T, which introduced the Cisco 800 series platforms, the modem over Basic Rate Interface (BRI) functionality, several voice features including call holding and retrieving, call waiting, three-way call conferencing, call transferring, and call forwarding (Sweden and Finland only). The features of 12.0(1)XB have been integrated into 12.0T starting with 12.0(3)T.	
Product Support	**Main Features**	**Platforms**
	Modem over BRI Voice over ISDN (see description above) Automatic Detection of ISDN Switch and SPIDs	Cisco 800 series routers including 801,802, 803, and 804
Synchronization Points with Major Releases	**Based On**	**Ported Into**
	Cisco IOS 12.0(1)T	12.0(3)T
	Cisco platforms currently running Cisco IOS XED software should consider upgrading to an equivalent software image of the CTED at or above the "ported into" revision level.	
Release Type	XED	
Target Market	SOHO, SMB, Enterprise	
Maintenance Releases	Cisco IOS 12.0(1)XB is a one-time release.	

Interim Builds				
Recommended Migration	**From**		**To**	
	Cisco IOS 12.0(1)XB		Cisco IOS 12.0(3)T or later	
	The recommended migration path is the logical superceding release, which provides additional features and hardware support to the network without loss of previously configured functionality.			
Life Cycle	**Milestones**	**Y2K Compliance**	**Certification**	**Other Dates**
	—	Yes	ED	FCS in November, 1998
	Short-lived			
Internet Addresses	For more information, consult the following web pages: • Release Notes of Cisco 800 at http://www.cisco.com/univercd/cc/td/doc/product/software/ios120/relnote/800ser/rn800xb.htm • Cisco IOS Software Release 12.0(1)XB Product Bulletin at http://www.cisco.com/warp/customer/cc/cisco/mkt/ios/rel/120/prodlit/810_pp.htm			
Comments	Continued maintenance software features introduced by XED is performed on the major release CTED.			

Cisco IOS Release 12.0(2)XC

Description	Cisco IOS 12.0(2)XC is an XED that introduced advanced voice and cable features. 12.0(2)XC is based on Cisco IOS 12.0(2)T and delivered new features for the Cisco 2600, Cisco 3600, uBR7200, and uBR900 platforms. The features include L2TP, DHCP, IPSec, NAP/PAT, FE Quake, and Firewall features for the small-office/home-office (SOHO) market. The BRI functionality includes support for carrying both incoming and outgoing analog calls over BRI. Cisco IOS 12.0(2)XC also introduces Cisco uBR900 and support for the MC016 Modem Card, which enables volume deployments of cable modems.	
Product Support	**Main Features**	**Platforms**
	L2TP, DHCP, IPSec	Cisco 2600, Cisco 3600
	NAT/PAT, Firewall features, modem over BRI, and the MC-16 Modem Card	uBR7200 and uBR900
	Voice and cable features	
	Analog calls over BRI	
Synchronization Points with Major Releases	**Based On**	**Ported Into**
	Cisco IOS 12.0(2)T	Cisco IOS 12.0(3)T
	Cisco platforms currently running Cisco IOS XED software should consider upgrading to an equivalent software image of the CTED at or above the "ported into" revision level.	

Release Type	XED			
Target Market	SOHO and Cable modem customers			
Maintenance Releases	Cisco IOS 12.0(2)XC is a one-time release.			
Interim Builds				
Recommended Migration	**From**		**To**	
	12.0(2)XC		12.0(3)T or later	
	The recommended migration path is the logical superceding release, which provides additional features and hardware support to the network without loss of previously configured functionality.			
Life Cycle	**Milestones**	**Y2K Compliance**	**Certification**	**Other Dates**
	—	Yes	ED	FCS in January, 1999
	Short-lived			
Internet Addresses	For more information, consult the following web pages: • http://www.cisco.com/warp/customer/cc/cisco/mkt/ios/rel/120/prodlit/843_pp.htm			
Comments	Continued maintenance software features introduced by XED are performed on the major release CTED.			

Cisco IOS Release 12.0(2)XD

Description	Cisco IOS 12.0(2)XD is an XED based on 12.0(2)T. It delivers support for a double density line card on the AS5300 as well as ISDN BRI Voice Interface Card (VIC) for the Cisco 2600 and the Cisco 3600 Series routers. The ISDN BRI VIC operates within the Voice Network Module on Cisco 26xx and 36xx platforms. Additionally, Cisco IOS 12.0(2)XD provides narrow band digital voice connectivity in VoIP and VoFR environments. On the AS5300, 12.0(2)XD also introduced the eight Primary Rate Interface (PRI) card plus four T1 serial interfaces and support for 240 modems. The features of 12.0(2)XD have been integrated into 12.0T starting with 12.0(3)T.	
Product Support	**Main Features**	**Platforms**
	ISDN BRI VIC	Cisco 2600 and 3600 series routers
	Eight PRI card	Cisco 5300
	New drivers, new NEAT, E1/T1, firmware	

<table>
<tr><td rowspan="3">Synchronization Points with Major Releases</td><td colspan="2">Based On</td><td colspan="2">Ported Into</td></tr>
<tr><td colspan="2">Cisco IOS 12.0(2)T</td><td colspan="2">Cisco IOS 12.0(3)T</td></tr>
<tr><td colspan="4">Cisco platforms currently running Cisco IOS XED software should consider upgrading to an equivalent software image of the CTED at or above the "ported into" revision level.</td></tr>
<tr><td>Release Type</td><td colspan="4">XED</td></tr>
<tr><td>Target Market</td><td colspan="4">Selected platforms</td></tr>
<tr><td>Maintenance Releases</td><td colspan="4">Cisco IOS 12.0(2)XD is a one-time release.</td></tr>
<tr><td>Interim Builds</td><td colspan="4"></td></tr>
<tr><td rowspan="3">Recommended Migration</td><td colspan="2">From</td><td colspan="2">To</td></tr>
<tr><td colspan="2">Cisco IOS 12.0(2)XD</td><td colspan="2">Cisco IOS 12.0(3)T or later</td></tr>
<tr><td colspan="4">The recommended migration path is the logical superceding release, which provides additional features and hardware support to the network without loss of previously configured functionality.</td></tr>
<tr><td rowspan="3">Life Cycle</td><td>Milestones</td><td>Y2K Compliance</td><td>Certification</td><td>Other Dates</td></tr>
<tr><td>—</td><td>Yes</td><td>ED</td><td>CCO FCS in December, 1998</td></tr>
<tr><td colspan="4">Short-lived</td></tr>
<tr><td>Internet Addresses</td><td colspan="4">For more information, consult the following web pages:
• New Features in 12.0-Based Limited Lifetime Releases at http://www.cisco.com/univercd/cc/td/doc/product/software/ios120/120newft/120limit/index.htm</td></tr>
<tr><td>Comments</td><td colspan="4">Continued maintenance software features introduced by XED are performed on the major release CTED.</td></tr>
</table>

Cisco IOS Release 12.0XE

<table>
<tr><td>Description</td><td>Cisco IOS 12.0XE is a series of short-lived XED releases based on the different maintenance revisions of 12.0T. They are used to deliver Enterprise-specific software and hardware features.

Additionally, selected features first deployed in Cisco IOS 12.0(x)XE will be carried into Cisco IOS 12.0(x)S. For example, features of 12.0(1)XE appeared in 12.0(5)S. Moreover, it is expected that features of 12.0W5 ported into 12.0XE pre-integration. This will lay the foundation for a later unified Workgroup/Enterprise Cisco IOS software release, 12.1E.</td></tr>
</table>

Product Support	Main Features	Platforms
	Sonetization, CH-OC-12, 7576, ICT3 Multichannel DS1/PRI and E1/PRI E1 VOIP Network Based Application Recognition (NBAR) E1 Support for Two-Port T1/E1 High-Capacity Digital Voice Port Adapter for Cisco 7200 series routers Two-Port T1/E1 High Capacity Digital Voice port adapter for Cisco 7200 series routers Inverse Multiplexing over ATM (IMA) port adapter Distributed Traffic Shaping Cisco 7100 Series VPN routers New Network Processing engines Two-Port Multichannel DS1/PRI and Multichannel E1/PRI port adapters Internet Key Exchange (IKE) mode configuration Frame Relay enhancements for K2 scalability NPE-300, Gigabit Ethernet, Cisco 7576 Support, CT3, CE3, Cisco 7100, 7200 and 7500, Voice Card, VPN features The complete list of features is available at http://www.cisco.com/univercd/cc/td/doc/product/software/ios120/120newft/120limit/120xe/index.htm.	Cisco 7100 Series - as of 12.0(4)XE Cisco 7200 Series Cisco 7500 Series Catalyst 6000 Series (NOTE: 12.0(3)XE is an unrelated branch of the 12.0XE families until 12.0(7)XE.)
Feature Integration	New features and functionality have been added to subsequent maintenance revisions.	
Synchronization Points with Major Releases	Based On	Ported Into
	Cisco IOS 12.0T	Cisco IOS 12.0T
	Each release is sync to maintenance to the corresponding 12.0T maintenance revision.	
Release Type	Multiple XED release	
Target Market	Enterprise/Workgroup, multiservice	

<table>
<tr><th>Maintenance Releases</th><td colspan="4">This release inherits bug fixes as needed from Cisco IOS 12.0(x)T.</td></tr>
<tr><th>Interim Builds</th><td colspan="4">—</td></tr>
<tr><th rowspan="9">Recommended Migration</th><th colspan="2">From</th><th colspan="2">To</th></tr>
<tr><td colspan="2">12.0(x)XE</td><td colspan="2">12.1(1)E</td></tr>
<tr><td colspan="2">12.0(5)XE</td><td colspan="2">12.0(5)XEx (where x=1,2,3,4,5…)</td></tr>
<tr><td colspan="2">12.0(4)XE</td><td colspan="2">12.0(7)T</td></tr>
<tr><td colspan="2">12.0(3)XE</td><td colspan="2">12.0(7)XE (cat6000)/12.0(7)T</td></tr>
<tr><td colspan="2">12.0(2)XE</td><td colspan="2">12.0(3)T</td></tr>
<tr><td colspan="2">12.0(1)XE</td><td colspan="2">12.0(2)XE (7200VXR/NPE-300 Only)</td></tr>
<tr><td colspan="4">The recommended migration path is the logical superceding release, which provides additional features and hardware support to the network without loss of previously configured functionality.</td></tr>
<tr><th rowspan="2">Life Cycle</th><th>Milestones</th><th>Y2K Compliance</th><th>Certification</th><th>Other Dates</th></tr>
<tr><td>—</td><td>Yes</td><td>ED</td><td>CCO FCS of 12.0(1)XE in December, 1998</td></tr>
<tr><th>Internet Addresses</th><td colspan="4">For more information, consult the following web pages:
• Release Notes at http://www.cisco.com/univercd/cc/td/doc/product/software/ios120/relnote/7000fam/rn120xe.htm
• Release Notes for Cisco 7000 Family for Cisco IOS Release 12.0 XE at http://www.cisco.com/univercd/cc/td/doc/product/software/ios120/relnote/7000fam/rn120xe.htm</td></tr>
<tr><th>Comments</th><td colspan="4">12.0(1)XE
• IETF-PPP over ATM PA-A3
• Cisco 7200 series VXR router
• NPE-300
12.0(2)XE
• Gigabit Ethernet Interface Processor (GEIP)
• Cisco 7576 router
• PA-MC-T3 Multichannel T3 port adapter
• PA-MC-E3 Multichannel E3 synchronous serial port adapter
• PA-MC-8EI/120 port adapter</td></tr>
</table>

	12.0(4)XE • Cisco 7100 series VPN routers • NPE-175 and NPE-225 • Two-port multichannel DS1/PRI and multichannel E1/PRI port adapters—PA-MC-4T1, PA-MC-8T1, and PA-MC-8DSX1 • Inverse multiplexing for ATM port adapters • Memory scan • Frame Relay enhancements for K2 scalability

Cisco IOS Release 12.0(2)XF

Description	Cisco IOS 12.0(2)XF is an XED based on 12.0(2)T. It introduced the IOS supported ATM OC-3 LANE of the Catalyst 2900 XL series. This ATM module provides support for Multiple virtual LANs, Emulated LAN, and RFC-1483 PVC.			
Product Support	**Main Features**		**Platforms**	
	LANE client and RFC 1483 Ethernet to ATM switching Multiple virtual LANs, Emulated LAN		Catalyst 2900XL ATM OC-3	
Synchronization Points with Major Releases	**Based On**		**Ported Into**	
	Cisco IOS 12.0(2)T		Cisco IOS 12.0(4)T	
	Cisco platforms currently running Cisco IOS XED software should consider upgrading to an equivalent software image of the CTED at or above the “ported into” revision level.			
Release Type	XED			
Target Market	Enterprise, Workgroup, SMB			
Maintenance Releases	Cisco IOS 12.0(2)XF is a one-time release.			
Interim Builds				
Recommended Migration	**From**		**To**	
	Cisco IOS 12.0(2)XF		Cisco IOS 12.0(4)T	
	The recommended migration path is the logical superceding release, which provides additional features and hardware support to the network without loss of previously configured functionality.			
Life Cycle	**Milestones**	**Y2K Compliance**	**Certification**	**Other Dates**
	—	Yes	ED	CCO FCS in April, 1999
	Short-lived			

Internet Addresses	For more information, consult the following web pages: • http://www.cisco.com/univercd/cc/td/doc/product/lan/c2900xl/c29xlatm/78549501.htm • Cisco IOS Software Release 12.0(2)XF at http://www.cisco.com/warp/customer/cc/cisco/mkt/ios/rel/120/prodlit/914_pp.htm
Comments	Continued maintenance software features introduced by XED are performed on the major release CTED.

Cisco IOS Release 12.0(3)XG

Description	Cisco IOS 12.0(3)XG is an XED based on 12.0(3)T. It introduced enhancements to the BRI Voice Module of the Cisco MC3810 Multi Access Concentrator as well as new features such as support for Frame Relay Forum FRF.11 for voice data fragmentation, and FRF.12 for compressed voice in Frame Relay. The Frame Relay voice features were introduced on the Cisco MC3810, 2600, and 3600 series routers.	
Product Support	**Main Features**	**Platforms**
	BRI Voice module Frame Relay Forum FRF.11 for voice data fragmentation Frame Relay Forum FRF.12 for compressed voice in Frame Relay	Cisco MC3810 Cisco 2600 and 3600 series routers
	Voice over Frame Relay Using FRF.11 and FRF.12 ISDN BRI Voice on the Cisco MC3810 QSIG Digit Forwarding on the Cisco MC3810	
Synchronization Points with Major Releases	**Based On**	**Ported Into**
	Cisco IOS 12.0(3)T	Cisco IOS 12.0(4)T
	Cisco platforms currently running Cisco IOS XED software should consider upgrading to an equivalent software image of the CTED at or above the "ported into" revision level.	
Release Type	XED	
Target Market	SOHO, SMB, ISP	
Maintenance Releases	Cisco IOS 12.0(3)XG is a one-time release.	
Interim Builds		

Recommended Migration	From		To	
	Cisco IOS 12.0(3)XG		Cisco IOS 12.0(4)T	
	The recommended migration path is the logical superceding release, which provides additional features and hardware support to the network without loss of previously configured functionality.			
Life Cycle	Milestones	Y2K Compliance	Certification	Other Dates
	—	Yes	ED	CCO FCS in February, 1999
	Short-lived			
Internet Addresses	For more information, consult the following web pages: • Cisco IOS Software Release 12.0(3)XG at http://www.cisco.com/warp/customer/cc/cisco/mkt/ios/rel/120/prodlit/889_pp.htm • New Features in Release 12.0 XG at http://www.cisco.com/univercd/cc/td/doc/product/software/ios120/120newft/120limit/120xg/index.htm			
Comments	Continued maintenance software features introduced by XED are performed on the major release CTED.			

Cisco IOS Release 12.0(2)XH

Description	Cisco IOS 12.0(2)XH is an XED based on 12.0(2)T. It introduced support for the voice Digital Signal Processing (DSP), DSPM-549 on existing voice carrier cards of the Cisco AS5300 platform. It also includes functionality that doubles the number of T1, E1, and Primary Rate Interface (PRI) ports from the previous limit of two. In other words, the AS5300 will now support up to 96 voice calls in T1/PRI configurations or up to 120 voice calls in E1/PRI configurations when configured with AS53-VOXD (T1 549-based) voice cards and running Cisco IOS 12.0(2)XH or later. Additionally, this release also delivers initial support for the G.723.1 and G.729a voice coders including out-of-band dual-tone multifrequency (DTMF) transport for coders that do not transport DTMF or codec negotiation.

<table>
<tr><th rowspan="2">Product Support</th><th colspan="2">Main Features</th><th colspan="2">Platforms</th></tr>
<tr><td colspan="2">DSP (DSPM-549)
Increased support for voice calls
G.723.1 and G729a voice coders
Higher port density
H.323 Version 2 support
Single Density Voice support with DSPM-542
High Density Voice support with DSPM-549
Open Settlements Protocol (OSP) for IP Telephony
Debit Card Accounting and New RADIUS Attributes for IP Telephony
Interactive Voice Response (IVR)</td><td colspan="2">Cisco AS5300</td></tr>
<tr><th rowspan="3">Synchronization Points with Major Releases</th><th colspan="2">Based On</th><th colspan="2">Ported Into</th></tr>
<tr><td colspan="2">Cisco IOS 12.0(2)T</td><td colspan="2">Cisco IOS 12.0(5)T</td></tr>
<tr><td colspan="4">Cisco platforms currently running Cisco IOS XED software should consider upgrading to an equivalent software image of the CTED at or above the “ported into” revision level.</td></tr>
<tr><th>Release Type</th><td colspan="4">XED</td></tr>
<tr><th>Target Market</th><td colspan="4">Access Server, ISP, NSP</td></tr>
<tr><th>Maintenance Releases</th><td colspan="4">Cisco IOS 12.0(2)XH is a one-time release.</td></tr>
<tr><th>Interim Builds</th><td colspan="4"></td></tr>
<tr><th rowspan="3">Recommended Migration</th><th colspan="2">From</th><th colspan="2">To</th></tr>
<tr><td colspan="2">Cisco IOS 12.0(2)XH</td><td colspan="2">Cisco IOS 12.0(5)T or later</td></tr>
<tr><td colspan="4">The recommended migration path is the logical superceding release, which provides additional features and hardware support to the network without loss of previously configured functionality.</td></tr>
<tr><th rowspan="3">Life Cycle</th><th>Milestones</th><th>Y2K Compliance</th><th>Certification</th><th>Other Dates</th></tr>
<tr><td>—</td><td>Yes</td><td>ED</td><td>CCO FCS in June, 1999</td></tr>
<tr><td colspan="4">Short-lived</td></tr>
</table>

Internet Addresses	For more information, consult the following web pages: • Release Notes at http://www.cisco.com/univercd/cc/td/doc/product/software/ios120/relnote/5300as/rn5300xh.htm • Cisco IOS Software Release 12.0(2)XH Product Bulletin at http://www.cisco.com/warp/public/cc/cisco/mkt/ios/rel/120/prodlit/887_pb.htm
Comments	Continued maintenance software features introduced by XED is performed on the major release CTED.

Cisco IOS Release 12.0(4)XH

Description	Cisco IOS 12.0(4)XH is an XED based on 12.0(4)T. It introduced support for Test Command Language (TCL), scripting language, and other enhanced Voice features. TCL scripting ability within the Cisco IOS software environment provides a flexible way to create, update, and modify the Interactive Voice Response (IVR) call flow. The Cisco IOS 12.0(4)XH also introduced the Pre-Paid (DebitCard) application which adds the ability to perform pre-paid calling services whereby calls are pre-rated and terminated at the end of the talk time. The 12.0(4)XH also expanded RADIUS Authentication, Authorization, and Accounting (AAA) to support Vendor Specific Attribute (VSA) options. Finally, Cisco IOS 12.0(4)XH integrated the Open Settlement Protocol (OSP) client software which enables service providers to use Cisco Open Packet Telephony to communicate directly with a Clearinghouse. OSP is an ETSI TIHPON approved standard.	
Product Support	**Main Features**	**Platforms**
	IVR, TCL Support OSP, AAA support of VSA On the 5300: • H.323 Version 2 support • Single Density Voice support with DSPM-542 • High Density Voice support with DSPM-549 • Open Settlements Protocol (OSP) for IP Telephony • Debit Card Accounting and New RADIUS Attributes for IP Telephony • Interactive Voice Response (IVR)	AS5300, 2600, 3600

<table>
<tr><td></td><td colspan="2">On the 2600 and 3600:
• Settlements for Packet Voice
• Debit Card for Packet Telephony on Cisco Access platforms
• TCLWare
• Interactive Voice Response (IVR)
• H.323 Version 2 support</td><td colspan="2"></td></tr>
<tr><td rowspan="3">Synchronization Points with Major Releases</td><td colspan="2">Based On</td><td colspan="2">Ported Into</td></tr>
<tr><td colspan="2">Cisco IOS 12.0(4)T</td><td colspan="2">Cisco IOS 12.0(7)T</td></tr>
<tr><td colspan="4">Cisco platforms currently running Cisco IOS XED software should consider upgrading to an equivalent software image of the CTED at or above the "ported into" revision level.</td></tr>
<tr><td>Release Type</td><td colspan="4">XED</td></tr>
<tr><td>Target Market</td><td colspan="4">Access Servers, Network service providers, Dial, ISP, and SOHO</td></tr>
<tr><td>Maintenance Releases</td><td colspan="4">Cisco IOS 12.0(4)XH is a one-time release.</td></tr>
<tr><td>Interim Builds</td><td colspan="4"></td></tr>
<tr><td rowspan="3">Recommended Migration</td><td colspan="2">From</td><td colspan="2">To</td></tr>
<tr><td colspan="2">Cisco IOS 12.0(4)XH</td><td colspan="2">Cisco IOS 12.0(6)T or later</td></tr>
<tr><td colspan="4">The recommended migration path is the logical superceding release, which provides additional features and hardware support to the network without loss of previously configured functionality.</td></tr>
<tr><td rowspan="3">Life Cycle</td><td>Milestones</td><td>Y2K Compliance</td><td>Certification</td><td>Other Dates</td></tr>
<tr><td>—</td><td>Yes</td><td>ED</td><td>CCO FCS in July, 1999</td></tr>
<tr><td colspan="4">Short-lived</td></tr>
<tr><td>Internet Addresses</td><td colspan="4">For more information, consult the following web pages:
• AS5300 Release Notes at http://www.cisco.com/univercd/cc/td/doc/product/software/ios120/relnote/5300as/rn5300xh.htm
• Cisco 2600 Release Notes at http://www.cisco.com/univercd/cc/td/doc/product/software/ios120/relnote/2600ser/rn2600xh.htm
• Cisco 3600 Release Notes at http://www.cisco.com/univercd/cc/td/doc/product/software/ios120/relnote/3600ser/rn3600xh.htm</td></tr>
<tr><td>Comments</td><td colspan="4">Continued maintenance software features introduced by XED are performed on the major release CTED.</td></tr>
</table>

Cisco IOS Release 12.0(4)XI

Description	Cisco IOS 12.0(4)XI is an XED based on 12.0(4)T. It introduced support for several new software and hardware features including: • The Cisco 1400 series router for Digital Subscriber Line (DSL) networks that connects small businesses and remote branch offices to the Internet or to corporate networks. • The uBR 924 subscriber-end cable access router that provides small-office/home-office customers with IP data and voice service through a provider's fiber/coax network. • TelcoReturn and Enhanced Spectrum Management support on uBR 7200. • Resource Pooling Manger on the Cisco AS5200, AS5300, and AS5800. Resource pooling allows the user to maximize the use of available modems, terminal adapters, or voice channels by using configurable Customer Profiles. • Support for H.245 Coder Negotiation, G723.1 Codec, dual tone multifrequency (DTMF) Digit Relay via RTP, and G.729 Bit Ordering Compliance on the Cisco AS5300 platform.	
Product Support	**Main Features**	**Platforms**
		Cisco 1400 series
	uBR924 features:	uBR 924
	Cable Device MIB	uBR 7200
	Cisco Standard MIBs	Cisco AS5200, AS5300, and AS5800 routers
	Cisco Voice MIBs	
	Full and DOCSIS-Compliant bridging	
	Home Office with Voice support	
	Network Address Translation and Port Address Translation (NAT/PAT)	
	Radio Frequency Interface MIB	
	Routing (RIP V2)	
	7200 features:	
	Additional or Changed Show commands	
	Additional Vendor-Proprietary RADIUS attributes	
	Automated Double authentication	
	Burst Profile configuration	
	Cable Modem and Multicast Authentication using RADIUS	
	DHCP Relay Subscriber ID Insertion	

	Downstream Quality of Service handling compliant to MCNS requirements Encrypted Baseline Privacy Key Exchange Improved and Extended Command-Line interface Improved MAC Scheduler Improved Parameter configuration Improved Upstream Quality of Service IP Type of Service and Precedence for GRE tunnels MIB enhancements Microsoft Point-to-Point Compression (MPPC) Multiple ISDN switch types Named Method Lists for AAA authorization and accounting National ISDN switch types for BRI and PRI Per-Modem and Per-Host Access List support Quality of Service configuration Quality of Service profile enforcement Read/Create Implementation of Quality of Service table Spectrum Management enhancements Upstream traffic shaping VPDN MIB and Syslog facility Resource Pooling Manger H.245 Coder Negotiation, G723.1 Codec and DTMF Digit Relay via RTP, G.729 Bit Ordering Compliance Dual tone multifrequency (DTMF)	
Synchronization Points with Major Releases	**Based On**	**Ported Into**
	Cisco IOS 12.0(4)T	Cisco IOS 12.0(5)T
	Cisco platforms currently running Cisco IOS XED software should consider upgrading to an equivalent software image of the CTED at or above the "ported into" revision level.	

<table>
<tr><td>Release Type</td><td colspan="4">XED</td></tr>
<tr><td>Target Market</td><td colspan="4">Branch Office/Remote Offices SOHO, SMB, LEC, CLES</td></tr>
<tr><td>Maintenance Releases</td><td colspan="4">XED</td></tr>
<tr><td>Interim Builds</td><td colspan="4"></td></tr>
<tr><td rowspan="3">Recommended Migration</td><td colspan="2">From</td><td colspan="2">To</td></tr>
<tr><td colspan="2">Cisco IOS 12.0(4)XI</td><td colspan="2">Cisco IOS 12.0(5)T</td></tr>
<tr><td colspan="4">The recommended migration path is the logical superceding release, which provides additional features and hardware support to the network without loss of previously configured functionality.</td></tr>
<tr><td rowspan="3">Life Cycle</td><td>Milestones</td><td>Y2K Compliance</td><td>Certification</td><td>Other Dates</td></tr>
<tr><td>—</td><td>Yes</td><td>ED</td><td>CCO FCS in May, 1999</td></tr>
<tr><td colspan="4">Short-lived</td></tr>
<tr><td>Internet Addresses</td><td colspan="4">For more information, consult the following web pages:
• Cisco 1400 Release Notes at http://www.cisco.com/univercd/cc/td/doc/product/software/ios120/relnote/1400ser/rn1400xi.htm
• Cisco uBR7200 Release Notes at http://www.cisco.com/univercd/cc/td/doc/product/software/ios120/relnote/ubr7200/rn7200xi.htm
• Cisco IOS Software Release 12.0(4)XI at http://www.cisco.com/warp/customer/cc/cisco/mkt/ios/rel/120/prodlit/912_pp.htm</td></tr>
<tr><td>Comments</td><td colspan="4">Continued maintenance software features introduced by XED are performed on the major release CTED.</td></tr>
</table>

Cisco IOS Release 12.0(4)XJ

<table>
<tr><td>Description</td><td colspan="2">Cisco IOS 12.0(4)XJ is an XED which focuses on functionality for the dial access market by delivering time-proven features and functionality for Cisco Access Products. It is based on Cisco IOS 12.0(4)T and incorporates all features of 12.0T up to 12.0(4)T including features from 11.3AA and 11.3NA. Cisco IOS 12.0(4)XJ supports the AS5200, AS5300 and the AS5800 including the NPE-300 CPU.</td></tr>
<tr><td rowspan="4">Product Support</td><td>Main Features</td><td>Platforms</td></tr>
<tr><td>Access features of 12.0T</td><td>Cisco AS5200</td></tr>
<tr><td>Internet fax store and forward</td><td>Cisco AS5300</td></tr>
<tr><td>New NPE-300 CPU</td><td>Cisco AS5800</td></tr>
</table>

<table>
<tr><th rowspan="2">Synchronization Points with Major Releases</th><th colspan="2">Based On</th><th colspan="2">Ported Into</th></tr>
<tr><td colspan="2">Cisco IOS 12.0(4)T</td><td colspan="2">Cisco IOS 12.1(2)</td></tr>
<tr><th>Release Type</th><td colspan="4">XED</td></tr>
<tr><th>Target Market</th><td colspan="4">ISP/Dial, Access, and remote Access market, CLEC, LEC</td></tr>
<tr><th>Maintenance Releases</th><td colspan="4">Cisco IOS 12.0(4)XJ is a short-lived release. However, in an effort to achieve very high stability and quality requirements of the ISP market, it will deploy several software rebuilds labeled as 12.0(4)XJ1, 12.0(4)XJ2, etc.</td></tr>
<tr><th>Interim Builds</th><td colspan="4"></td></tr>
<tr><th rowspan="3">Recommended Migration</th><th colspan="2">From</th><th colspan="2">To</th></tr>
<tr><td colspan="2">Cisco IOS 12.0(4)XJ</td><td colspan="2">Cisco IOS 12.0(4)XJx or 12.1</td></tr>
<tr><td colspan="4">The recommended migration path is the logical superceding release, which provides additional features and hardware support to the network without loss of previously configured functionality.</td></tr>
<tr><th rowspan="3">Life Cycle</th><th>Milestones</th><th>Y2K Compliance</th><th>Certification</th><th>Other Dates</th></tr>
<tr><td>—</td><td>Yes</td><td>ED</td><td>CCO FCS in June, 1999</td></tr>
<tr><td colspan="4">Short-live</td></tr>
<tr><th>Internet Addresses</th><td colspan="4">For more information, consult the following web pages:
• Cisco IOS Software Release 12.0(4)XJ Product Bulletin at http://www.cisco.com/warp/customer/cc/cisco/mkt/ios/rel/120/prodlit/916_pp.htm
• AS5800 Release Notes at http://www.cisco.com/univercd/cc/td/doc/product/software/ios120/relnote/5800as/rn5800xj.htm
• AS5300 Release Notes at http://www.cisco.com/univercd/cc/td/doc/product/software/ios120/relnote/5300as/rn5300xj.htm</td></tr>
<tr><th>Comments</th><td colspan="4">Cisco IOS 12.0(4)XJ focuses on delivering time-proven features with stringent quality criteria.</td></tr>
</table>

Cisco IOS Release 12.0(5)XK

<table>
<tr><td>Description</td><td colspan="2">Cisco IOS 12.0(5)XK is an XED release based on 12.0(5)T. It introduced several new software features and hardware modules for the Cisco 2600, 3600, and MC3810 series routers. These features include:
• Video over ATM SVCs and PVC on the Cisco MC3810.
• Voice over ATM SVCs on the Cisco MC3810.
• FRF.5 enhancements on the Cisco MC3810.
• FRF.8 on the Cisco MC3810.
• Digital T1 packet voice trunk network modules on the Cisco 2600 and 3600 series routers.
• Multiport T1/E1 ATM network modules with inverse multiplexing over ATM on the Cisco 2600 and 3600 series routers.</td></tr>
<tr><td rowspan="2">Product Support</td><td>Main Features</td><td>Platforms</td></tr>
<tr><td>Video over ATM SVCs, Voice over ATM SVCs, FRF.5 enhancements, FRF.8
Multiport T1/E1 ATM network modules with inverse multiplexing over ATM
Digital T1 Packet Voice Trunk Network Modules</td><td>Cisco MC3810
Cisco 2600 and 3600 series routers</td></tr>
<tr><td rowspan="3">Synchronization Points with Major Releases</td><td>Based On</td><td>Ported Into</td></tr>
<tr><td>Cisco IOS 12.0(5)T</td><td>Cisco IOS 12.0(6)T</td></tr>
<tr><td colspan="2">Cisco platforms currently running an XED release should upgrade to a Cisco IOS image of the CTED at or above the synchronization point.</td></tr>
<tr><td>Release Type</td><td colspan="2">XED</td></tr>
<tr><td>Target Market</td><td colspan="2">ISP, Telco, LEC, CLEC</td></tr>
<tr><td>Maintenance Releases</td><td colspan="2">Cisco IOS 12.0(5)XK is a one-time release.</td></tr>
<tr><td>Interim Builds</td><td colspan="2"></td></tr>
<tr><td rowspan="3">Recommended Migration</td><td>From</td><td>To</td></tr>
<tr><td>Cisco IOS 12.0(5)XK</td><td>Cisco IOS 12.0(6)T</td></tr>
<tr><td colspan="2">The recommended migration path is the logical superceding release, which provides additional features and hardware support to the network without loss of previously configured functionality.</td></tr>
</table>

Life Cycle	Milestones	Y2K Compliance	Certification	Other Dates
	—	Yes	ED	CCO FCS in July, 1999
	Short-lived			
Internet Addresses	For more information, consult the following web pages: • Cisco IOS 12.0(5)XK Product Bulletin at http://www.cisco.com/warp/customer/cc/cisco/mkt/ios/rel/120/prodlit/949_pb.htm • Release Notes at http://www.cisco.com/univercd/cc/td/doc/product/software/ios120/relnote/3600ser/rn3600xk.htm			
Comments	Continued maintenance on software features introduced by XED is performed on the major release CTED.			

Cisco IOS Release 12.0(7)XK

Description	Cisco IOS 12.0(7)XK is an XED based on the 12.0(7) software branch. It introduced several features and hardware modules of the Cisco 2600, 3600, and MC3810 series routers. The new features of Cisco IOS 12.0(7)XK include Q.SIG, Q.SIG Prime, and transparent signaling support for the Primary Rate Interface (PRI) in the Symphony architecture for the Cisco 2600, 3600, and MC3810 products. In addition to Simple Gateway Control Protocol (SGCP) 1.1 support, it also include several enhancements for Voice over IP (VoIP) and Voice over Frame Relay (VoFR). Hardware features include an increased number of supported network modules for the Cisco 3660 with enhanced online insertion and removal (OIR) functionality. It also combines functionality of existing network modules into a new module with enhanced WAN and voice interface cards (WICs/VICs) for the Cisco 2600 and 3600 platforms.	
Product Support	Main Features	Platforms
	Transparent signaling support Primary Rate Interface (PRI) Voice over Frame Relay Using FRF.11 and FRF.12 on the Cisco 2600 and 3600 Series Routers Voice Port Enhancements on the Cisco 2600 and 3600 Series Routers QSIG and Transparent CCS on the Cisco 2600 and 3600 Series Routers Voice over ATM on the Cisco 3600 Series Routers	Cisco MC3810 Cisco 2600 and 3600 series routers

	QSIG and Transparent CCS on the Cisco MC3810 QSIG and Transparent CCS on the Cisco 7200 Series Routers Transparent signaling support Primary Rate Interface (PRI) Voice over IP (VoIP) Voice over Frame Relay (VoFR)			
Synchronization Points with Major Releases	**Based On**		**Ported Into**	
	Cisco IOS 12.0(7)T		Cisco IOS 12.1 / 12.1T	
	Cisco platforms currently running an XED release should upgrade to a Cisco IOS image of the CTED at or above the synchronization point.			
Release Type	XED			
Target Market	ISP, Telco			
Maintenance Releases	Cisco IOS 12.0(7)XK is a one-time release.			
Interim Builds				
Recommended Migration	**From**		**To**	
	Cisco IOS 12.0(7)XK		Cisco IOS 12.1 or 12.1T	
	The recommended migration path is the logical superceding release, which provides additional features and hardware support to the network without loss of previously configured functionality.			
Life Cycle	**Milestones**	**Y2K Compliance**	**Certification**	**Other Dates**
	—	Yes	ED	CCO FCS in December, 1999
	Short-lived			
Internet Addresses	For more information, consult the following web pages: • Cisco IOS 12.0(7)XK Product Bulletin at http://www.cisco.com/warp/customer/cc/cisco/mkt/ios/rel/120/prodlit/			
Comments	Continued maintenance support for the features introduced by XED software is provided on the major release CTED.			

Cisco IOS Release 12.0(4)XL

Description	Cisco IOS 12.0(4)XL is an XED based on 12.(4)T. It introduced high density VoIP applications on the Cisco AS5800. The VoIP function gives the Cisco AS5800 the ability to be an H.323 Gateway (Public Switched Telephone Network (PSTN) to VoIP networks. Cisco IOS 12.0(4)XL supports up to one T3's of voice channels over four Voice Feature Cards (672 for T3, and 720 for two E1 cards). Traditional Cisco AS5800 modem and ISDN data features continue to be supported in mixed voice/data mode.	
Product Support	**Main Features**	**Platforms**
	Two-stage dial toll bypass PSTN voice traffic and fax traffic offload Universally accessible voice mail and fax mail services DS58-192VOX (T1 C549 DSP-based Voice feature card) Up to 1344 VoIP calls, in a split-dial shelf configuration with Voice Detection (VAD)/ silence suppression turned on Multiple voice coders including G.723.1, G.729a, G.726, G.728 as well as the existing G.711, and G.729 Fax relay up to 14.4 Kbps	Cisco AS5800
Synchronization Points with Major Releases	**Based On**	**Ported Into**
	Cisco IOS 12.0(4)T	Cisco IOS 12.0(7)T
	Cisco platforms currently running Cisco IOS XED software should consider upgrading to an equivalent software image of the CTED at or above the "ported into" revision level.	
Release Type	XED	
Target Market	ISP, Telco, LEC	
Maintenance Releases	Cisco IOS 12.0(4)XL is a one-time release.	
Interim Builds		
Recommended Migration	**From**	**To**
	Cisco IOS 12.0(4)XL	Cisco IOS 12.0(7)T
	The recommended migration path is the logical superceding release, which provides additional features and hardware support to the network without loss of previously configured functionality.	

Life Cycle	**Milestones**	**Y2K Compliance**	**Certification**	**Other Dates**
	—	Yes	ED	CCO FCS in July, 1999
	Short-lived			
Internet Addresses	For more information, consult the following web pages: • Cisco IOS Software Release 12.0(4)XL at http://www.cisco.com/warp/customer/cc/cisco/mkt/ios/rel/120/prodlit/933_pp.htm • Cisco IOS 12.0(4)XL Release Notes at http://www.cisco.com/univercd/cc/td/doc/product/software/ios120/relnote/5800as/rn5800xl.htm			
Comments	Cisco IOS 12.0(4)XL and 12.0(4)XH are from the same source code branch.			

Cisco IOS Release 12.0(4)XM

Description	Cisco IOS 12.0(4)XM is an XED based on 12.0(4)T which introduced support for the Cisco 805 serial router. The Cisco 805 serial router provides small offices with secure and reliable Internet access via Frame Relay, leased line, X.25, or asynchronous dialup. The Cisco 805 router features an Ethernet port and a serial port that supports synchronous serial connections of up to 512 kbps or asynchronous serial dialup (up to 115 kbps) with an external modem. While running the IOS firewall feature set, it offers a secure and manageable multiprotocol solution for remote network access.	
Product Support	**Main Features**	**Platforms**
	Various security options, including Firewall feature set and IPSec	Cisco 805 serial router
	Frame Relay, leased line, X.25, or asynchronous dialup options	
	Virtual Private Networks (VPNs), point-of-sale (POS) services	
Synchronization Points with Major Releases	**Based On**	**Ported Into**
	Cisco IOS 12.0(4)T	Cisco IOS 12.0(7)T
	Cisco platforms currently running Cisco IOS XED software should consider upgrading to an equivalent software image of the CTED at or above the "ported into" revision level.	
Release Type	XED	
Target Market	SOHO, remote office, branch offices	
Maintenance Releases	Cisco IOS 12.0(4)XM is a one-time release	
Interim Builds		

Recommended Migration	**From**		**To**	
	Cisco IOS 12.0(4)XM		Cisco IOS 12.0(6)T	
	The recommended migration path is the logical superceding release, which provides additional features and hardware support to the network without loss of previously configured functionality.			
Life Cycle	**Milestones**	**Y2K Compliance**	**Certification**	**Other Dates**
	—	Yes	ED	CCO FCS in June, 1999
	Short-lived			
Internet Addresses	For more information, consult the following web pages: • Cisco IOS 12.0(4)XM Release Notes at http://www.cisco.com/univercd/cc/td/doc/product/software/ios120/relnote/800ser/rn800xm.htm • Cisco IOS Software Release 12.0(4)XM Product Bulletin at http://www.cisco.com/warp/customer/cc/cisco/mkt/ios/rel/120/prodlit/926_pb.htm • Cisco 800 Series at http://www.cisco.com/warp/customer/cc/cisco/mkt/access/800/index.shtml			
Comments	Continued maintenance of software features introduced by XED is performed on the major release CTED.			

Cisco IOS Release 12.0(5)XN

Description	Cisco IOS 12.0(5)XN is an XED based on 12.(5)T. It introduced the newly developed SNA Switching services (SNASw) and features for Cisco Transaction Connection (CTRC). It provides IBM Advanced Peer-to-Peer Networking (APPN) switching for traditional IBM 3270 sessions and distributed Advanced Program-to-Program Communications (APPC) including transaction routing to Customer Information Control Systems (CICS) via the Cisco Transaction Connection (CTRC). SNA Switch will replace the APPN features in Cisco IOS software starting with 12.1 software releases. SNASw provides an easier way to design and implement networks with Systems Network Architecture (SNA) routing requirements. CTRC is a software gateway TCP-IP client connecting directly to IBM host resident CICS transactions and DB2 applications. CTRC extends Cisco dbconn functionality to support CICS and could be used to replace IBM SP2 gateway requesters to host resident Application Servers. SNA Switching Services implements IBM APPN and High Performance Routing (HPR) End Node (EN), together with Dependent Logical Unit requester (DLUr), Branch Extender (BrNN), and Enterprise Extender (EE).

Product Support	**Main Features**		**Platforms**	
	SNA Switch services		2500 series	
	CTRC		2600 series	
	Dynamic CP Name Generation support		4000 series	
	Dynamic SNA BTU size		4700 series	
	DLUR Connect-Out		RSP series	
	Responsive Mode Adaptive Rate-Based flow control		7200 series	
	User-Settable port limits			
	HPR capable			
	SNA routing services			
	Branch extender			
	Enterprise extender (HPR/IP)			
	Usability features			
	Management enhancements			
	LAN and IP-Focused connection types			
Synchronization Points with Major Releases	**Based On**		**Ported Into**	
	Cisco IOS 12.0(5)T		Cisco IOS 12.1(1)	
	SNA Switch was introduced in 12.0(5)XN and committed to the pre-integration branch of 12.1.			
Release Type	XED			
Target Market	Enterprise, SNA networks			
Maintenance Releases	Cisco IOS 12.0(5)XN is a one-time release.			
Interim Builds				
Recommended Migration	**From**		**To**	
	Cisco IOS 12.0(5)XN		12.0(7)T and 12.1(1)	
	The recommended migration path is the logical superceding release, which provides additional features and hardware support to the network without loss of previously configured functionality.			
Life Cycle	**Milestones**	**Y2K Compliance**	**Certification**	**Other Dates**
	—	Yes	ED	CCO FCS in September, 1999
	Short-lived			

Internet Addresses	For more information, consult the following web pages: • Release Notes for 12.0(5)XN at http://www.cisco.com/univercd/cc/td/doc/product/software/ios120/relnote/xnrelnt.htm
Comments	SNA Switching Services (SNASw) functionality supersedes all functionality previously available in the APPN feature set of the Cisco IOS software. SNASw configuration will not accept the previous APPN configuration syntaxes. Existing APPN users should reconfigure APPN functionality using the new SNASw commands. Continued maintenance of software features introduced by XED is performed on the major release CTED.

Cisco IOS Release 12.0(5)XQ

Description	Cisco IOS 12.0(5)XQ is an XED based on 12.0(5)T. It introduced the Cisco 1750 platform. The Cisco 1750 is a voice-enabled derivative of the 1720 platform. It provides extensive voice capabilities with interchangeable modular WAN and Voice Interface Cards (WIC/VIC).	
Product Support	**Main Features**	**Platforms**
	Support for Cisco 1750 router Two WIC/VIC slots and one VIC slot Supports same WICs as 1720 (1T, 2T, 2A/S, 1BRI-S/T, 1BRI-U, 1DSU-FT1, 1DSU-56k) Analog VICs (2FXS, 2FXO, 2E&M) One DSP slot (supports 1 to 3 DSP's) Supports G.711 and G.729 codecs and Fax-Relay	Cisco 1750
Synchronization Points with Major Releases	**Based On**	**Ported Into**
	Cisco IOS 12.0(5)T	Cisco IOS 12.0(7)T
	Cisco 1750 was introduced in 12.0(5)XQ and committed to the pre-integration branch of 12.0(6)T.	
Release Type	XED	
Target Market	Enterprise, small offices, remote offices, branch offices, SOHO, SMB	
Maintenance Releases	Cisco IOS 12.0(5)XQ is a one-time release.	
Interim Builds		

Recommended Migration	**From**		**To**	
	Cisco IOS 12.0(5)XQ		Cisco IOS 12.1(1)	
	The recommended migration path is the logical superceding release, which provides additional features and hardware support to the network without loss of previously configured functionality.			
Life Cycle	**Milestones**	**Y2K Compliance**	**Certification**	**Other Dates**
	—	Yes	ED	CCO FCS in September, 1999
	Short-lived			
Internet Addresses	For more information, consult the following web pages: • Cisco IOS 12.0(5)XQ Product Bulletin at http://www.cisco.com/warp/customer/cc/cisco/mkt/ios/rel/120/prodlit/959_pp.htm • Cisco 1750 Release Notes at http://www.cisco.com/univercd/cc/td/doc/product/software/ios120/relnote/1700ser/c1750/rn1750xq.htm			
Comments				

Cisco IOS Release 12.0(5)XP

Description	Cisco IOS 12.0(5)XP is an XED based on 12.0(5)T and optimized for the Catalyst family of switches. It introduced support ATM modules on the Cisco Catalyst 2900 and the 3500 series platforms.	
Product Support	**Main Features**	**Platforms**
	ATM Modules	Catalyst 1900
	Extended Cluster Member functionality	Catalyst 2900 series XL 8-MB
	RMON Support	Catalyst 3500
	Management VLAN configuration	
	IEEE 802.1p Quality of Service	
Synchronization Points with Major Releases	**Based On**	**Ported Into**
	Cisco IOS 12.0(5)T	Cisco IOS 12.1(1)WC or 12.1E
Release Type	XED	
Target Market	Enterprise workgroup, branch offices, SOHO, Network service providers	
Maintenance Releases	Cisco IOS 12.0(5)XP is a one-time release.	
Interim Builds		

Recommended Migration	**From**		**To**	
	Cisco IOS 12.0(5)XP		Cisco IOS 12.1(1)WB or 12.1E	
	The recommended migration path is the logical superceding release, which provides additional features and hardware support to the network without loss of previously configured functionality.			
Life Cycle	**Milestones**	**Y2K Compliance**	**Certification**	**Other Dates**
	—	Yes	ED	CCO FCS in October, 1999
	Short-lived			
Internet Addresses	For more information, consult the following web pages: • Release Notes For Cisco IOS 12.0(5)XP at http://www.cisco.com/univercd/cc/td/doc/product/lan/c2900xl/29_35xp/ • Catalyst 2900 and 3500 Release Notes at http://www.cisco.com/univercd/cc/td/doc/product/lan/c2900xl/29_35xp/index.htm			
Comments	This release does not support the Catalyst 2900 series XL 4 MB switches. 1.2(8)SA6.			

Cisco IOS Release 12.0(7)XR

Description	Cisco IOS 12.0(7)XR is an XED based on the 12.0(7)T software branch. It introduced dial access and voice over IP features on the Cisco 2600, the uBR7200, the uBR924 and the AS5300 platforms. One of the main features of 12.0(7)XR is the Media Gateway Control Protocol (MGCP). MGCP is an interface protocol used for controlling VoIP Gateways from external call control elements. The MGCP architecture assumes call control intelligence, which resides outside the gateways and is handled by external call control elements. This Cisco IOS software release also provides support for the NTT (Japanese system) SS7 variant. It provides the 2600-SLT with the ability to terminate NTT SS7 links using the V.35 interface. The NTT MTP-1 and MTP-2 are terminated on the 2600 and MTP-3 with upper layers backhauled to the virtual switch controller (VSC). A CII to V.35 conversion box is required to connect the 2600 to NTT CII equipment. Features and functionality of this release will be ported to 12.1(1)T or later.

<table>
<tr><td rowspan="8">Product Support</td><td colspan="2">Main Features</td><td colspan="2">Platforms</td></tr>
<tr><td colspan="2">Cable Interface Bundling
MC16 Modem Card for the Cisco uBR7200
Data-over-Cable Service Interface Specification (DOCSIS) 1.0+
Broadband Wireless Point-to-Point
Media Gateway Control Protocol (MGCP)
SS7 support for H.323 voice calls via SC2200
Cisco Signaling Link Terminal (SLT)</td><td colspan="2">uBR7200 DOCSIS 1+ Compliant
uBR924
2600 series
AS5300</td></tr>
</table>

Synchronization Points with Major Releases	**Based On**		**Ported Into**	
	Cisco IOS 12.0(7)T		Cisco IOS 12.1(1)T	
	Features introduced by 12.0(7)XR are committed to the pre-integration branch of 12.1(1)T.			
Release Type	XED			
Target Market	Interexchange Carriers (IXCs), Local Exchange Carriers (LECs), Competitive Local Exchange Carriers (CLECs), Worldwide PTTs/Carriers, ISPs			
Maintenance Releases	Cisco IOS 12.0(7)XR is a one-time release.			
Interim Builds				
Recommended Migration	**From**		**To**	
	Cisco IOS 12.0(7)XR		Cisco IOS 12.1(1)T	
	The recommended migration path is the logical superceding release, which provides additional features and hardware support to the network without loss of previously configured functionality.			
Life Cycle	**Milestones**	**Y2K Compliance**	**Certification**	**Other Dates**
	—	Yes	ED	FCS: January 2000
	Short-lived			
Internet Addresses	For more information, consult the following web pages: • CCO at www.cisco.com • Product Bulletin: http://www.cisco.com/warp/customer/cc/cisco/mkt/ios/rel/120/prodlit/1001_pp.htm • Release Notes For SLT: http://www.cisco.com/univercd/cc/td/doc/product/software/ios120/120newft/120limit/120xr/tcslt6xr.htm			
Comments				

Cisco IOS Release 12.0(5)XS

<table>
<tr><td>Description</td><td colspan="4">Cisco IOS 12.0(5)XS is an XED which introduced support for the OC-12 ATM module for the Catalyst 6000 family of switches. In addition to being compliant with RFC1483, this software also supports LANE, Traffic Shaping, and MPOA.</td></tr>
<tr><td rowspan="2">Product Support</td><td colspan="2">Main Features</td><td colspan="2">Platforms</td></tr>
<tr><td colspan="2">OC-12 ATM Uplink
LAN Emulation (LANE)
Multiprotocol over ATM (MPOA)—MPC support only
RFC 1483 SNAP/LLC Bridged format
Fast PHY switchover
PVC traffic shaping</td><td colspan="2">Catalyst 6000 series</td></tr>
<tr><td rowspan="2">Synchronization Points with Major Releases</td><td colspan="2">Based On</td><td colspan="2">Ported Into</td></tr>
<tr><td colspan="2">Cisco IOS 12.0(5)T</td><td colspan="2">Cisco IOS 12.1(1)E and 12.1(3)T</td></tr>
<tr><td>Release Type</td><td colspan="4">XED</td></tr>
<tr><td>Target Market</td><td colspan="4">Enterprise, Workgroup, Network service providers</td></tr>
<tr><td>Maintenance Releases</td><td colspan="4">Cisco IOS 12.0(5)XS is a one-time release.</td></tr>
<tr><td>Interim Builds</td><td colspan="4"></td></tr>
<tr><td rowspan="3">Recommended Migration</td><td colspan="2">From</td><td colspan="2">To</td></tr>
<tr><td colspan="2">Cisco IOS 12.0(5)XS</td><td colspan="2">12.1(1)E, 12.1(3)T</td></tr>
<tr><td colspan="4">The recommended migration path is the logical superceding release, which provides additional features and hardware support to the network without loss of previously configured functionality.</td></tr>
<tr><td rowspan="3">Life Cycle</td><td>Milestones</td><td>Y2K Compliance</td><td>Certification</td><td>Other Dates</td></tr>
<tr><td>—</td><td>Yes</td><td>LD</td><td>CCO FCS in September, 1999</td></tr>
<tr><td colspan="4">Short-lived</td></tr>
<tr><td>Internet Addresses</td><td colspan="4">For more information, consult the following web pages:
• Cisco IOS Product Bulletin at http://www.cisco.com/warp/customer/cc/cisco/mkt/gen/bulletin/soft/ios_120/index.shtml
• Catalyst 6000 ATM Modules at http://www.cisco.com/univercd/cc/td/doc/product/lan/cat6000/relnotes/atm_rns/78_10108.htm</td></tr>
</table>

Comments	ATM release 12.0(5)XS requires that the Supervisor Engine is running software release 5.3.2 or later. Supervisor Engine software release 5.3.1 will recognize the ATM module but does not support it. Do not use Supervisor Engine Software Release version 5.3.1. The Multilayer Switch Module software release version must be 12.0(4a)WX5(11) or later to support the OC-12 ATM module.

Cisco IOS Release 12.0(7)XV

Description	Cisco IOS 12.0(7)XV is an XED optimized for Cisco 800 series routers (801 and 803). It introduces support for Common-Application Programming Interface (CAPI) 2.0 (as opposed to a socket-based interface) that is designed to provide support for a wider variety of clients. CAPI and Remote CAPI (RCAPI) provide the Windows application programming interface standard used by access ISDN equipment connected to basic rate interfaces (BRIs) and primary rate interfaces (PRIs). CAPI was initially deployed as a standard application-programming interface (API) on PCs equipped with ISDN equipment (such as ISDN-terminal adapter (TA) cards). Using a PC equipped with an ISDN network connection and CAPI drivers, end-user communications applications are provided that run on multi-vendor ISDN hardware. The new ANSI C-compliant source code is compiled in the Windows environment into a C Library and C DLL binaries. The Cisco 800 provides low-end Cisco IOS Software-based router solutions. It is the natural upgrade for the Cisco 1003, Cisco 1004, and Cisco 700 series routers.	
Product Support	**Main Features**	**Platforms**
	Basic call features, such as call setup and tear-down Multiple B channels for data and voice connections Multiple logical data link connections within a physical connection Selection of different services and protocols during connection setup and on answering incoming calls Transparent interface for protocols above Layer 3	Cisco 801 and 803 routers

	One or more BRIs as well as PRI on one or more ISDN adapters Multiple applications Operating-systems-independent messages Operating-system-dependent exchange mechanism for optimum operating system integration Asynchronous event driven mechanism, resulting in high throughput Multiple supplementary services			
Synchronization Points with Major Releases	**Based On**		**Ported Into**	
	Cisco IOS 12.0(5)T		Cisco IOS 12.1(1)E and 12.1(3)T	
Release Type	XED			
Target Market	Enterprise, Network Service Providers, ISP, SOHO			
Maintenance Releases	Cisco IOS 12.0(7)XV is a one-time release.			
Interim Builds	None			
Recommended Migration	**From**		**To**	
	Cisco IOS 12.0(7)XV		12.1(3)T	
	The recommended migration path is the logical superceding release, which brings additional features and hardware support to the network without loss of previously configured functionality			
Life Cycle	**Milestones**	**Y2K Compliance**	**Certification**	**Other Dates**
	—	Yes	ED	CCO FCS in January, 2000
	Short lived			
Internet Addresses	For more information, consult the following web pages: • Cisco IOS Product Bulletin: http://www.cisco.com/warp/customer/cc/cisco/mkt/ios/rel/120/prodlit/1022_pp.htm • Release Notes: http://www.cisco.com/univercd/cc/td/doc/product/software/ios120/relnote/800ser/rn800xv.htm			
Comments				

PART III

The Hardware-Software Relationship

CHAPTER 8

Hardware Architectures and Cisco IOS Software

The central focus of this chapter is to provide information on how Cisco IOS software utilizes the router's physical resources as logical entities to forge an extensive service offering. Here, you'll find concise specifications for router architecture and how IOS uses processor resources, memory resources, and other physical attributes of the networking device. The chapter will end with a step-by-step booting process of selected Cisco hardware, highlighting how the IOS software is used to extend hardware capability while offering continuous enhanced network and Internetwork services.

Cisco Routers and Switches

Cisco IOS provides multidimensional support for routers, bridges, and switches alike. Support includes all standards for LAN media and WAN protocols, and includes support for network services including routing, switching, signaling, IBM protocols, video streaming, voice/fax applications, protocol translation, and many other integrated applications (see Figure 8-1).

Figure 8-1 *Cisco IOS Services*

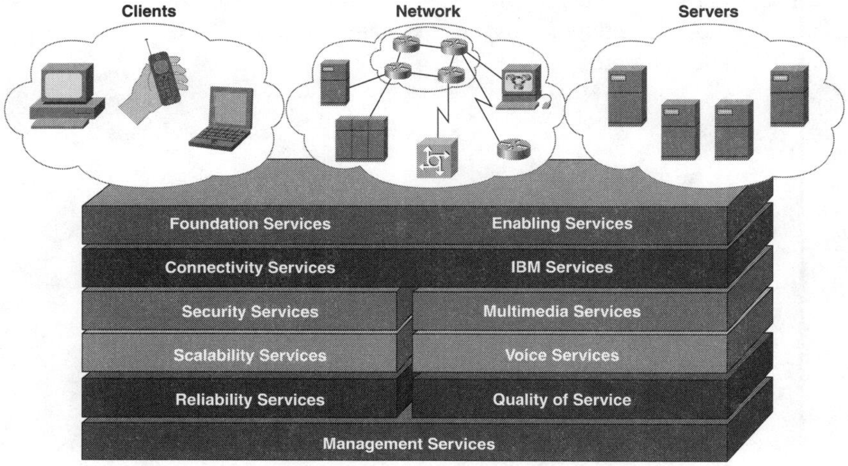

You're probably familiar with the OSI model, as illustrated in Figure 8-2. Routers and switches perform various functions in different layers of the OSI model.

Figure 8-2 *OSI Reference Model*

Layer	Name	Function
7	Application Layer	Manages the communication between applications
6	Presentation Layer	Identifies structure used in the data
5	Session Layer	Adds control mechanisms to the data flow
4	Transport Layer	Provides higher level of service to application, including end-end error recovery and flow control
3	Network Layer	End-to-end routing and data flow
2	Data Link Layer	Transmission, framing, and error control
1	Physical Layer	Electrical/Mechanical Interface

Basic Router Functions

A router (or a switch with a routing module) is an intelligent link between networks, which looks at header information (that is, layer 3 addresses) to determine the final destination of the packet, then determines which path is best for the packet to take (see Figure 8-3). This makes routing a processor-intensive activity. Most routers running Cisco IOS software use a variety of layer 3 switching mechanisms to increase performance and reduce overhead activity. Cisco IOS switching mechanisms include fast switching, optimum switching, silicon switching, and more advanced switching such as Cisco Express Forwarding (CEF) and NetFlow Switching.

Figure 8-3 *Packet Flow in a Router*

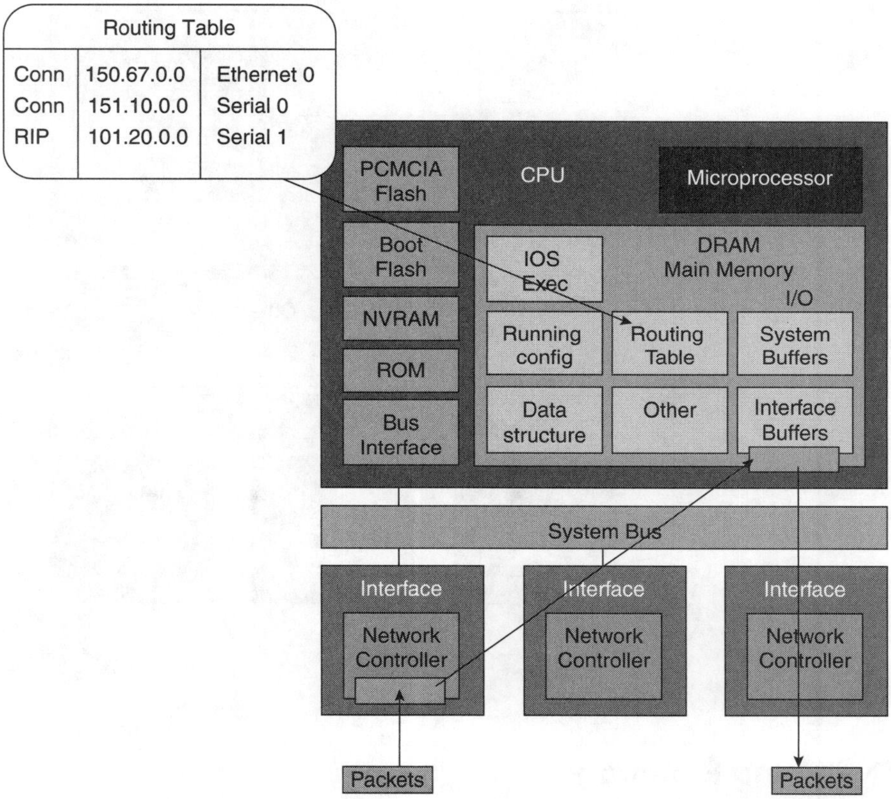

As mentioned earlier, routers operate at the network layer of the OSI model. They move data between different network segments by looking into layer 3 information of a packet header to determine the best path for the packet to travel (see Figure 8-4). It then selects the optimal route for the message, based upon destination, routing protocol, quality of service (QoS), administrative policy, and traffic considerations. In contrast, traditional switches need only to look at OSI model layer 2 information to make forwarding decisions. Using the intelligence built into the Cisco IOS software, increasingly both routers and switches are looking at layer 4 and above to implement advanced QoS and security policies. In recent years, the distinction between bridges, switches, and routers has become blurred as Cisco IOS software can be used to configure the functions of any of these devices to perform the services found in all of them. However, routers make up the backbone of any modern corporate network and constitute the nervous system of today's Internet.

Figure 8-4 *Layer 3 Switching*

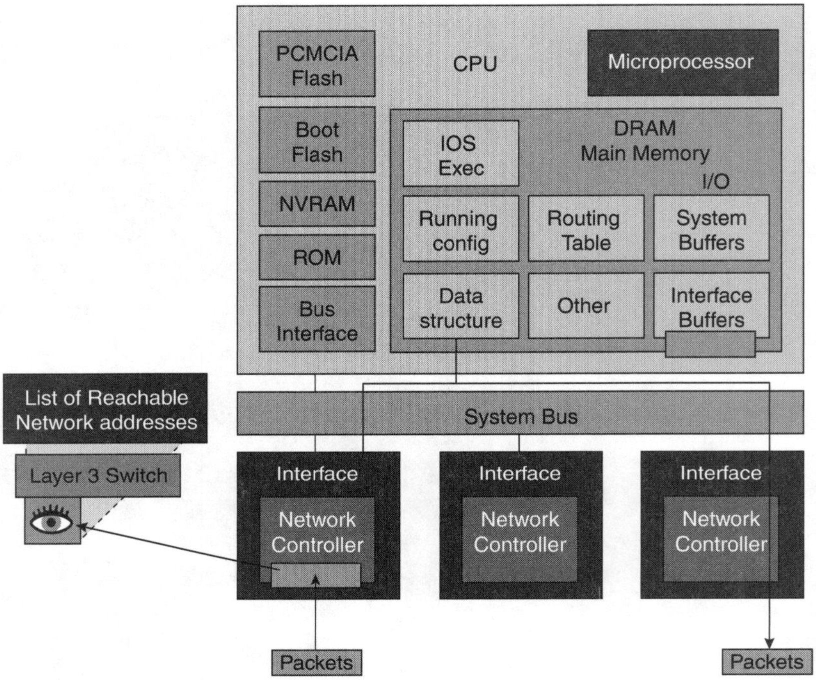

Basic Switching Function

Both bridges and switches operate at layer 2 of the OSI reference model, the data link layer, shown in Figure 8-5. Switching is the process of transferring data from an interface where data is received to another interface, which houses the destination host. Conceptually, a LAN switch is a multi-port bridge. While the use of switches has increased substantially, bridges are almost extinct.

Figure 8-5 *Operation Layers of Repeaters, Bridge/Switches, and Routers*

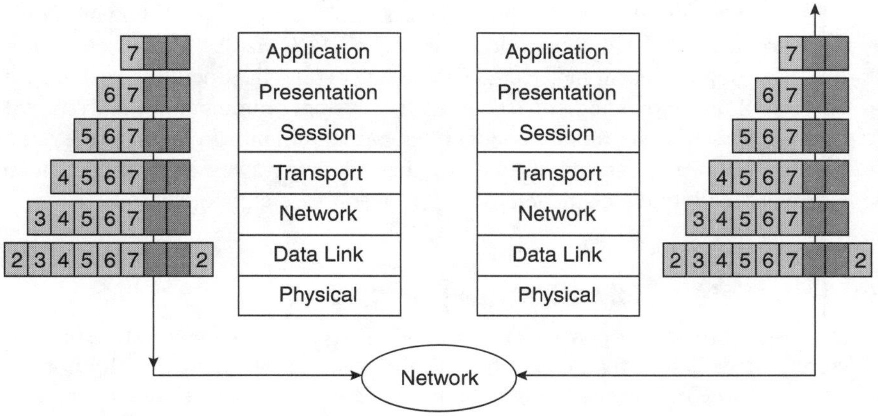

NOTE Cisco IOS software techniques allow switching at layer 3.

Today's switches are devices that improve network performance by segmenting the network and reducing competition for bandwidth. When a switched port receives data packets, it forwards those packets only to the appropriate port for the intended recipient. This further reduces competition for bandwidth between clients, servers, or workgroups connected to each switch port. Some Cisco switches equipped with the appropriate hardware module perform both routing and layer 3 switching services. The Cisco Catalyst 5000, equipped with the route switch module (RSM) board running Cisco IOS software, or the Cisco 8500 series multiservice routers, provide that capability. Figure 8-6 illustrates the basic switching mechanism.

Figure 8-6 *Basic Switching Mechanism*

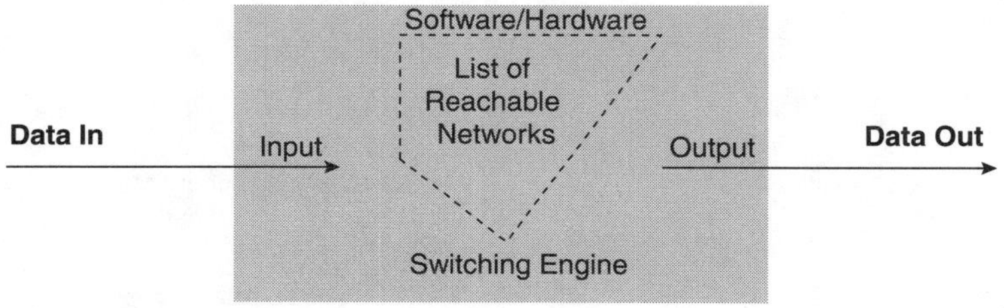

The Software Components of a Typical Router

A typical Cisco router (or switch) utilizes a combination of the following three types of software: the ROM Monitor, which is stored in EPROMs; the boot loader or boot software image, which is present in selected Cisco routers; and the operating system, which can be Cisco IOS software (another Cisco operating system prominent in Catalyst Switches). The rxboot software is another component that is found in most routers. However, newer generations of modular routers and switches are doing away with rxboot. The following sections highlight the characteristics of each software component.

Boot ROM System (ROM Monitor)

Boot ROM software is contained in an EPROM which permanently stores platform-specific startup diagnostic software. The boot ROM is also known as ROM Monitor (ROMMON) or bootstrap code. At power up, the boot ROM software verifies that the hardware is fully functional and that a more intelligent software image exists. In some routers, the more intelligent software image can be the boot image or the full IOS image. For example, in the 2500 series, there is not a boot image, so the ROMMON loads the Cisco IOS image. However, on the 7500 series or the 4500 series, the ROMMON will look for the boot image instead. In any case, if ROMMON fails to identify a valid software image (boot image or IOS image), it has the ability to handle those exceptions and take appropriate remedial action or provide the user with a prompt for further troubleshooting. If all is well, it proceeds to load the next software component, the boot loader or the fully qualified Cisco IOS image.

Identifying ROMMON

Starting with Cisco IOS version 12.0, the Cisco ROMMON based on Cisco IOS software branches use the generalized convention illustrated in Figure 8-7.

Figure 8-7 *The Convention for Identifying the ROMMON*

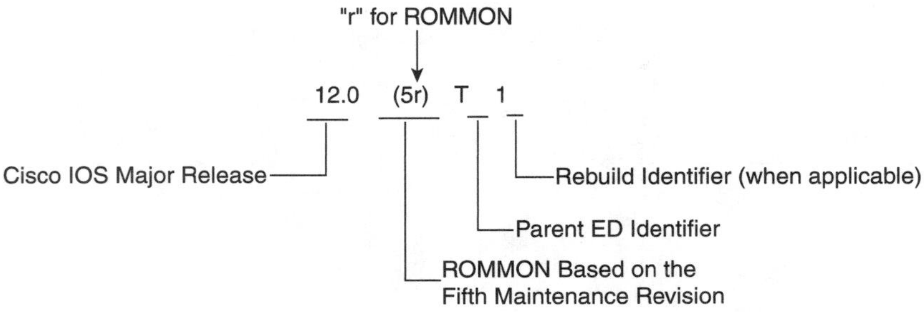

The output of a **show version** command will show the following ROMMON Banner information consistent with the format shown in Figure 8-7:

ROM: System Bootstrap, Version <version_number>, <banner_string> RELEASE SOFTWARE

The Cisco IOS Boot Software (Boot Loader/rxboot)

Cisco IOS boot software images, also known as boot loaders, are different from ROMMON. ROMMON are stored in EPROM and become part of the hardware structure. Upgrading a boot ROM requires swapping some hardware components. Boot software images, however, are soft images that are loaded in a router in the same way as the regular Cisco IOS software image. It should be noted that not all Cisco routers support boot images. For example, the Cisco 2500, 2600, and 3600 series routers have no software boot images, while the Cisco 7000, 7200, 7500, 12000, and the 45000 series routers require the presence of a boot image or boot loader. The boot image is responsible for parsing the configuration, identifying, and loading the fully qualified Cisco IOS image according to the configuration register setting and the **boot system** parameters configured by the user. The functions of the boot loader are streamlined and included in the ROMMON of the routers that do not have an explicit boot system software image. Boot images also contain the function of rxboot (see RXboot).

Identifying Cisco IOS Boot Software Images

The Cisco IOS boot images are clearly distinguishable from the regular Cisco IOS software with the word "boot" inserted in the image name. The boot files names follow the format:

PPPP-boot-MM

where PPPP is the platform identifier and MM is the fully qualified Cisco IOS maintenance revision number. (See Appendix A, "Cisco IOS Image Name Reference," for more information.)

For example, the boot image of the Cisco 4500 series routers based on Cisco IOS 12.0(5)T will be named as c4500-boot-mz.120-5.T.bin. Similarly, the boot image of the Cisco 6400 NRP based on Cisco IOS software revision 12.0(3)DC1 will be named c6400r-boot-mz.120-3.DC1.bin. The naming structure shown in Figure 8-8 further illustrates the Cisco IOS boot image naming convention.

Figure 8-8 *Cisco IOS Boot Image Naming Convention*

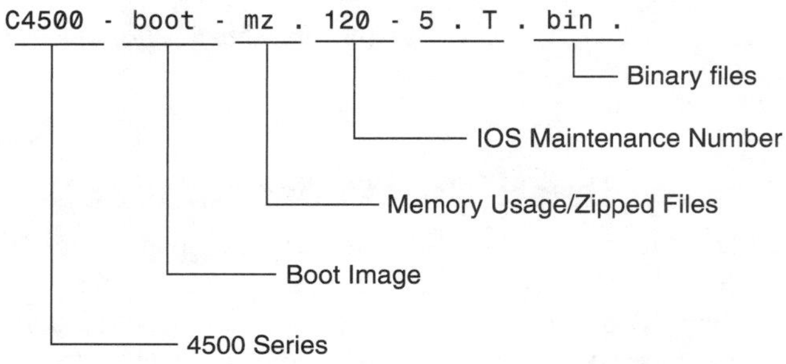

The Rxboot

Among others, the rxboot software provides a recovery mechanism in case of damage to the operating system binary image. When the boot ROM fails to locate the IOS executable file, or if it detects that the present IOS file is corrupted, it calls on the rxboot. Rxboot loads and configures the physical interface's driver and starts querying the network for a valid IOS binary. If a valid IOS is detected on one of the network servers, it is downloaded into the router's flash and executed. Routers that do not provide rxboot functionality have transferred this recovery mechanism to one of the asynchronous ports.

Rxboot is also known as boot helper image, helper IOS, or bootstrap image (or just bootstrap, which confuses it with the ROMMON). It is located on boot ROM, or boot Flash depending upon platform and in most cases is loaded into processor memory (DRAM) for execution.

The Operating System (IOS)

The Cisco IOS software is a highly specialized operating system that provides Kernel services, network services, platform-specific services and integrated applications. In terms of router resource management, the IOS also provides process scheduler, memory manager, and parser functions. Cisco IOS runs on most Cisco routers and switches as well as selected hardware from third-party vendors.

Summary of Router Boot Process

At startup, the software components of a router are executed in the following order:

1 **ROM Monitor**—Performs the hardware diagnostic check, sets up the console, and sizes the memory. It checks the configuration registers and loads the rxboot, or stays in ROMMON in case of failure. [rommon>]

2 **The Rxboot**—Builds the basic data structures, sets up the interfaces, sets up the router host mode, and checks startup-configuration file. It then loads the IOS binary image for execution, or stays in rxboot in case of failure. [router(boot)>]

3 **The IOS Image**—Builds up data structures, sets up physical and logical interfaces, and allocates buffers, then parses the startup-configuration file to complete boot process according to instructions contained in the configuration file. [router>]

Cisco Router Architecture

This section gives a brief description of the generic Cisco router architecture. It provides a background for understanding how these resources are viewed and utilized by the IOS operating systems. The next section provides information on how Cisco IOS leverages available physical resources of a router to optimize service offerings.

Basic Router Architecture

The basic architecture of a Cisco router is composed of the following four elements, shown in Figure 8-9. Some routers might vary slightly from what is shown.

- Central processing unit
- System bus
- Network interfaces
- Memory space

As mentioned in the introduction to this chapter, the most important of these components from the IOS point of view is the memory space in which it executes. The definitions and specifications for Cisco routers listed in this chapter include information about the other three components only as they are related to the way in which IOS uses their resources.

Figure 8-9 *Basic Router Architecture*

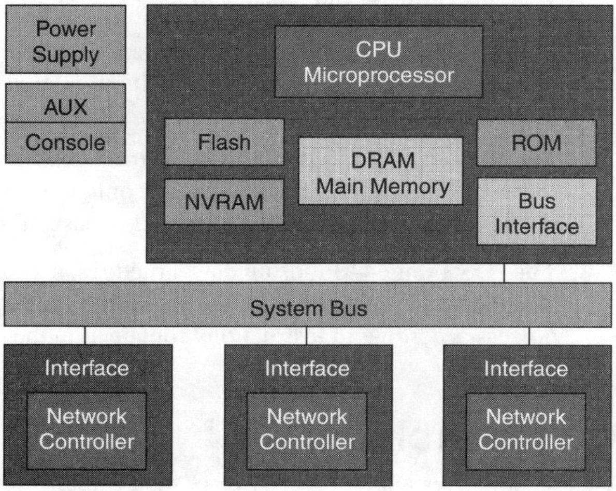

The Central Processing Unit (CPU)

The processor executes instructions coded in the IOS software. These translate into basic operations of the router's functions. These processors differ in features such as RISC/CISC, clock speed, data, and address bus width.

Generally, the processor and its related components are on one board called a CPU board. Some routers can support multiple processor cards, which are usually for distributing functionality or, less frequently, for providing redundancy.

The System or CPU Bus

The three types of buses in the Cisco router have different but related functions. The specifications of Cisco routers generally includes the type of buses used:

- **The CPU Bus** is used by the CPU for accessing various components of the system and transferring instructions and data to or from specified memory addresses. Characteristics of the CPU Bus (such as data bits, address bits, or frequency) depend upon the processor.
- **The I/O Bus** may be used on the CPU board of some routers for slower I/O functionality, so that the CPU Bus is used for high-speed operations only.
- **The System Bus** is used for communication between the CPU board and the interface boards (and others). A System Bus Controller arbitrates access conflicts among the various processes.

Cisco routers use different industry standard buses (such as MultiBus or PCI) and proprietary buses (such as CxBus or CyBus) for system bus functionality.

Network Interfaces

Network interfaces are used for receiving and forwarding data packets based upon various protocols at different layers and media types. Within most Cisco routers, the interface functions are placed on separate boards for modularity. In some cases, interface modules might communicate via CPU Bus rather than a System Bus.

The Memory Space

Memory is used in various forms for several purposes including storing the IOS image, storing the configuration files, and storing the bootstrap code. Router memory is also used for packets buffering and building routing tables. There are four or five main components to the memory space of a typical Cisco router. They include the main memory, the NVRAM, the boot Flash memory, and the boot ROM. As with most memory components, the architecture of the memory space is categorized by its physical and logical characteristics. The following main memory spaces can be identified:

- Main Memory
- Flash Memory
- NVRAM
- Boot ROM (ROM)
- Other Memory

Each of these memory spaces varies somewhat in size, division, and construction based on the router series.

Cisco IOS provides a command line method for extracting information about the system's memory. Use the following syntax to find out the full memory, Flash, and other memory components.

```
show memory
show buffers
show flash [all] ...
show flash devices
show bootflash
show region
```

Please refer to IOS documentation for exact use of IOS commands.

Main Memory

The main memory component consists of one of two types of physical RAM: dynamic RAM (DRAM) or static RAM (SRAM).

In some routers, DRAM is logically divided in main processor memory and shared I/O memory. Shared I/O memory is shared among interfaces for temporary storage of packets.

Some routers have separate DRAM SIMMs for main processor and shared I/O memory.

- Runtime executable IOS (and its subsystems)
- Routing tables
- Switching cache
- Configuration file(s) storage
- Packets buffering
- Main Processor memory
- Shared I/O memory is shared among interfaces for temporary storage of input and output packets

With either DRAM or SRAM, the router's processor generally has direct access to the main memory components via the CPU bus. Either configuration might also include the addition of an external or internal hardware cache to speed up data transfers to and from the processor.

Flash Memory

Flash memory exists in one of two forms: PCMCIA Flash memory or EEPROM (electronically erasable programmable ROM) Flash memory.

- **EEPROM Flash memory** is used for permanent storage of either the full IOS or a subset of IOS on boot Flash memory in some routers. Flash memory is installed by SIMMs which vary in speed among platforms. Some Flash are also user configurable for size.
- **PCMCIA Flash memory** is used for more flexibility in permanently storing and moving full IOS, backup configuration files, or any other files. PCMCIA Flash is implemented via type 2 PCMCIA cards. It is portable, easily serviceable, and overcomes the size limitations of Flash SIMMs.

NVRAM

NVRAM is used for writable permanent storage of the startup configuration. It can be either a battery-backed SRAMor an EEPROM.

Boot ROM

Boot ROM is an EPROM used for permanently storing startup diagnostic code (also known as ROM Monitor). In some routers a subset of IOS (or even full IOS in some cases) is also stored on boot ROM. Boot ROMs rarely need to be replaced in a router, except in a case when a new hardware feature requires the upgrade.

Other Memory Units

Other EPROM are used on almost every router board for various purposes such as permanent storage of hardware revision and identification information, or allocated MAC addresses. For the most part, they are registers.

Registers are small, fast memory units used for storing special purpose information, such as interrupt status or instructions for code execution. The location of registers depends upon their use. For example, the main processor contains an instruction register and other control registers, which are fast memories used by the processor during the execution of programs. Router DUART contains its own status register such as I/O devices, or data read/write registers on various components.

FIFO is First-In, First-Out memory used for buffering of high-speed data. FIFO memory is usually located on the router interface controllers.

The Identification Programmable Read Only Memory (IDPROM) is a portion of memory used by Cisco or a third-party router developer. This component usually contains system and installation information needed for troubleshooting or the internal operation of the router. End users do not access this area of memory.

Overview of Hardware Memory Configuration

As stated in the preceding section, Cisco IOS re-maps or otherwise optimizes existing hardware resources to improve performance and reliability. The next few sections outline the levels of the memory configuration per families of routers. In an effort to cover the broadest range of router families, the routers are categorized in two main groups: low/mid-range routers and high-end routers.

Cisco Low-End/Mid Range Routers Configuration

Cisco routers can be divided into several series groups: 2500 series, 3600 series, 4000/4500 series, and 7*x*00 series. These series are classified into ranges of low- to high-end based on the aggregation capability, speed, and other physical and logical attributes. Figure 8-10 shows the hardware configuration for the 1600 series router, and Figure 8-11 illustrates the hardware configuration for the 2500 series. Most low/mid-range Cisco routers have similar memory configuration.

Figure 8-10 *Cisco 1600 Series Hardware Configuration*

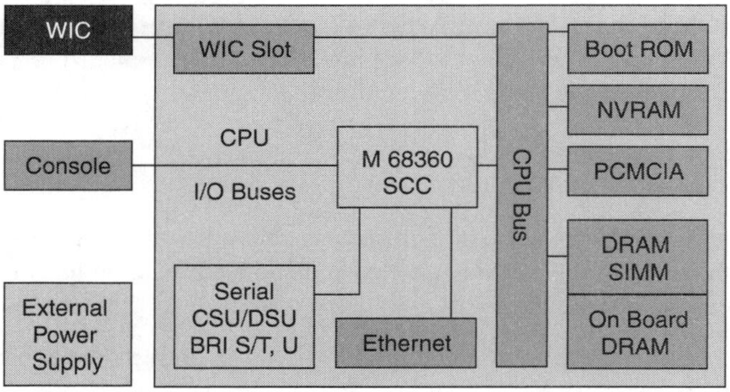

Figure 8-11 *Cisco 2500 Series Hardware Configuration*

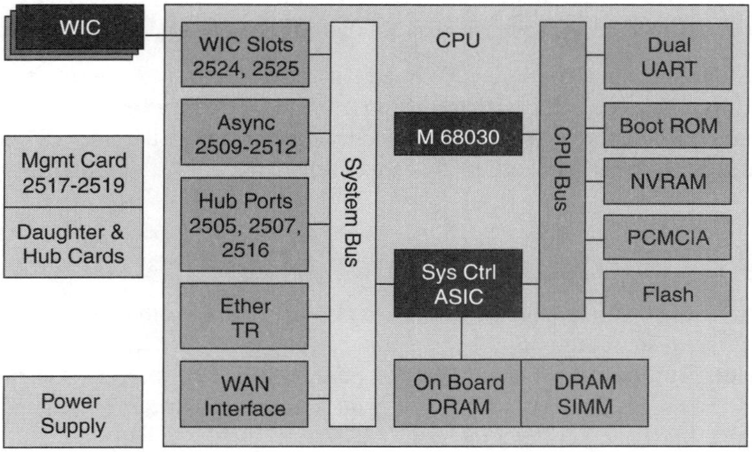

Figure 8-12 shows the hardware configuration for the 4700 series.

Figure 8-12 *Cisco 4700 Hardware Configuration*

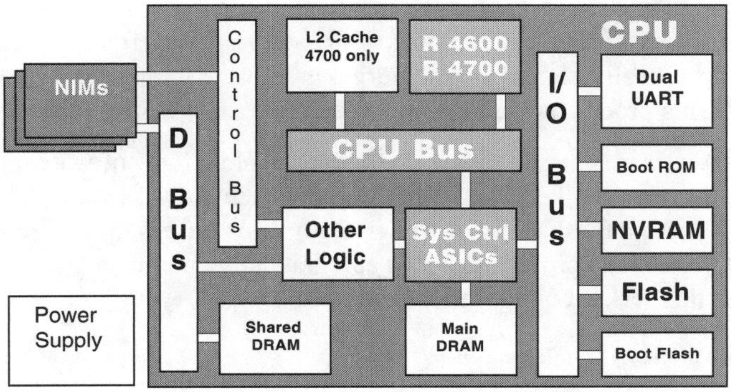

Typical Low to Mid Range Router Logical Memory Representation

At execution time, the IOS software re-maps the physical memory configuration to logical areas. Figure 8-13 illustrates a generic example applicable to low- to mid-range routers.

Figure 8-13 *Typical Memory Configuration for Low to Mid Range Routers*

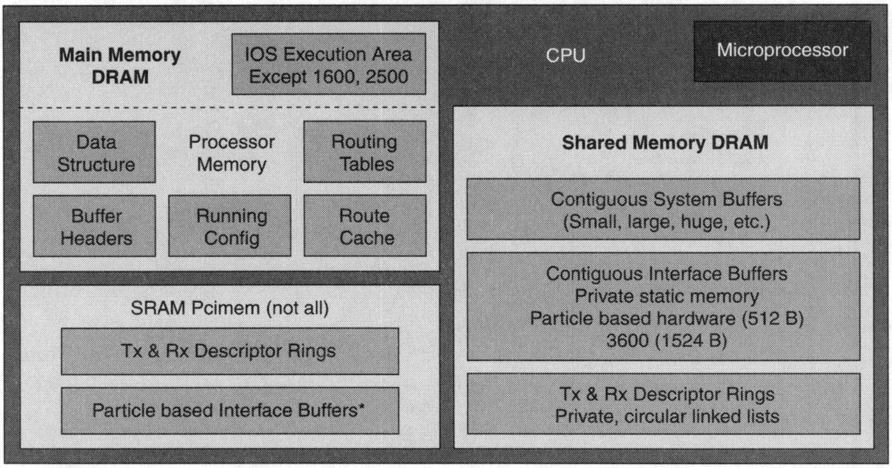

The following examples illustrate Cisco IOS resource management for specific families of routers.

The Cisco 2500 Series

In the particular case of the 2500 series routers, main memory is typically divided into two logical components: main processor memory and shared I/O memory. In this case, though, the main processor memory can borrow unused resources from the shared I/O memory as needed. Specifically, shared I/O memory is used for temporary storage of packets in system buffers during process switching, and interface buffers during fast switching.

The 2500 series routers run IOS from Flash with older IOS software releases. In newer IOS releases, they can run IOS from DRAM if sufficient DRAM is available. If the router is running IOS from Flash, copying a new IOS image requires the router to be in rxboot mode. Newer IOS versions provide this step automatically and transparently. Figure 8-14 illustrates this series' configuration using IOS.

Figure 8-14 *Cisco 2500 Memory Configuration*

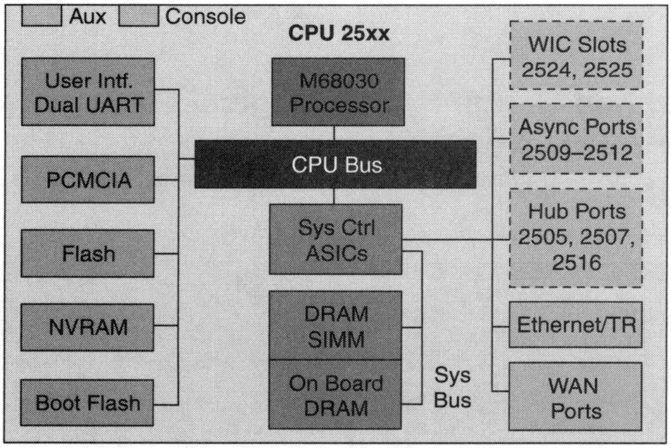

The Cisco 36xx Series

In the 3600 series of Cisco routers, Flash memory serves as permanent storage of the full IOS image. Note that 36x0 platforms have no Boot Flash, and no rxboot (see Figure 8-15). So, net_booting is not possible, and having a good IOS image on Flash or PCMCIA Flash is important.

Figure 8-15 *Cisco 3600 Memory Configuration*

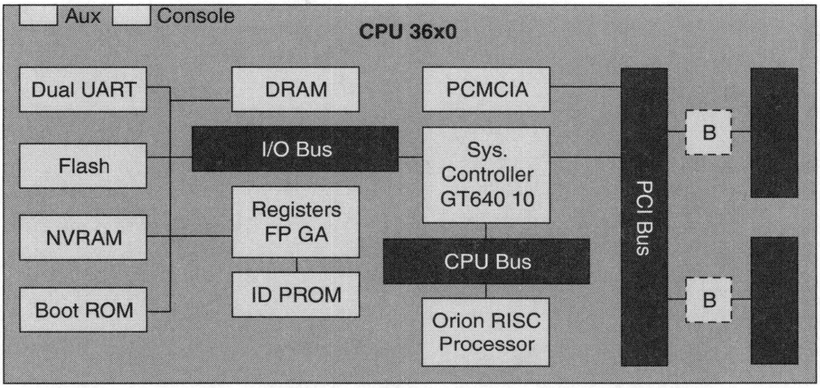

As with the 26xx series, NVRAM in the 36x0 routers serves as writable permanent storage of the startup configuration and is a battery backed SRAM.

Because of the absence of rxboot, the boot ROM of the 36x0 routers is much smaller than that of the 25xx series, 512 KB versus 2 MB.

Cisco High-End Routers Memory Configuration

Let's use the Cisco 7x00 router series to illustrate IOS resource management in the high-end category. The 7x00 routers have two primary divisions based on the type of processor. These two processors affect the components that are formatted to work with them, and their capabilities are not the same.

- Cisco 7000 series routers use the *Route Processor* (RP), which has a more limited functionality.
- Cisco 7500 series routers use the *Route Switch Processor* (RSP), which is a board that runs IOS and interfaces with switches. Using RSP increases the flexibility of the router through various interfaces, including the VIP.
- The *Virtual Interface Processor* (VIP) is an added-value processor card that can be plugged into the RSP to work with a broader variety of components.

The following examples are based on the RSP7500 series routers. Figure 8-16 illustrates the Cisco RSP7500 series router architecture.

Figure 8-16 *The Cisco RSP7500 Series Router Architecture*

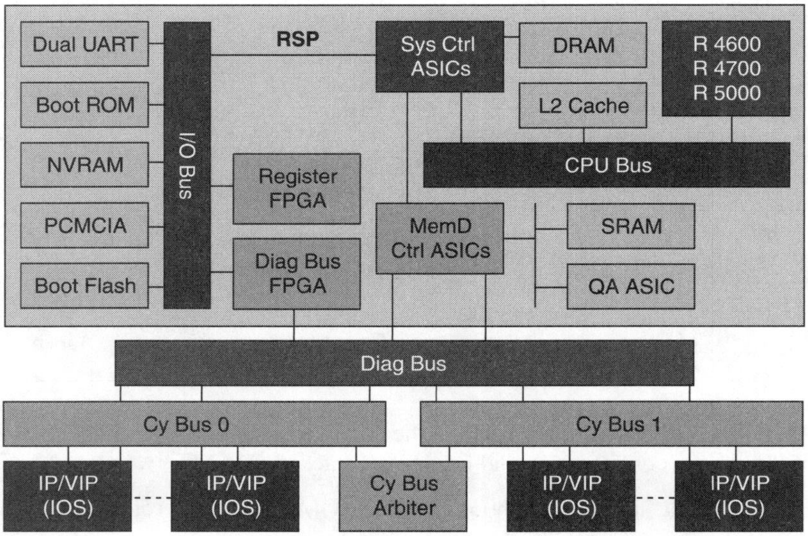

How Cisco IOS Uses High-End Router Resources

As with other routers, the processor loads instructions defined in IOS from main processor memory and executes them, which basically involves some manipulation of data. Figure 8-17 illustrates how the following elements are affected by IOS:

- **The Local Processor**—The Local Processor of the VIP card runs its own version of IOS software and has the ability to make independent data flow and optional high speed Distributed Switching decisions. This frees the main processor (RSP) from attending every packet. Only fast or process switched packets still require the attention of the main processor.
- **Local memory**—The local memory of the VIP card is used for various purposes. It is composed of DRAM, SRAM, boot ROM, special buffers, and registers. DRAM (8 MB to 64 MB possible) holds the small VIP OS (Microcode-like) during execution on the Local Processor. It also holds the Distributed Switching cache when configured.
- **SRAM**—The SRAM is used for temporary storage of packets for transfers between memories and network interface logic on Port Adapters.

Figure 8-17 *RSP7500 Series Routers Run Multiple IOS Software Distributed on the VIPs*

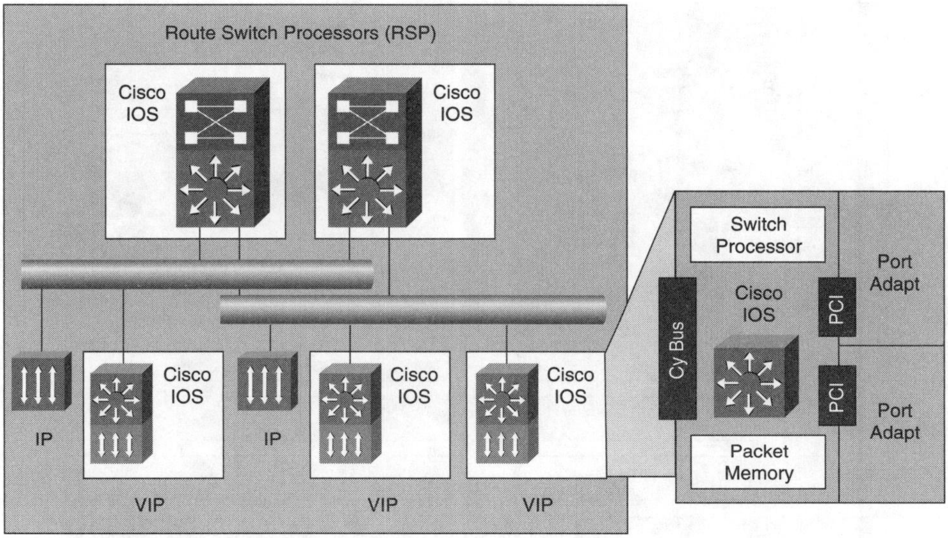

Cisco 7500 Series Memory Allocated to IOS

The memory component of the RSP7x00 consists of the following (see Figure 8-18):

- **Main memory**—The main memory is composed of both DRAM and SRAM. SRAM holds interface buffers and is shared among interface processors for storing packets during autonomous or fast switching.
- **Boot ROM**—The boot ROM (256 KB EPROM) is used for storing ROMMON.
- **Flash memory**—The Flash memory has the following specs:
  - — **Boot Flash** (8 MB SIMM) stores rxboot (Boot Image).
  - — **PCMCIA Flash** has two slots. PCMCIA Flash stores the full IOS.
- **NVRAM**—The NVRAM is 128 KB of battery-backed SRAM.

Figure 8-18 *RSP7500 Series Memory Configuration*

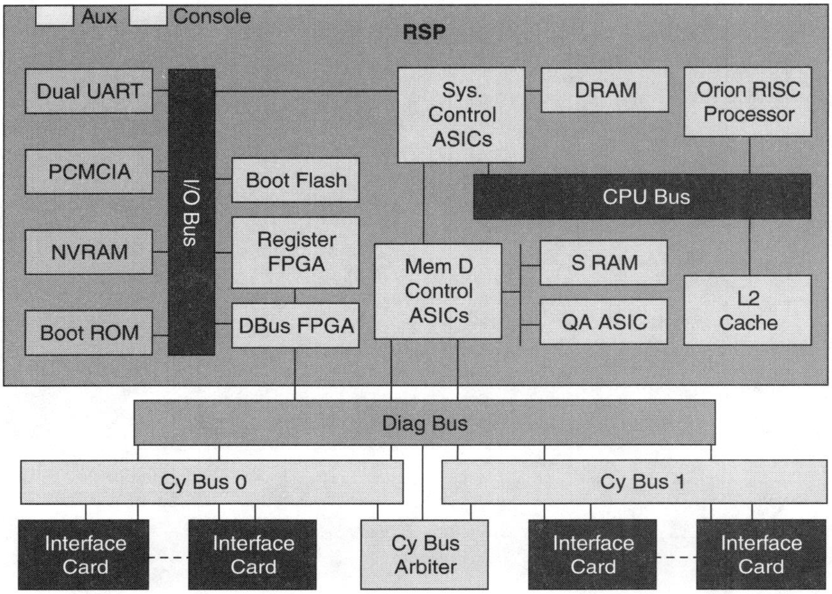

How IOS Software Views Memory Space

A significant advantage of IOS software is its capability to interface with a variety of platforms. In order for Cisco IOS to maintain the ability to be easily ported to non-native platforms, it divides existing physical memory into consistent logical mapping. In other words, the IOS software *maps* the configuration of SIMMs and other PC board memory chips into consistent logical memory divisions. This mapping ability enables the IOS to access specific memory components at a consistent address. Where applicable, software can map these physical memory addresses to non-existing virtual addresses for various implementations or portability to other systems. Knowledge of a router's memory map helps identify points of failure during the IOS troubleshooting. Cisco hardware documentation provides maps of the router physical and logical memory mapping specific to your hardware. Table 8-1 lists physical memory resources and how Cisco IOS uses these resources through memory mapping.

Table 8-1 *Summary of Basic Hardware Memory Configuration*

Physical	Usage
Main DRAM (Logically or physically separated from Shared DRAM—division decided at boot time)	Execute IOS software Execute rxboot (4500, 4700, 7200, RSP7000, 7500) Sets IOS Variables Stores Running Config, Routing Table, Route Cache, Buffer Headers andSystem Buffers (7000/7500)
Shared DRAM (1000, 1600, 2500, 4x00, 3600, 7200)	Used as System & Interface Buffers Used as Interface Particle Buffers (7200 x 3600)
SRAM (7000 SP/SSP, 7500) (7200 except NPE100)	Used as Interface Buffers Used as Interface Particle Buffers (For High BW PAs only)
EPROM (Except 1000, 1600)	Stores Rev Info, ID, MAC addresses
NVRAM Battery backed SRAM or EEPROM	Stores Startup Config and Rev Info, ID, MAC addr (1000, 1600)
Boot ROM (Flash PROM in RSP4)	Contains ROMMON Contains Executable rxboot (1000) Contains Executable rxboot (1600, 2500, 4000) Contains Subset of IOS (7000 RP)
Boot Flash (4500, 4700, 7200, RSP7000, 7500)	Stores rxboot or boot loader
PCMIA Flash (1000, 1600, 3600, 7200, RSP7000, 7500)	Stores IOS images Executes IOS (1600) Contains Other files: Config & HTML
Flash (4x00, 2500, 7000 RP)	Stores IOS images Execute IOS (2500)

PART IV

Appendixes

APPENDIX A

Cisco IOS Image Name Reference

This appendix lists the platform and feature set identifiers contained in the IOS software images. The information provided in this appendix should be cross-referenced with the section on Cisco IOS Image Naming Convention in Chapter 3, "Characteristics of Cisco IOS: Definitions, Naming Convention, Versioning, Numbering, and Feature Packaging."

In general, Cisco IOS image names follow this syntax:

PPPPP-FFFF-MM

IOS images for boards follow this syntax:

BBB-PPPP-MM

For either syntax, the parts are defined as follows:

BBB = Board
PPPPP = Platform
FFFF = Features
MM = Run-time memory and compression format

Cisco IOS Image Platforms (PPPP) and Board (BBB) Code Definitions

Code Identifiers	Definition
as5200	5200
ca1003	CiscoAdvantage™ 1003
ca1005	CiscoAdvantage™1005
cpa1003	CiscoPro 1003,4
cpa1005	CiscoPro 1005
cpa25	CiscoPro 2500

Code Identifiers	Definition
cpa3620	CiscoPro 3620
cpa3640	CiscoPro 3640
cpa45	CiscoPro 4500
cs	Communication server
cs500	cs500
c1000	1003,4
c1005	1005
c1600	1600
c2500	25xx, 3xxx, 5100, AO (11.2 and later only)
c25fx	Fixed FRAD
c2600	2600 Quake
c2800	Catalyst 2800
c2900	2910, 2950
c29atm	2900 ATM
c3620	3620
c3640	3640
c3800	3800
c4000	4000 (11.2 and later—earlier releases use xx)
c4500	4500, 4700
c5rsfc	Catalyst 5000 series
c5rsm	Catalyst 5k RSP
c5atm	Catalyst ATM
c6400s	6400 NSP
c6400r	6400 NRP
c6msm	Catalyst

Code Identifiers	Definition
c7000	7000, 7010 (11.2 and later only)
c7200	7200
igs	IGS, 25xx, 3xxx, 5100, AP
gs3	Gateway server (AGS, AGS+)
gs7	Gateway server (7000, 7010)
gsr	Gigabit switch router (12000)
ls1010	LightStream 1010
mc3810	Ardent Multiservice Cisco 3810
p<n	Partners' platform n
pt	Protocol translator
rpm	MGX 8850
rsp	75xx
ubr7200	Universal Broadband Router 7200
ubr900	Universal Broadband Router 900
ubr920	Universal Broadband Router 920
vcw	Voice card ware
xx	4000
igsetx	2500 (media specific image that supports only Ethernet, Token Ring, and X.25)

Code Identifiers	Definition
das	Dial shelf feature board
dsc	Dial shelf controller board platforms

Cisco IOS Image Feature Identifiers Definition (FFFF)

a

a	APPN
a2	ATM
a3	APPN replacement called SNA Switch (12.0(4)XN and 12.1)

b

b	AppleTalk
boot	Boot image

c

c	CommServer/Remote Access Server (RAS) subset (SNMP, IP, Bridging, IPX, AppleTalk, DECnet, FR, HDLC, PPP, X.25, ARAP, tn3270, PT, XRemote, LAT) (non-CiscoPro)
c	CommServer lite (CiscoPro)
c2	CommServer/Remote Access Server (RAS) subset (SNMP, IP, Bridging, IPX, AppleTalk, DECnet, FR, HDLC, PPP, X.25, ARAP, tn3270, PT, XRemote, LAT) (CiscoPro)
c3	Clustering

d

d	Desktop subset (SNMP, IP, Bridging, WAN, Remote Node, Terminal Services, IPX, AppleTalk, ARAP) (11.2 - DECnet)
d2	Reduced desktop subset (SNMP, IP, IPX, AppleTalk, ARAP)
diag	IOS based diagnostic images

e

e	IPeXchange (prior to 11.3) StarPipes DB2 Access—Enables Cisco IOS to act as a "gateway" to all IBM DB2 products for downstream clients/servers in 11.3T
eboot	Ethernet boot image for mc3810 platform

f

f	FRAD subset (SNMP, FR, PPP, SDLLC, STUN)
f2	Modified FRAD subset, EIGRP, Pcbus, Lan Mgr removed, OSPF added

g

g	ISDN subset (SNMP, IP, Bridging, ISDN, PPP, IPX, AppleTalk)
g2	Gatekeeper proxy, voice, and video
g3	ISDN subset for c800 (IP, ISDN, FR)

h

h	For Malibu (2910), 8021D, switch functions, IP Host
hdiag	Diagnostics image for Malibu (2910)

i[1]

i	IP subset (SNMP, IP, Bridging, WAN, Remote Node, Terminal Services)
i2	Subset similar to IP subset for system controller image (3600)
i3	Reduced IP subset with BGP/MIB, EGP/MIB, NHRP, DIRRESP removed.
i4	Subset of IP (available on 5200)

1. These are not used for low-end routers.

j

j	Enterprise subset (formerly bpx, includes protocol translation) Note that this was not used until 10.3

k

k	Kitchen sink (enterprise for high-end) (same as bx) (not used after 10.3)
k1	Baseline Privacy key encryption (On 11.3 and later)
k2	High-end enterprise w/CIP2 ucode (not used after 10.3)
k2	Triple DES (on 11.3 and later)
k3	56 bit encryption with secured shell (ssh)
k4	168 bit encryption with secured shell (ssh)
k5	Reserved for future encryption capabilities (on 11.3 and later)
k6	Reserved for future encryption capabilities (on 11.3 and later)
k7	Reserved for future encryption capabilities (on 11.3 and later)
k8	Reserved for future encryption capabilities (on 11.3 and later)
k9	Reserved for future encryption capabilities (on 11.3 and later)

l

l	IPeXchange (IPX), static routing, gateway

m

m	RMON (11.1 only)
m	For 11.2, Catalyst 2820-kernel, parser, ATM signaling, LANE Client, Bridging

n

n	IPX

o

• o	• Firewall (formerly IPeXchange Net Management)
• o2	• Firewall (3xx0)
• o3	• Firewall with ssh (36x0 26x0)

p

p	Service Provider (IP RIP/IGRP/EIGRP/OSPF/BGP, CLNS ISIS/IGRP)
p2	Service Provider w/CIP2 ucode
p3	as5200 Service Provider
p4	5800 (Nitro) Service Provider

q

q	Async
q2	IPeXchange Async

r

r	IBM base option (SRB, SDLLC, STUN, DLSW, QLLC)—used with i, in, d
r2	IBM variant for 1600 images
r3	IBM variant for Ardent images (3810)
r4	Reduced IBM subset with BSC/MIB, BSTUN/MIB, ASPP/MIB, RSRB/MIB removed.

s

<table>
<tr><td>s</td><td colspan="2">Source route switch (SNMP, IP, Bridging, SRB) (10.x releases)</td></tr>
<tr><td rowspan="10">s</td><td colspan="2">11.2(only) division by platform</td></tr>
<tr><td>c1000</td><td>(OSPF, PIM, SMRP, NLSP, ATIP, ATAURP, FRSVC, RSVP, NAT)</td></tr>
<tr><td>c1005</td><td>(X.25, full WAN, OSPF, PIM, NLSP, SMRP, ATIP, ATAURP, FRSVC, RSVP, NAT)</td></tr>
<tr><td>c1600</td><td>(OSPF, IPMULTICAST, NHRP, NTP, NAT, RSVP, FRAME_RELAY_SVC)
AT "s" images also have: (SMRP, ATIP, AURP)
IPX "s" images also have: (NLSP, NHRP)</td></tr>
<tr><td>c2500</td><td>(NAT, RMON, IBM, MMP, VPDN/L2F)</td></tr>
<tr><td>c2600</td><td>(NAT, IBM, MMP, VPDN/L2F, VoIP and ATM)</td></tr>
<tr><td>c3620</td><td>(NAT, IBM, MMP, VPDN/L2F) In 11.3T added VoIP</td></tr>
<tr><td>c3640</td><td>(NAT, IBM, MMP, VPDN/L2F) In 11.3T added VoIP</td></tr>
<tr><td>c4000</td><td>(NAT, IBM, MMP, VPDN/L2F)</td></tr>
</table>

	c4500	(NAT, ISL, LANE, IBM, MMP, VPDN/L2F)
	c5200	(PT, v.120, managed modems, RMON, MMP, VPDN/L2F)
	c5300	(MMP, VPDN, NAT, Modem Management, RMON, IBM)
	c5rsm	(NAT, LANE, VLANs)
	c7000	(ISL, LANE, IBM, MMP, VPDN/L2F)
	c7200	(NAT, ISL, IBM, MMP, VPDN/L2F)
	rsp	(NAT, ISL, LANE, IBM, MMP, VPDN/L2F)

t

t	AIP w/ modified Ucode to connect to Teralink 1000 Data (11.2)
t	Telco return (12.0)

u

u	IP with VLAN RIP (Network Layer 3 Switching Software, rsrb, srt, srb, sr/tlb)

v

v	VIP and dual RSP (HSA) support
v2	Voice V2D
v3	Voice feature card

w

w	WBU Feature Sets (11.3WA and 12.0W5 releases)	
	i	IISP
	l	LANE and PVC
	p	PNNI
	v	PVC traffic shaping
w2	Cisco Advantage ED Train Feature Sets	
	a	IPX, static routing, gateway
	b	Net management
	c	FR/X25
	y	Async
w3	Distributed director feature sets	

x

x	X.25 in 11.1 and earlier releases. Also available in 12.0T on c800 series.
x	FR/X.25 in 11.2 (IPeXchange)
x	H.323 Gatekeeper/Proxy in 11.3 and later releases for 2500, 3620, 3640, mc3810.

y[1]

y	Reduced IP (SNMP, IP RIP/IGRP/EIGRP, Bridging, ISDN, PPP) (C1003/4)
y	Reduced IP (SNMP, IP RIP/IGRP/EIGRP, Bridging, WAN - X.25) (C1005) (11.2 - includes X.25) (c1005)
y	IP variant (no Kerberos, Radius, NTP, OSPF, PIM, SMRP, NHRP) (c1600)
y2	IP variant (SNMP, IP RIP/IGRP/EIGRP, WAN - X.25, OSPF, PIM) (C1005)
y2	IP Plus variant (no Kerberos, Radius, NTP, ...) (c1600)
y3	IP/X.31
y4	Reduced IP variant (Cable, Mibs, DHCP, EZHTTP)
y5	Reduced IP variant (Cable, Mibs, DHCP, EZIP) Home Office
y6	Reduced IP variant (c800)

1. These are used for low-end routers.

z

z	Managed modems

0-9

40	40 bit encryption
56	56 bit encryption
56i	56 bit encryption with IPSEC

Obsolete

h	Reduced desktop subset (SNMP, IP RIP/IGRP/EIGRP, Bridging, ISDN, PPP, IPX, AppleTalk) 1003/4
h	Reduced desktop subset (SNMP, IP RIP/IGRP/EIGRP, Bridging, WAN - X.25, IPX, AppleTalk) 1005

Available Cisco IOS Images

There are literally hundreds of IOS images. Some of them are obsolete, but are still in use in customer networks. The following lists identify the available and existing IOS images.

Images for Routers and Boards

Special Images

Some Cisco IOS images have been customized and built for selected customers. As an administrator, it is possible that you will encounter an image that does not fit in the Cisco model. Examples of these are listed below.

xx-r-m is xx-ir-mz minus BGP, EGP, OSPF, IP multicast, CDP, PPP, CHAT, ISDN, SMDS, X.25, and FRAME_RELAY

igs-inr2-l is igs-inr-l minus SMDS, EGP/BGP, LEX, DHCP, NTP

c1005-xy2-m is c1005-xy-m plus OSPF/MIBS and PIM/MIBS/fast-switching, minus bridging/MIBS

Obsolete Images

h - reduced desktop subset (SNMP, IP RIP/IGRP/EIGRP, Bridging, ISDN, PPP, IPX, AppleTalk) for 1003/4/5

Existing or Changed Cisco IOS Images

The tables in this section list numerous Cisco IOS images. Some of these image names have changed or have been replaced by other images as the releases continued to evolve.

Table A-1 lists some of the basic images and their descriptions. Table A-2 shows image names that have changed.

Table A-1 *Cisco IOS Image Descriptions for Router Images*

Pre-10.2	10.2	10.3	Description
gs7-k		gs7-k-m or gs7-k-mz	Enterprise 70x0
gs3-k		gs3-k-m	Enterprise AGS+
cs3-k		cs3-c-m	CommServer ASM
igs-bpx	igs-bpx-l	igs-j-l	Enterprise 3xxx
igs-bfpx	igs-bpx-l	igs-j-l	Enterprise 25xx/3xx
	igs-cd-l	igs-c-l	CommServer RAS
igs-df	igs-d-l	Desktop 25xx	
igs-if	igs-i-l	IP 25xx	
igs-isdn	igs-g-l	ISDN 2503/4I	
igs-frad	igs-f-l	FRAD 2501/2CF	
xx-k	(*obsolete*)		
xx-bpx		xx-j-m or xx-j-mz	Enterprise 4000
c4500-k	(*obsolete*)		
c4500-bpx	c4500-bpx	c4500-j-m or c4500-j-mz	Enterprise 4500
c4500-i	c4500-i-m		IP 4500
c4500-d	c4500-d-m		Desktop 4500
cs500-k	cs500-c-m		CommServer CS500
igs-rxboot		igs-boot-r	Boot 2500/3xxx
xx-rxboot		xx-boot-r	Boot 4000
c4500-xboot		c4500-boot-m	Boot 4500

Table A-2 *Cisco IOS Image Names That Have Changed*

10.3(3)+	11.0(4)+	Description
c1000-h-m	c1000-bny	Reduced DT 1003
c1005-h-m	c1005-bny	Reduced DT w/reduced WAN 1005
c1005-x-m	c1005-bnxy	Reduced DT w/X.25 1005
c1005-y-m	c1005-xy	Reduced IP 1005

continues

Table A-2 *Cisco IOS Image Names That Have Changed (Continued)*

11.0	11.1	Description
gs7-k-mz	gs7-j-mz	Enterprise 70xx
gs7-ak-mz	gs7-aj-mz	Enterprise/APPN 70xx
rsp-k-mz	rsp-j-mz	Enterprise 75xx
rsp-ak-mz	rsp-aj-mz	Enterprise/APPN 75xx

Table A-3 lists the image names that changed from 11.1 to 11.2; however, the only new functionality in each case are the new 11.2 features. The table is segmented by platform groupings.

Table A-3 *Cisco IOS Image Names That Have Changed from 11.1 to 11.2*

11.1	11.2
c1005-bnxy-mz	c1005-bny-mz
c1005-bxy-mz	c1005-by-mz
c1005-nxy-mz	c1005-ny-mz
c1005-xy-mz	c1005-y-mz
c1005-xy2-mz	c1005-y2-mz
igs-ainr-l	c2500-ainr-l
igs-c-l	c2500-c-l
igs-d-l	c2500-d-l
igs-f-l	c2500-f-l
igs-fin-l	c2500-fin-l
igs-g-l	c2500-g-l
igs-i-l	c2500-i-l
igs-jm-l	c2500-js-l
igs-j-l	c2500-j-l
igs-p-l	c2500-p-l
xx-ainr-mz	c4000-ainr-mz
xx-d-mz	c4000-d-mz
xx-ir-mz	c4000-is-mz
xx-j-mz	c4000-j-mz

Table A-3 *Cisco IOS Image Names That Have Changed from 11.1 to 11.2 (Continued)*

11.1	11.2
xx-p-mz	c4000-p-mz
c4500-ir-mz	c4500-is-mz ***
gs7-aj-mz	c7000-ajs-mz
gs7-ajv-mz	c7000-ajsv-mz
gs7-jv-mz	c7000-jsv-mz
gs7-j-mz	c7000-js-mz
gs7-pv-mz	c7000-pv-mz
c7200-aj-mz	c7200-ajs-mz
c7200-dr-mz	c7200-ds-mz
c7200-j-mz	c7200-js-mz
rsp-ajv-mz	rsp-ajsv-mz
rsp-jv-mz	rsp-jsv-mz

Table A-4 lists the replacement images for 11.1 images that are no longer available in 11.2. (That is, the new image has new functionality and the previous functionality no longer exists.)

Table A-4 *Cisco IOS Image Replacements in 11.2 for Obsolete 11.1 Images*

11.1 Images Obsoleted	11.2 Replacement
as5200-jmz-l	c5200-js-l
as5200-dz-l	c5200-ds-l
as5200-iz-l	c5200-is-l
c1005-by-mz	c1005-by-mz
igs-aj-l	c2500-ajs-l
igs-dr-l	c2500-ds-l
igs-im-l	c2500-is-l
igs-imn-l	c2500-ds-l
igs-imnr-l	c2500-ds-l

continues

Table A-4 *Cisco IOS Image Replacements in 11.2 for Obsolete 11.1 Images (Continued)*

11.1 Images Obsoleted	11.2 Replacement
igs-imr-l	c2500-is-l
igs-in-l	c2500-d-l
igs-ir-l	c2500-is-l
igs-inr-l	c2500-ds-l
xx-aj-mz	c4000-ajs-mz
xx-dr-mz	c4000-ds-mz
xx-in-mz	c4000-d-mz
xx-inr-mz	c4000-ds-mz
xx-ir-mz	c4000-is-mz
c4500-aj-mz	c4500-ajs-mz
c4500-dr-mz	c4500-ds-mz
c4500-in-mz	c4500-d-mz
c4500-inr-mz	c4500-ds-mz
c4500-ir-mz	c4500-is-mz
c7200-inu-mz	c7200-inu-mz
rsp-aj-mz	rsp-ajsv-mz
rsp-j-mz	rsp-jsv-mz

Images Added to Various Releases

This section includes tables listing images as they were added to several Cisco IOS releases, beginning with release 10.2(2) and beyond. Tables A-5 through A-19 list the various added image names, their descriptions, and specific platforms affected. The end of the section includes single-column lists of images added to specific releases.

Table A-5 *Cisco IOS Image Names Added for 10.2(2) and Beyond*

Added Image	Feature Set and Platform
igs-in-l	IP/IPX 2500
xx-in-mz	IP/IPX 4000
c4500-in-m	IP/IPX 4500
igs-ir-l	IP/IBM 2500
xx-ir-mz	IP/IBM 4000
c4500-ir-m	IP/IBM 4500

Table A-5 *Cisco IOS Image Names Added for 10.2(2) and Beyond (Continued)*

Added Image	Feature Set and Platform
igs-inr-l	IP/IPX/IBM 2500
xx-inr-mz	IP/IPX/IBM 4000
c4500-inr-m	IP/IPX/IBM 4500
igs-dr-l	DT/IBM 2500
xx-dr-mz	DT/IBM 4000
c4500-dr-m	DT/IBM 4500
gs7-s-m	Source Route Switch 70x0
c1000-y-m	Reduced IP 1003
rsp-k-m	Enterprise 7500
igs-p-l	Service Provider 25xx
xx-p-mz	Service Provider 4000
c4500-p-mz	Service Provider 4500
gs3-p-m	Service Provider AGS+
gs7-p-mz	Service Provider 70xx
rsp-p-mz	Service Provider 75xx
rsp-ak-mz	Enterprise/APPN 7500
gs7-ak-mz	Enterprise/APPN 7000
gs3-ak-mz	Enterprise/APPN AGS+
igs-aj-l	Enterprise/APPN 2500
igs-ainr-l	IP/IPX/IBM/APPN 2500
xx-aj-mz	Enterprise/APPN 4000
xx-ainr-mz	IP/IPX/IBM/APPN 4000
c4500-aj-mz	Enterprise/APPN 4500
c4500-ainr-mz	IP/IPX/IBM/APPN 4500
cpa25-y-l	Reduced IP CiscoPro
cps25-cg-l	RAS/ISDN CiscoPro
igs-im-l	IP/RMON 2500
igs-imr-l	IP/IBM/RMON 2500
igs-imn-l	IP/IPX/RMON 2500
igs-imnr-l	IP/IPX/IBM/RMON 2500

continues

Table A-5 *Cisco IOS Image Names Added for 10.2(2) and Beyond (Continued)*

Added Image	Feature Set and Platform
igs-jm-l	Enterprise+RMON 2500
xx-r-mz	IBM no-frills 4000
c1000-by-m	IP, AT, ISDN 1003,4
c1000-ny-m	IP, IPX, ISDN 1003,4
c1005-bxy-m	IP, AT, X.25 1005
c1005-nxy-m	IP, IPX, X.25 1005
c1005-by-m	IP, AT, WAN - X.25 1005
c1005-ny-m	IP, IPX, WAN - X.25 1005
igs-fin-l	LANFRAD 252x
c1005-qy-m	IP, WAN - X.25 w/Async 1005
c1005-nqy-m	IP, IPX, WAN - X.25 w/Async 1005
rsp-ajv-mz	Enterprise/APPN/VIP 7500
rsp-jv-mz	Enterprise/VIP 7500
rsp-pv-mz	Service Provider/VIP 75xx
rsp-dr-mz	Desktop/IBM 75xx
rsp-drv-mz	Desktop/IBM/VIP 75xx
rsp-i-mz	IP 75xx
rsp-iv-mz	IP/VIP 75xx
igs-inr2-l	IP/IPX/IBM(4MB) 25xx
c1005-xy2	IP/OSPF/PIM 1005
as5200-iz-l	IP w/managed modems 5200
as5200-dz-l	Desktop w/managed modems 5200
as5200-jm-l	Enterprise+ RMON w/managed modems 5200
c7200-j-mz	Enterprise 7200
c7200-aj-mz	Enterprise+APPN 7200
c7200-dr-mz	Desktop/IBM 7200
c7200-inu-mz	Network Layer 3 Switching Software 7200
c3640-ainr-mz	IP/IPX/IBM/APPN 3640
c3640-aj-mz	Enterprise/APPN 3640
c3640-d-mz	Desktop 3640

Table A-5 *Cisco IOS Image Names Added for 10.2(2) and Beyond (Continued)*

Added Image	Feature Set and Platform
c3640-dr-mz	Desktop/IBM 3640
c3640-i-mz	IP 3640
c3640-in-mz	IP/IPX 3640
c3640-inr-mz	IP/IPX/IBM 3640
c3640-ir-mz	IP/IBM 3640
c3640-j-mz	Enterprise 3640
c3640-p-mz	Service Provider 3640
c3620-ainr-mz	IP/IPX/IBM/APPN 3620
c3620-aj-mz	Enterprise/APPN 3620
c3620-d-mz	Desktop 3620
c3620-dr-mz	Desktop/IBM 3620
c3620-i-mz	IP 3620
c3620-in-mz	IP/IPX 3620
c3620-inr-mz	IP/IPX/IBM 3620
c3620-ir-mz	IP/IBM 3620
c3620-j-mz	Enterprise 3620
c3620-p-mz	Service Provider 3620
c1600-y-l	IP 1600
c1600-sy-l	IP/Plus 1600
c1600-ny-l	IP/IPX 1600
c1600-nsy-l	IP/IPX/Plus 1600
c1600-by-l	IP/AT 1600
c1600-bsy-l	IP/AT/Plus 1600
c1600-bny-l	IP/IPX/AT 1600
c1600-bnsy-l	IP/IPX/AT/Plus 1600

Table A-6 *Cisco IOS Image Names Added for 11.2(1) and Beyond*

Added Image	Platform
c1000-bnsy-mz	1003/4
c1000-bnsy40-mz	1003/4

continues

Table A-6 *Cisco IOS Image Names Added for 11.2(1) and Beyond (Continued)*

Added Image	Platform
c1000-bnsy56-mz	1003/4
c1005-bnsy-mz	1005
c1005-bnsy40-mz	1005
c1005-bnsy56-mz	1005
c2500-ajs-l	25XX
c2500-ajs40-l	25XX
c2500-ajs56-l	25XX
c2500-ds-l	25XX, AP
c2500-ds40-l	25XX, AP
c2500-ds56-l	25XX, AP
c2500-is-l	25XX, AP
c2500-is40-l	25XX, AP
c2500-is56-l	25XX, AP
c2500-js40-l	25XX, AP
c2500-js56-l	25XX, AP
c4000-ajs-mz	4000
c4000-ajs40-mz	4000
c4000-ajs56-mz	4000
c4000-ds-mz	4000
c4000-ds40-mz	4000
c4000-ds56-mz	4000
c4000-is-mz	4000
c4000-is40-mz	4000
c4000-is56-mz	4000
c4000-js-mz	4000
c4000-js40-mz	4000
c4000-js56-mz	4000

Table A-6 *Cisco IOS Image Names Added for 11.2(1) and Beyond (Continued)*

Added Image	Platform
c4500-ajs-mz	4500, 4700
c4500-ajs40-mz	4500, 4700
c4500-ajs56-mz	4500, 4700
c4500-ds-mz	4500, 4700
c4500-ds40-mz	4500, 4700
c4500-ds56-mz	4500, 4700
c4500-is-mz	4500, 4700
c4500-is40-mz	4500, 4700
c4500-is56-mz	4500, 4700
c4500-js-mz	4500, 4700
c4500-js40-mz	4500, 4700
c4500-js56-mz	4500, 4700
c5200-d-l	as5200
c5200-ds-l	as5200
c5200-i-l	as5200
c5200-is-l	as5200
c5200-j-l	as5200
c5200-js-l	as5200
c7000-p-mz	RP (70X0)
c7200-ads-mz	7200
c7200-is-mz	7200
c7200-p-mz	7200
rsp-adsv-mz	RSP(75XX)
rsp-ajsv40-mz	RSP(75XX)
rsp-ajsv56-mz	RSP(75XX)

continues

Table A-6 *Cisco IOS Image Names Added for 11.2(1) and Beyond (Continued)*

Added Image	Platform
rsp-dsv-mz	RSP(75XX)
rsp-dsv40-mz	RSP(75XX)
rsp-dsv56-mz	RSP(75XX)
rsp-isv-mz	RSP(75XX)
rsp-isv40-mz	RSP(75XX)
rsp-isv56-mz	RSP(75XX)
rsp-jsv40-mz	RSP(75XX)
rsp-jsv56-mz	RSP(75XX)
rsp-p-mz	RSP(75XX)

Table A-7 *Cisco IOS Image Names Added for 11.1(9) and 11.2(4)M/P/F and Beyond*

Added Image	Platform
igs-f2in-l	25XX
c2500-f2in-l	25XX

Table A-8 *Cisco IOS Image Names Added for 11.2(4)P/F and Beyond*

Added Image	Platform
c3800-ainr-mz	3800
c3800-f-mz	3800
c3800-j-mz	3800

Table A-9 *Cisco IOS Image Names Added for 11.2(4)F and Beyond*

Added Image	Platform
c1000-l-mz	1000
c1000-lo-mz	1000
c1005-lx-mz	1005
c1005-lox-mz	1005
c1005-lq2-mz	1005
c2500-de-l	25XX
c2500-des-l	25XX
c2500-des40-l	25XX

Table A-9 *Cisco IOS Image Names Added for 11.2(4)F and Beyond*

Added Image	Platform
c2500-des56-l	25XX
c1000-y3-mz	1000 IP/X.31 image for X25 over ISDN D channel

Table A-10 *Cisco IOS Image Names Added for 11.2(5)P/F and Beyond*

Added Image	Platform
c3800-fin-mz	3800
c3800-i-mz	3800
c3800-ajs-mz	3800
c1600-y-l	1600
c1600-sy-l	1600
c1600-sy40-l	1600
c1600-sy56-l	1600
c1600-by-l	1600
c1600-bsy-l	1600
c1600-bsy40-l	1600
c1600-bsy56-l	1600
c1600-ny-l	1600
c1600-nsy-l	1600
c1600-nsy40-l	1600
c1600-nsy56-l	1600
c1600-bny-l	1600
c1600-bnsy-l	1600
c1600-bnsy40-l	1600
c1600-bnsy56-l	1600
c3620-ainr-mz	3620
c3620-ajs-mz	3620
c3620-d-mz	3620
c3620-ds-mz	3620

continues

Table A-10 *Cisco IOS Image Names Added for 11.2(5)P/F and Beyond (Continued)*

Added Image	Platform
c3620-i-mz	3620
c3620-is-mz	3620
c3620-j-mz	3620
c3620-js-mz	3620
c3620-p-mz	3620
c3640-ainr-mz	3640
c3640-ajs-mz	3640
c3640-d-mz	3640
c3640-ds-mz	3640
c3640-i-mz	3640
c3640-is-mz	3640
c3640-j-mz	3640
c3640-js-mz	3640
c3640-p-mz	3640

Table A-11 *Cisco IOS Image Names Added for 11.2(6) and Beyond*

Image Name	Feature/Platform
c5200-p3-l	Service Provider image for 5200

Table A-12 *Cisco IOS Image Names Added for 11.2(6)P/F and Beyond*

Image Name	Feature/Platform
ls1010-wp-mz	LightStream 1010
c25fx-f-l	Fixed FRAD platform, FRAD image
c25fx-fin-l	Fixed FRAD platform, LAN FRAD image
c25fx-f2in-l	Fixed FRAD platform, OSPF LAN FRAD image

Table A-13 *Cisco IOS Image Names Added for 11.2(7)P/F and Beyond*

Image Name	Feature Set/Platform
c2800-m-mx	2800

Table A-13 *Cisco IOS Image Names Added for 11.2(7)P/F and Beyond (Continued)*

Image Name	Feature Set/Platform
c5rsm-i-mz	Cat 5K rsp IP image
c5rsm-d-mz	Cat 5K rsp desktop image
c7200-ajs40-mz	7200
c7200-ajs56-mz	7200
c7200-is40-mz	7200
c7200-is56-mz	7200
c7200-ds40-mz	7200
c7200-ds56-mz	7200
c7200-js40-mz	7200
c7200-js56-mz	7200
c3800-ainr-mz	3801
c3800-f-mz	3801
c3800-j-mz	3801
c3800-fin-mz	3801

Table A-14 *Cisco IOS Image Names Added for 11.2(8)P and Beyond*

Image Name	Platform
c7200-ads40-mz	7200
c7200-ads56-mz	7200
c1600-nr2y-l	1600
c1600-nr2sy-l	1600
c1600-nr2sy40-l	1600
c1600-nr2sy56-l	1600
rsp-itv-mz	7500

Table A-15 *Cisco IOS Image Names Added for 11.2(9)P/11.3 and Beyond*

Image Name	Platform
c1600-y-mz	1605
c1600-sy-mz	1605
c1600-sy40-mz	1605
c1600-sy56-mz	1605
c1600-by-mz	1605
c1600-bsy40-mz	1605
c1600-bsy56-mz	1605
c1600-bsy-mz	1605
c1600-ny-mz	1605
c1600-nsy-mz	1605
c1600-nsy40-mz	1605
c1600-nsy56-mz	1605
c1600-bny-mz	1605
c1600-bnsy-mz	1605
c1600-bnsy40-mz	1605
c1600-bnsy56-mz	1605
c1600-nr2y-mz	1605
c1600-nr2sy-mz	1605
c1600-nr2sy40-mz	1605
c1600-nr2sy56-mz	1605
c5rsm-jsv-mz	Cat5K
c5rsm-isv-mz	Cat5K
c5rsm-dsv-mz	Cat5K
c5rsm-dsv40-mz	Cat5K[1]
c5rsm-dsv56-mz	Cat5K
c5rsm-jsv40-mz	Cat5K[1]
c5rsm-jsv56-mz	Cat5K
c5rsm-isv40-mz	Cat5K[1]
c5rsm-isv56-mz	Cat5K

Table A-15 *Cisco IOS Image Names Added for 11.2(9)P/11.3 and Beyond*

Image Name	Platform
c3620-inu-mz	3620
c3640-inu-mz	3640
c4000-inu-mz	4000[2]
c4500-inu-mz	4500

1. These encryption images are for testing only.
2. For testing purposes only in 11.2P.

Table A-16 *Cisco IOS Images Added in 11.2(9)GS and 11.3 and Later Releases*

Image Name	Platform
gsr-p-mz	GSR
gsr-diag-mz	GSR

Table A-17 *Cisco IOS Images Added in 11.2(10)P and Later Releases*

Image Name	Platform
c5300-d-l	5300
c5300-i-l	5300
c5300-j-l	5300
c5300-ds-l	5300
c5300-is-l	5300
c5300-js-l	5300
c5300-p3-l	5300

Table A-18 *Cisco IOS Images Added in 11.3(1) and 11.3(1)P*

Image Name	Platform
c1600-bnr2y-l	1600
c1600-bnr2sy-l	1600
c1600-bnr2sy40-l	1600
c1600-bnr2sy56-l	1600

Table A-19 *Cisco IOS Images Added in 11.3(1)MA*

Image Name	Platform
mc3810-inr3-mz	3810
mc3810-a2inr3-mz	3810
mc3810-inr3v2-mz	3810
mc3810-a2inr3v2-mz	3810

Images Added in 11.3(2)T

c2500-ai3r4-l

Images added in 11.3(3)T

c4500-aejs-mz
c4500-aejs40-mz
c4500-aejs56-mz

c7200-aejs-mz
c7200-aejs40-mz
c7200-aejs56-mz

rsp-aejsv-mz
rsp-aejsv40-mz
rsp-aejsv56-mz

New Board and Router Images Introduced in 11.3AA

dsc-c5800-mz
das-c5800-mz
c5800-p4-mz
c3640-c2is-mz

Images Added for 11.3(3)T and Forwards

c2600-i-mz
c2600-is-mz
c2600-c-mz
c2600-d-mz
c2600-ds-mz
c2600-js-mz

c2600-ajs-mz
c2600-p-mz

ubr7200-p-mz

XXXX-*56i-* (All platforms 1600 and up have multiples of this image.)

Images Added for 11.3(2)NA

c2500-ix-l
c3620-ix-mz
c3640-ix-mz

NOTE IOS feature sets are constantly added to the list. Consult CCO for the latest list of feature sets.

APPENDIX **B**

Cisco IOS Software Product Numbering System

The Cisco IOS software maintenance releases are packaged and labeled to allow customers to order the IOS image of their choice. The product numbers contain information that helps the customer identify the platform, the feature set, the maintenance revision number, and the IOS release train of their choice. Figure B-1 shows the various identifiers in the syntax of a product number (SKU).

Figure B-1 *Identifiers in the Syntax of a Product Number*

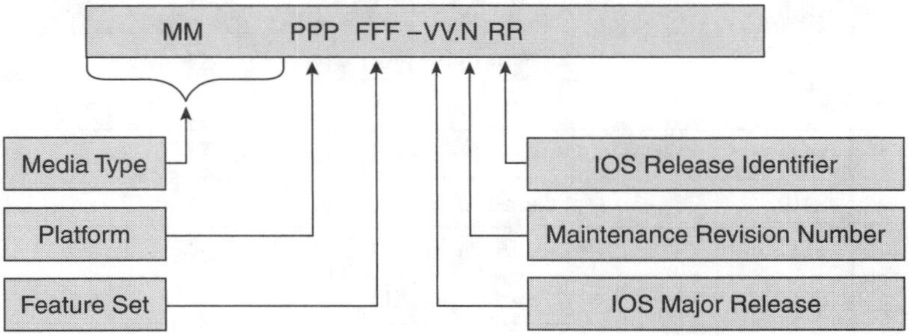

Example: S72CL-12.0.4XE

Where:

MM = S = Software in Flash

PPP = 72 = 7200 platform

FFF = CL where C is IP only feature set and L is 56 bit IPSEC encryption

VV.N =12.0.4 (The dots have been removed starting with 12.1(1). See product number for 12.1.)

RR = XE

Table B-1 and Table B-2 list the designators for the media types (MM) for pre- and post-12.0 media definitions. Table B-3 lists the feature set designators for the FFF placeholders.

Table B-1 *Cisco IOS Software Media Designators Used for Product Numbers Pre-12.0 Release*

Designator	Media Type
SF	System Flash
SFxxxx=	System Flash Spares
SW	System Floppy
SWxxxxx=	System Floppy Spares
FLxxxxx=	Feature License
FR	Feature License (Obsolete)
INT	Crypto Export Upgrade

Table B-2 *Cisco IOS Software Media Designators Used for Product Numbers Starting with Cisco IOS version 12.0*

Designator	Media Type
S	System Flash or Floppy
Sxxxx=	System Flash Spares
Sxxxxx=	System Floppy Spares
FLxxxxx=	Feature License
FR	Feature License (Obsolete)
I	Crypto Export Upgrade

Table B-3 *Cisco IOS Feature Designators Used for Product Numbers*

Feature Designator	Description	Platforms by Major IOS Releases					
		11.0	11.1	11.2	11.3	12.0	12.0T
A	Enterprise			2500, 3620, 3640, 3800, 4500, 4700, 5rsm, as5200, as5300, 7200, 7500			
A	IP/IPX/AT			1600, 1605			
B	Desktop			7200			
B	IP/IPX/AT			1000, 1005			
B	IP/IPX/AT/DEC			2500, 3620, 3640, 4500, 4700, 5rsm, as5200, as5300			
B	IP/IPX			1600, 1605			
C	IP			all	all	all	

Table B-3 *Cisco IOS Feature Designators Used for Product Numbers (Continued)*

Feature Designator	Description	Platforms by Major IOS Releases					
		11.0	11.1	11.2	11.3	12.0	12.0T
C6	Home Office						UBR900
C7	Telecommuter - contains non-ECRA crypto (Basic)	-	-	-	-	-	UBR900
C8	Small Office	-	-	-	-	-	UBR900
C9	IP/Bridging	-	-	-	-	-	UBR900
D	IP/IPX/IBM			3620, 3640, 3800			
D2	Distributed Director	-	-	-	-	2500	2500
E	RAS			2509 - 2525			
E	IP/AT			1600, 1605			
E2	SS7	-	-	-	-	-	2600
F	FRAD			2500			
F	CFRAD			3800			
F1	Fixed FRAD-Serial				25fx	25fx	
F2	Fixed FRAD-LAN FRAD/OSPF				25fx	25fx	
F2	IP/AT/X.25	1003, 1005			-	-	
F3	Fixed FRAD-LAN FRAD/EIGRP				25fx	25fx	
F1	FRAD-Serial				2500	2500	
F2	FRAD-LAN FRAD/OSPF				2500	2500	
F3	LAN FRAD/EIGRP				2500	2500	
F4	LAN FRAD				-	2500	
FRAD1	Fixed FRAD-Serial			25fx	-	-	-

Table B-3 *Cisco IOS Feature Designators Used for Product Numbers (Continued)*

Feature Designator	Description	Platforms by Major IOS Releases					
		11.0	11.1	11.2	11.3	12.0	12.0T
FRAD2	Fixed FRAD-LAN FRAD/EIGRP			25fx	-	-	-
FRAD3	Fixed FRAD-LAN FRAD/OSPF			25fx	-	-	-
G	SOHO (7500)			-			
G	ACIP			7500			
G2	IP/IPX/X25	1003, 1005	1003, 1005	-			
G3	NA			-			
H	IP/ASYNCH (3810)			-			
H	FIREWALL			1600, 1605, 2500	x	x	
I	ISDN			2500			
J	IP/IPX/Asynch	1003, 1005	-	-			
J2	IP/IPX/Asynch	1003, 1005					
J3	NRP	-	-	-	6400		
J4	NSP	-	-	-	6400		
J5	NRP - SSG						
J6	NRP - SSG with Web Dashboard						
K	40-bit crypto (No Plus)			7200, 7500			
K2	3DES (Triple DES)	-	-	-	-	all	
K3	SECURED SHELL 56						7200, 7500, gsr
K4	Baseline Privacy						ubr900, ubr7200
K5	SECURED SHELL 3DES						7200, 7500, gsr

Table B-3 *Cisco IOS Feature Designators Used for Product Numbers (Continued)*

Feature Designator	Description	Platforms by Major IOS Releases					
		11.0	11.1	11.2	11.3	12.0	12.0T
L	56-bit IPSEC (and/or PLUS)			7200, 7500	X	X	
L	56-bit IPSEC PLUS			not 7200, 7500	X	X	
L	LAN			3800			
M	PIM (1005)						
M	IP/IPX/IBM			1600, 1605	X		
M2	ATM					3810	
M3	MCNS TWO-WAY						ubr7200
M4	OC-3 ATM UPLINK MODULE FOR CATALYST 2900 XL					29atm	
M4	ATM OC-3 LANE					2800	
N				all	all		
N2	APPN/DBCONN					X	X
O	OSFP			2500	-		
O2	Subtending	-	-	-	-	-	6200
O3	ATM QoS	-	-	-	-	-	6200
O4	Redundancy	-	-	-	-	-	6200
O5	ATM Signaling	-	-	-	-	-	6200
O6	O2 to O5 Bundle	-	-	-	-	-	6200
P	Plus			all	all	all	
Q	IP/IPX/IBM (1600)			-			
Q	IP/IPX/AT/IBM			1600, 1605			
R	Network Layer 3 Switching		7200	-			
R1	SNA Switching Services					core	core
R2	PNNI for MSR	-	-	-	-	-	cat85x0

Table B-3 *Cisco IOS Feature Designators Used for Product Numbers (Continued)*

Feature Designator	Description	Platforms by Major IOS Releases					
		11.0	11.1	11.2	11.3	12.0	12.0T
R3	Layer 3 for CSR	-	-	-	-	-	cat85x0
S	IBM			2500, 3620, 3640, 7500			
S2	Desktop/IBM	7500					
T	56-bit crypto (No Plus)			7200, 7500			
T	TELCO	-	-	-	-	-	3660
T2	Telco Return	-	-	-	-	-	ubr7200
U	MCM			-		3810	3810
V	Voice					all	all
V	VIP			all	all	-	-
W	Plus 40			1600, 1605, 2500, 3620, 3640, 4500, 4700			
W2	LIGHTSTREAM 1010 IISP AND PNNI					ls1010	ls1010
X	NA*						
Y	Plus 56			all	all		
Z	NA			1600, 1605, 2500, 3620, 3640, 4500, 4700			
Z	Base System Software			gsr			
Y	Plus 56			all	all		
Y	Plus 56			all	all		

*NA = Not assigned at the time this book was written.

Cisco IOS Product Numbers and Feature Set Definition

Product numbers (SKU) of Cisco IOS Software starting 12.1, 12.1T, and STED derivative of 12.1 and 12.1T releases, will be formed without using the dot (.) separator. This move allows the SKU numbers to grow without increasing the total number of character fields. Here are a few examples:

Convention before 12.1	New Convention starting with 12.1(1)
S26CHL-12.0.7	S26CHL-12101
S38M3PU-12.0.7T	S38M3PU-12101T
SU7M3PT2-12.0.7XR=	SU72M3PT2-12101XR=

The following table applies to Cisco IOS software 12.1(1)

NOTE Future Product Numbering format is subject to change.

Platform	Software Feature Set Description	IOS Image Name	New SKU for 12.1(1)
800	IP	c800-y6-mw	S8CA-12101
800	IP PLUS	c800-sy6-mw	S8CD-12101
800	IP/FW PLUS	c800-osy6-mw	S8CM-12101
800	IP/FW PLUS IPSEC 56	c800-osy656i-mw	S8CN-12101
800	IP/IPX FW PLUS IPSEC 56	c800-nosy656i-mw	S8BA-12101
800	IP/IPX PLUS	c800-nsy6-mw	S8BB-12101
805	IP	c805-y6-mw	S8CA-12101
805	IP PLUS	c805-sy6-mw	S8CD-12101
805	IP/IPX PLUS	c805-nsy6-mw	S8BB-12101
1400	IP	c1400-ny-mz	S14CA-12101
1400	IP/FW PLUS IPSEC 56	c1400-osy56i-mz	S14CN-12101
1400	IP/IPX	c1400-ny-mz	S14BF-12101
1400	IP/IPX PLUS	c1400-nsy-mz	S14BB-12101
1400	IP/IPX/FW PLUS	c1400-nosy-mz	S14BL-12101

Platform	Software Feature Set Description	IOS Image Name	New SKU for 12.1(1)
1601-1604	IP	c1600-y-l	S160CA-12101
1601-1604	IP PLUS	c1600-sy-l	S160CD-12101
1601-1604	IP PLUS 40	c1600-sy40-l	S160CE-12101
1601-1604	IP PLUS 56	c1600-sy56-l	S160CF-12101
1601-1604	IP PLUS IPSEC 56	c1600-sy56i-l	S160CH-12101
1601-1604	IP/FW	c1600-oy-l	S160CL-12101
1601-1604	IP/FW PLUS IPSEC 56	c1600-osy56i-l	S160CN-12101
1601-1604	IP/IPX	c1600-ny-l	S160BF-12101
1601-1604	IP/IPX/AT/IBM	c1600-bnr2y-l	S160BG-12101
1601-1604	IP/IPX/AT/IBM PLUS	c1600-bnr2sy-l	S160BH-12101
1601-1604	IP/IPX/AT/IBM/FW PLUS IPSEC 56	c1600-bnor2sy56i-l	S160BI-12101
1601-1604	IP/IPX/FW PLUS	c1600-nosy-l	S160BL-12101
1601R-1605R	IP	c1600-y-mz	S16RCA-12101
1601R-1605R	IP PLUS IPSEC 56	c1600-sy56i-mz	S16RCH-12101

Platform	Software Feature Set Description	IOS Image Name	New SKU for 12.1(1)
1601R-1605R	IP/FW	c1600-oy-mz	S16RCL-12101
1601R-1605R	IP/FW PLUS IPSEC 56	c1600-osy56i-mz	S16RCN-12101
1601R-1605R	IP/IPX	c1600-ny-mz	S16RBF-12101
1601R-1605R	IP/IPX/AT/IBM PLUS	c1600-bnr2sy-mz	S16RBH-12101
1601R-1605R	IP/IPX/AT/IBM/FW PLUS IPSEC 56	c1600-bnor2sy56i-mz	S16RBI-12101
1601R-1605R	IP/IPX/FW PLUS	c1600-nosy-mz	S16RBL-12101
1700	IP	c1700-y-mz	S17CA-12101
1700	IP PLUS IPSEC 3DES	c1700-k2sy-mz	S17CG-12101
1700	IP PLUS IPSEC 56	c1700-sy56i-mz	S17CH-12101
1700	IP/IPX	c1700-ny-mz	S17BF-12101
1700	IP/IPX/AT/IBM PLUS	c1700-bnr2sy-mz	S17BH-12101
2500FRAD	FRAD	c2500-f-l	S25EJ-12101
2500FRAD	LAN FRAD	c2500-fin-l	S25EN-12101
2500FRAD	LAN FRAD/OSPF	c2500-f2in-l	S25EO-12101
2501-2525	ENTERPRISE PLUS	c2500-js-l	S25AE-12101
2501-2525	ENTERPRISE PLUS IPSEC 56	c2500-js56i-l	S25AI-12101
2501-2525	ENTERPRISE/FW PLUS IPSEC 56	c2500-jos56i-l	S25AL-12101

Platform	Software Feature Set Description	IOS Image Name	New SKU for 12.1(1)
2501-2525	IP	c2500-i-l	S25CA-12101
2501-2525	IP PLUS	c2500-is-l	S25CD-12101
2501-2525	IP PLUS IPSEC 56	c2500-is56i-l	S25CH-12101
2501-2525	IP/FW	c2500-io-l	S25CL-12101
2501-2525	IP/FW PLUS IPSEC 56	c2500-ios56i-l	S25CN-12101
2501-2525	IP/H323	c2500-ix-l	S25CQ-12101
2501-2525	IP/IPX/AT/DEC	c2500-d-l	S25BM-12101
2501-2525	IP/IPX/AT/DEC PLUS	c2500-ds-l	S25BA-12101
2501-2525	IP/IPX/AT/DEC/FW PLUS	c2500-dos-l	S25BC-12101
2501-2525	ISDN	c2500-g-l	S25EM-12101
2501-2525	REMOTE ACCESS SERVER	c2500-c-l	S25EQ-12101
25FX	FIXED FRAD-SERIAL	c25fx-f-l	SFRADEG-12101
25FX	FIXED LAN FRAD/EIGRP	c25fx-fin-l	SFRADEH-12101
25FX	FIXED LAN FRAD/OSPF	c25fx-f2in-l	SFRADEI-12101
2610-2621	ENTERPRISE PLUS	c2600-js-mz	S26AE-12101

Platform	Software Feature Set Description	IOS Image Name	New SKU for 12.1(1)
2610-2621	ENTERPRISE PLUS IPSEC 3DES	c2600-jk2s-mz	S26AH-12101
2610-2621	ENTERPRISE PLUS IPSEC 56	c2600-js56i-mz	S26AI-12101
2610-2621	ENTERPRISE/FW/IDS PLUS IPSEC 3DES	c2600-jk2o3s-mz	S26AP-12101
2610-2621	ENTERPRISE/FW/IDS PLUS IPSEC 56	c2600-jo3s56i-mz	S26AQ-12101
2610-2621	IP	c2600-i-mz	S26CA-12101
2610-2621	IP PLUS	c2600-is-mz	S26CD-12101
2610-2621	IP PLUS IPSEC 3DES	c2600-ik2s-mz	S26CG-12101
2610-2621	IP PLUS IPSEC 56	c2600-is56i-mz	S26CH-12101
2610-2621	IP/FW/IDS	c2600-io3-mz	S26CO-12101
2610-2621	IP/FW/IDS IPSEC 56	c2600-io3s56i-mz	S26CN-12101
2610-2621	IP/FW/IDS PLUS IPSEC 3DES	c2600-ik2o3s-mz	S26CP-12101
2610-2621	IP/H323	c2600-ix-mz	S26CQ-12101
2610-2621	IP/IPX/AT/DEC PLUS	c2600-ds-mz	S26BA-12101
2610-2621	IP/IPX/AT/DEC/FW/IDS PLUS	c2600-do3s-mz	S26BC-12101

Platform	Software Feature Set Description	IOS Image Name	New SKU for 12.1(1)
2610-2621	REMOTE ACCESS SERVER	c2600-c-mz	S26EQ-12101
3620	ENTERPRISE PLUS	c3620-js-mz	S362AE-12101
3620	ENTERPRISE PLUS IPSEC 3DES	c3620-jk2s-mz	S362H-12101
3620	ENTERPRISE PLUS IPSEC 56	c3620-js56i-mz	S362AI-12101
3620	ENTERPRISE/FW/IDS PLUS IPSEC 3DES	c3620-jk2o3s-mz	S362AP-12101
3620	ENTERPRISE/FW/IDS PLUS IPSEC 56	c3620-jo3s56i-mz	S362AQ-12101
3620	IP	c3620-i-mz	S362CA-12101
3620	IP PLUS	c3620-is-mz	S362CD-12101
3620	IP PLUS IPSEC 3DES	c3620-ik2s-mz	S362CG-12101
3620	IP PLUS IPSEC 56	c3620-is56i-mz	S362CH-12101
3620	IP/FW/IDS	c3620-io3-mz	S362CO-12101
3620	IP/FW/IDS PLUS IPSEC 3DES	c3620-ik2o3s-mz	S362CP-12101
3620	IP/FW/IDS PLUS IPSEC 56	c3620-io3s56i-mz	S362CN-12101
3620	IP/H323	c3620-ix-mz	S362CQ-12101
3620	IP/IPX/AT/DEC PLUS	c3620-ds-mz	S362BA-12101
3620	IP/IPX/AT/DEC/FW/IDS PLUS	c3620-do3s-mz	S362BC-12101
3640	ENTERPRISE PLUS	c3640-js-mz	S364AE-12101
3640	ENTERPRISE PLUS IPSEC 3DES	c3640-jk2s-mz	S364H-12101
3640	ENTERPRISE PLUS IPSEC 56	c3640-js56i-mz	S364AI-12101
3640	ENTERPRISE/FW/IDS PLUS IPSEC 3DES	c3640-jk2o3s-mz	S364AP-12101

Platform	Software Feature Set Description	IOS Image Name	New SKU for 12.1(1)
3640	ENTERPRISE/FW/IDS PLUS IPSEC 56	c3640-jo3s56i-mz	S364AQ-12101
3640	IP	c3640-i-mz	S364CA-12101
3640	IP PLUS	c3640-is-mz	S364CD-12101
3640	IP PLUS IPSEC 3DES	c3640-ik2s-mz	S364CG-12101
3640	IP PLUS IPSEC 56	c3640-is56i-mz	S364CH-12101
3640	IP/FW/IDS	c3640-io3-mz	S364CO-12101
3640	IP/FW/IDS PLUS IPSEC 3DES	c3640-ik2o3s-mz	S364CP-12101
3640	IP/FW/IDS PLUS IPSEC 56	c3640-io3s56i-mz	S364CN-12101
3640	IP/H323	c3640-ix-mz	S364CQ-12101
3640	IP/IPX/AT/DEC PLUS	c3640-ds-mz	S364BA-12101
3640	IP/IPX/AT/DEC/FW/IDS PLUS	c3640-do3s-mz	S364BC-12101
3660	ENTERPRISE PLUS	c3660-js-mz	S366AE-12101
3660	ENTERPRISE PLUS IPSEC 3DES	c3660-jk2s-mz	S366AH-12101
3660	ENTERPRISE PLUS IPSEC 56	c3660-js56i-mz	S366AI-12101
3660	IP	c3660-i-mz	S366CA-12101
3660	IP PLUS	c3660-is-mz	S366CD-12101
3660	IP PLUS IPSEC 3DES	c3660-ik2s-mz	S366G-12101
3660	IP PLUS IPSEC 56	c3660-is56i-mz	S366CH-12101
3660	IP/H323	c3660-ix-mz	S366CQ-12101
3660	IP/IPX/AT/DEC PLUS	c3660-ds-mz	S366BA-12101
3660	TELCO FEATURE SET	c3660-telco-mz	S366ES-12101
3660	TELCO PLUS FEATURE SET	c3660-telcoent-mz	S366ET-12101
4000	ENTERPRISE PLUS	c4000-js-mz	S4AE-12101

Platform	Software Feature Set Description	IOS Image Name	New SKU for 12.1(1)
4000	ENTERPRISE PLUS IPSEC 3DES	c4000-jk2s-mz	S4AH-12101
4000	ENTERPRISE PLUS IPSEC 56	c4000-js56i-mz	S4AI-12101
4000	IP	c4000-i-mz	S4CA-12101
4000	IP PLUS	c4000-is-mz	S4CD-12101
4000	IP PLUS 40	c4000-is40-mz	S4CE-12101
4000	IP PLUS IPSEC 3DES	c4000-ik2s-mz	S4CG-12101
4000	IP PLUS IPSEC 56	c4000-is56i-mz	S4CH-12101
4000	IP/IPX/AT/DEC	c4000-d-mz	S4BM-12101
4000	IP/IPX/AT/DEC Plus	c4000-ds-mz	S4BA-12101
4500-m / 4700 / 4700-m / 4500	ENTERPRISE PLUS	c4500-js-mz	S45AE-12101
4500-m / 4700 / 4700-m / 4500	ENTERPRISE PLUS IPSEC 3DES	c4500-jk2s-mz	S45AH-12101
4500-m / 4700 / 4700-m / 4500	ENTERPRISE PLUS IPSEC 56	c4500-js56i-mz	S45AI-12101
4500-m / 4700 / 4700-m / 4500	IP	c4500-i-mz	S45CA-12101
4500-m / 4700 / 4700-m / 4500	IP PLUS	c4500-is-mz	S45CD-12101

Platform	Software Feature Set Description	IOS Image Name	New SKU for 12.1(1)
4500-m / 4700 / 4700-m / 4500	IP PLUS 40	c4500-is40-mz	S45CE-12101
4500-m / 4700 / 4700-m / 4500	IP PLUS IPSEC 3DES	c4500-ik2s-mz	S45CG-12101
4500-m / 4700 / 4700-m / 4500	IP PLUS IPSEC 56	c4500-is56i-mz	S45CH-12101
4500-m / 4700 / 4700-m / 4500	IP/IPX/AT/DEC	c4500-d-mz	S45BM-12101
4500-m / 4700 / 4700-m / 4500	IP/IPX/AT/DEC PLUS	c4500-ds-mz	S45BA-12101
AS5200	DESKTOP	c5200-d-l	S52DA-12101
7200	DESKTOP/IBM	c7200-ds-mz	S72DD-12101
7200	DESKTOP/IBM 40	c7200-ds40-mz	S72DE-12101
7200	DESKTOP/IBM IPSEC 56	c7200-ds56i-mz	S72DF-12101
7200	DESKTOP/IBM/FW/IDS	c7200-do3s-mz	S72DG-12101
7200	DESKTOP/IBM/FW/IDS IPSEC 3DES	c7200-dk2o3s-mz	S72DH-12101
7200	DESKTOP/IBM/FW/IDS IPSEC 56	c7200-do3s56i-mz	S72DI-12101
7200	ENTERPRISE	c7200-js-mz	S72AA-12101

Platform	Software Feature Set Description	IOS Image Name	New SKU for 12.1(1)
7200	ENTERPRISE 40	c7200-js40-mz	S72AB-12101
7200	ENTERPRISE IPSEC 3DES	c7200-jk2s-mz	S72AC-12101
7200	ENTERPRISE IPSEC 56	c7200-js56i-mz	S72AD-12101
7200	ENTERPRISE/FW/IDS	c7200-jo3s-mz	S72AM-12101
7200	ENTERPRISE/FW/IDS IPSEC 3DES	c7200-jk2o3s-mz	S72AN-12101
7200	ENTERPRISE/FW/IDS IPSEC 56	c7200-jo3s56i-mz	S72AO-12101
7200	IP	c7200-is-mz	S72CA-12101
7200	IP 40	c7200-is40-mz	S72CC-12101
7200	IP IPSEC 3DES	c7200-ik2s-mz	S72CB-12101
7200	IP IPSEC 56	c7200-is56i-mz	S72CC-12101
7200	IP/FW/IDS	c7200-io3s-mz	S72CO-12101
7200	IP/FW/IDS IPSEC 3DES	c7200-ik2o3s-mz	S72CP-12101
7200	IP/FW/IDS IPSEC 56	c7200-io3s56i-mz	S72CN-12101
7200	NETWORK LAYER 3 SWITCHING	c7200-inu-mz	S72EP-12101
AS5200	DESKTOP PLUS	c5200-ds-l	S52DB-12101
AS5200	IP	c5200-i-l	S52CA-12101
AS5200	IP Plus	c5200-is-l	S52CD-12101
AS5300	DESKTOP	c5300-d-mz	S53DA-12101
AS5300	DESKTOP PLUS	c5300-ds-mz	S53DB-12101
AS5300	DESKTOP VOICE PLUS	c5300-ds-mz	S53DC-12101
AS5300	ENTERPRISE	c5300-j-mz	S53AA-12101
AS5300	ENTERPRISE PLUS	c5300-js-mz	S53AE-12101

Platform	Software Feature Set Description	IOS Image Name	New SKU for 12.1(1)
AS5300	ENTERPRISE PLUS 40	c5300-js40-mz	S53AF-12101
AS5300	ENTERPRISE PLUS IPSEC 3DES	c5300-jk2s-mz	S53AH-12101
AS5300	ENTERPRISE PLUS IPSEC 56	c5300-js56i-mz	S53AI-12101
AS5300	ENTERPRISE VOICE PLUS	c5300-js-mz	S53AJ-12101
AS5300	IP	c5300-i-mz	S53CA-12101
AS5300	IP PLUS	c5300-is-mz	S53CD-12101
AS5300	IP PLUS 40	c5300-is40-mz	S53CE-12101
AS5300	IP PLUS IPSEC 3DES	c5300-ik2s-mz	S53CG-12101
AS5300	IP PLUS IPSEC 56	c5300-is56i-mz	S53CH-12101
AS5300	IP VOICE PLUS	c5300-is-mz	S53CI-12101
AS5800	IP PLUS	c5800-p4-mz	S58CD-12101
AS5800	SERVICE PROVIDER IPSEC 56	c5800-p456i-mz	S58ER-12101
c5rsfc	ENTERPRISE PLUS	c5rsfc-js-mz	SC5RAE-12101
c5rsm	DESKTOP/IBM	c5rsm-dsv-mz	SC5DD-12101
c5rsm	DESKTOP/IBM 40	c5rsm-dsv40-mz	SC5DE-12101
c5rsm	DESKTOP/IBM IPSEC 56	c5rsm-dsv56i-mz	SC5DF-12101
c5rsm	ENTERPRISE	c5rsm-jsv-mz	SC5AA-12101
c5rsm	ENTERPRISE 40	c5rsm-jsv40-mz	SC5AB-12101
c5rsm	ENTERPRISE IPSEC 3DES	c5rsm-jk2sv-mz	SC5AC-12101
c5rsm	ENTERPRISE IPSEC 56	c5rsm-jsv56i-mz	SC5AD-12101
c5rsm	IP	c5rsm-isv-mz	SC5CA-12101
c5rsm	IP 40	c5rsm-isv40-mz	SC5CC-12101
c5rsm	IP IPSEC 3DES	c5rsm-ik2sv-mz	SC5CB-12101

Platform	Software Feature Set Description	IOS Image Name	New SKU for 12.1(1)
c5rsm	IP IPSEC 56	c5rsm-isv56i-mz	SC5CC-12101
c6msm	IP/IP-Multicast Routing	c6msm-in-mz	SC6CR-12101
Distributed Director 2501/2502	DISTRIBUTED DIRECTOR	c2500-w3-l	S25EA-12101
Distributed Director 4700M	DISTRIBUTED DIRECTOR	c4500-w3-mz	S47EA-12101
mc3810	ENTERPRISE PLUS	mc3810-js-mz	S38AE-12101
mc3810	ENTERPRISE PLUS ATM MCM H323	mc3810-a2jsx-mz	S38AG-12101
mc3810	ENTERPRISE/ATM PLUS	mc3810-a2js-mz	S38AK-12101
mc3810	IP	mc3810-i-mz	S38CA-12101
mc3810	IP PLUS	mc3810-is-mz	S38CD-12101
mc3810	IP PLUS ATM MCM H323	mc3810-a2isx-mz	S38I-12101
mc3810	IP/ATM PLUS	mc3810-a2is-mz	S38CK-12101
RPM	ENTERPRISE PLUS	rpm-js-mz	SRPMAE-12101
RSP7000 / 7500	DESKTOP/IBM	rsp-dsv-mz	S75DD-12101
RSP7000 / 7500	DESKTOP/IBM 40	rsp-dsv40-mz	S75DE-12101
RSP7000 / 7500	DESKTOP/IBM IPSEC 56	rsp-dsv56i-mz	S75DF-12101
RSP7000 / 7500	ENTERPRISE	rsp-jsv-mz	S75AA-12101

Platform	Software Feature Set Description	IOS Image Name	New SKU for 12.1(1)
RSP7000 / 7500	ENTERPRISE 40	rsp-jsv40-mz	S75AB-12101
RSP7000 / 7500	ENTERPRISE IPSEC 3DES	rsp-jk2sv-mz	S75AC-12101
RSP7000 / 7500	ENTERPRISE IPSEC 56	rsp-jsv56i-mz	S75AD-12101
RSP7000 / 7500	IP	rsp-isv-mz	S75CA-12101
RSP7000 / 7500	IP 40	rsp-isv40-mz	S75CC-12101
RSP7000 / 7500	IP IPSEC 3DES	rsp-ik2sv-mz	S75CB-12101
RSP7000 / 7500	IP IPSEC 56	rsp-isv56i-mz	S75CC-12101
ubr7200	DOCSIS 2-WAY	ubr7200-p-mz	SU7EB-12101
ubr7200	DOCSIS 2-WAY BPI	ubr7200-k1p-mz	SU7EC-12101
ubr7200	DOCSIS 2-WAY IP PLUS	ubr7200-is-mz	SU7ED-12101
ubr7200	DOCSIS 2-WAY IP+ TELCO-RETURN	ubr7200-ist-mz	SU7EE-12101
ubr7200	DOCSIS 2-WAY IP+ TELCO-RETURN W/BPI	ubr7200-ik1st-mz	SU7EF-12101
ubr900	HOME OFFICE	ubr900-k1y5-mz	SU9EK-12101
ubr920	BASE IP BRIDGING	ubr920-k1y5-mz	S92CS-12101
ubr920	HOME OFFICE	ubr920-k1y5-mz	S92EK-12101
ubr920	HOME OFFICE VOICE	ubr920-k1v4y5-mz	S92EL-12101
ubr920	TELECOMMUTER/IPSEC 56	ubr920-k1sy556i-mz	S92EU-12101

Platform	Software Feature Set Description	IOS Image Name	New SKU for 12.1(1)
ubr920	TELECOMMUTER/VOICE/IPSEC 56	ubr920-k1sv4y556i-mz	S92EV-12101
ubr920	TELECOMMUTER+/IPSEC 3DES	ubr920-k1k2sy5-mz	S92EW-12101
ubr920	TELECOMMUTER+/VOICE/ IPSEC 3DES	ubr920-k1k2sv4y5-mz	S92EX-12101

APPENDIX C

New Features of Cisco IOS 12.0T

The following is a maintenance-per-maintenance listing of major features committed into Cisco IOS 12.0T. Please note that the feature marketing name may be slightly different.

New Features of 12.0(1)T

64Bit SNMP counters
8Mbps Compression Advanced Interface Module (AIM)
Air Line Protocol System (ALPS) II - UTS support
APPN extender
ARP for LAM (local area mobility)
Ascend MIB support
Asymmetrical Windows/Packets support
Async over UDP
ATM PVC Traps/RFC2233 for ATM subinterfaces
CAR on GSR
Cisco 8510 OC-12 support
CLI string search
DHCP server
IETF compliant PPP over ATM scalability
IOS firewall feature set on mid-range platforms
IOS IEEE 802.1Q support
IOS STP enhancement
ISDN MIB RFC 2127
Layer 2 tunneling protocol (L2TP)
Mobile IP
New TDM Bus/ 2FE slots
OSPF Packet spacing
Parse bookmarks/CLI string search
PPP over Frame Relay
RSM/TR-VLAN
Timed-based access-lists
Triggered RIP

New Features of 12.0(2)T

1720 enhanced features (RMON, VINES, APPN, and so on)
7200 RPM blade integration with 8850/8650
ATM25 on 1600 routers
IPSec triple DES
MC3810 enhancement (QSIG voice signaling & PBX integration)

New Features of 12.0(3)T

2 ports FE for 2600 series
8T1/8E1/8DSX/4T1 potent cards for 7500/7200/7000
Analog modem support over BRI
Annex G (X.25 to Frame Relay Direct)
AS5300 8T1/E1 w/240 modem
ATM FUNI (ATM Frame-UNI) support (PVCs and SVCs)
Automatic protection switching (APS) and sonetization for GSR
Catalyst 8540 campus switch router support
CE3 port adapter support
Channelized OC-12 Packet over Sonet for GSR
Channelized T3 card for AS5800 (CT3)
Cisco 7576 support
Cisco 801, 802, 803, 804 routers introduction
CT3 port adaptor support
DistributedDirector Internet scaling application
DLSW+ enhancements (DLSW+/RSVP, Peer-group cluster)
Frame Relay encapsulation on Packet over SONET (POS) on GSR
Gigabit Ethernet for the 7x00 routers
H.323 Gatekeeper
IOS support for IP connection to SS7 signaling controller
IP ATM CoS enhancements
IP policy routing integrated in CEF and NetFlow
ISDN BRI VIC voice network module for 2600/3600
Large scale dial-out (centralized dial config via AAA Server)
Mapping of QoS between RSVP and ATM SVC
MC16 card on the uBR7200
MPC+ IBM channel protocol
MPLS on the GSR
Multilink inverse multiplexer
NPE-300 support for the 7200
OC-3 ATM modules for the 2600/3600
Process MIBs (enhanced CPU & memory stats)
Redundant dial shelf support for the AS5800

Response time reporter & Internet performance monitor (RPR/IPM) updates
Service provider features (IVR, RADIUS, RAS)
SNMPv3 provides MD5 authentication, DES encryption and a group-based administrative model
Tag switch controller (7500/7200/RPM) - MPLS features
The 6400 NSP support
TRLANE v2/MPOA - RFC1483 support for SRB token ring
uBR 904 multi media cable network service (MCNS)
Web cache control protocol (WCCP version 2)
WRED support for all flow (not just TCP)
X.25 calls can be load-balanced among all configured outgoing interfaces

New Features of 12.0(4)T

Dynamic multiple encaps allow dynamic assignment of encap type on ISDN B channels by Caller ID
Four port ISDN voice module for MC3810
Frame Relay fragmentation implementation agreement FRF.12
FRF.11 encapsulation, FRF.12 fragmentation, VoFR functionality on 2600,3600, 3810 & 7200
Internet fax - store and forward (ESMTP)
IOS client for Cisco directory services
ISDN LAPB-TA (X.75)
Resynchronize the connection on RPM and controller card (PXM)
SNMP over IPC for RPM
Voice over Frame Relay networks implementation agreement, FRF.11

New Features of 12.0(5)T

1E1ADSL-DMT CPE router on the 1417
4/8 port T1/E1 IMA ATM NM of 2600/3600
Airline protocol support - Phase III (MATIP support)
Async over UDP
ATM per VC MIB on the GSR ATM line cards
ATM per VC subinterface SNMP MIB
Cat 8500 CSR enhanced features
Catalyst 8540 multiservice switch router
Channelized DS3/E1 PAM for LS1010/Cat8540msr
Cisco 3660 (six slot router with an integrated TDM bus backplane and AIM slots)
Cisco IOS Firewall Feature Set - Phase II (context-based access control, Java blocking, denial of service detection and prevention, real-time alerts, and audit trail)
Class-based extension to IOS weighted fair queuing

CNS client for IOS (IPSec Policy Agent II)
Committed access rates with access lists on GSR
Common LS1010/Cat8540msr features
Distributed network load balancing for clusters of IP servers
DLSw+ Ethernet redundancy
DNS based X.25 routing
DSPM542 AS5300 (G.723.1 and G.729 and 14.4kb/s FAX Relay, as well as DTMF Digit Relay via RTP)
Extended voice support for Janeiro (AS5300)
Frame Relay switching on the GSR Packet over Sonet (POS)
Frame-relay end-to-end keepalive
Full resource pool management feature on a standalone NAS (Resource Pooling Phase 1)
GSR - IP Multicast on ATM (QOC3 & OC12)
GSR ATM SVCs (QOC3 & OC12)
H.323 version 2 protocol enhancement and feature additions (H.225, E.164, H.245)
HRSP for Gigabit Ethernet on the GSR router
IOS Firewall Feature Set/Intrusion Detection System (IDS) signature
IOS Subnet Bandwidth Manager (SBM)
IP Multicast MultiLayer Switching Route Processor Server on the RSM
IPX MultiLayer Switching Route Processor server on RSM
L2TP dial-out
LANE fast SSRP
Multiarea support for ISIS
Multicast routing monitor
OAM cell support on GSR QOC3 & OC12 ATM line cards
OC3ATM uplink module for Catalyst 2900 Series XL
PGM reliable transport protocol
PVC OAM management for the Quad OC3 ATM line card
RMON performance improvement
Router blade (supervisor daughter card) for Cat5K
RTR service provider features (Jitter-Path, UDP-Path, Voice Setup, HTTP Get/Put Probe)
SDH MPS on the GSR platforms sonet interfaces
Simple Gateway Control Protocol (SGCP) on the AS5300
Single port gigabit Ethernet line card for the GSR
Single port OC48 & Quad OC12 TTM Packet over SONET line cards for GSR
SONET OC48 regenerator on the GSR (SONET/SDH)
Tag switching virtual private networks and class of service
Telco Return Software Support with Spectrum Management
TN3270 server on the CIP
uBR924 Docsis cable modem with VoIP
Universal access concentrator (c6400NRP) - xDSL scaling

Weighted RED without Deficit Round Robin (DRR) on GSR
X.25 remote host fail detect based on VC diagnostic

New Features of 12.0(6)T

See 12.0(7)T

New Features of 12.0(7)T

AAA lists selection by DNIS and PPP configuration via the customer profile
C2600 Signaling Link Termination Device (SS7 FEP for the Cisco SC-2200)
Cisco 1750 voice enabled low-end router
Cisco 7100 router (VPN, QoS, firewall features)
Cisco 805 router
Debit Card Application for VoIP (AAA and IVR with Extension of TCL IVR functionality)
Dial video (RS-366) over ATM SVC and voice over ATM SVC for the MC3810
Digital T1 Packet Voice Trunk Module for the 2600/3600
Dual port T1/E1 (non-channelized) WAN interface card (Wic/Vic) for the 2600/3600
Dual port VoIP PA for 7xxx platforms
FS-CRTP Fast-Switched Compressed RTP (from 40 bytes to 2-5 bytes)
MC3810 FRF.8 support
MPLS traffic engineering (routing for resource reservation aka RRR)
Open settlement protocol for Packet voice
QSIG signaling for PBX interconnection on the 5300, with VoIP
RSP supporting Cz bus backplane protocol
RSP8 card support for the 75xx
SGCP Trunking & Residential Gateway (support for T1/CAS FGD-OS, SGCP version 1.1, SGCP MIB, and Fax/Modem Switchover)
SNA switching services (APPN, HPR, Distributed APPC)
VIP4 support
Voice feature board for AS5800
X.25 local acknowledgement (versus end to end)
X.25 Standard Closed User Group Service (CUG) service

GLOSSARY

A

Advanced Gateway Server See AGS.

Advanced Peer-to-Peer Networking See APPN.

AGS Advanced Gateway Server. One of Cisco's original products.

AppleTalk A series of communications protocols designed by Apple Computer. Two phases currently exist. Phase 1, the earlier version, supports a single physical network that can have only one network number and be in one zone. Phase 2, the more recent version, supports multiple logical networks on a single physical network and allows networks to be in more than one zone.

APPN Advanced Peer-to-Peer Networking. An enhancement to the original IBM SNA architecture. APPN handles session establishment between peer nodes, dynamic transparent route calculation, and traffic prioritization for APPC traffic.

Asynchronous Transfer Mode See ATM.

ATM Asynchronous Transfer Mode. An international standard for cell relay in which multiple service types (such as voice, video, or data) are conveyed in fixed-length (53-byte) cells. Fixed-length cells allow cell processing to occur in hardware, thereby reducing transit delays. ATM is designed to take advantage of high-speed transmission media such as E3, SONET, and T3.

B

Beta build An interim build performed prior to the initial FCS of a software release. The images produced are available for internal testing and for customers that are formally signed up (non-disclosure agreement signed and received by Cisco) to participate in the beta program for a release. Image banners from shadow build images will display "BETA TEST SOFTWARE".

BGP Border Gateway Protocol. An interdomain routing protocol that replaces EGP. BGP exchanges reachability information with other BGP systems. It is defined in RFC 1163.

Border Gateway Protocol See BGP.

Branch pull A term used when referring to the creation of a source code repository (or branch) from the contents of another repository (for example, the 12.0T branch was "pulled" from 12.0).

C

CAR Committed Access Rate.

CCO Cisco Connection Online: http://www.cisco.com.

CEF Cisco Express Forwarding.

CFRAD Compressed Frame Relay Access Device.

Cisco Connection Online See CCO.

Cisco Express Forwarding See CEF.

Classic release model Original Cisco IOS release model.

CLNS Connectionless Network Service. An OSI network layer service that does not require a circuit to be established before data is transmitted. CLNS routes messages to their destinations independently of any other messages.

Committed Access Rate See CAR.

Compressed Frame Relay Access Device See CFRAD.

Connectionless Network Service See CLNS.

Consolidated technology early deployment release See CTED.

CTED. Consolidated technology early deployment release. A release of software providing new features and cross-platform support from all business units. Consolidated technology releases mature to a mainline release and subsequently stop accepting new functionality.

CLEC Competitive Local Exchange Carriers

D

Data bus connector See DBCONN.

Data Encryption Standard See DES.

DBCONN Data bus connector. A type of connector used to connect serial and parallel cables to a data bus. DB connector names are of the format DB-*x*, where *x* represents the number of wires within the connector. Each line is connected to a pin on the connector, but in many cases, not all pins are assigned a function. DB connectors are defined by various EIA/TIA standards.

DECnet Group of communications products (including a protocol suite) developed and supported by Digital Equipment Corporation. DECnet/OSI (also called DECnet Phase V) is the most recent iteration and supports both OSI protocols and proprietary digital protocols. Phase IV Prime supports inherent MAC addresses that allow DECnet nodes to coexist with systems running other protocols that have MAC address restrictions.

Deferral The process of moving images containing serious customer impacting defects to a locked directory and removing them from CCO.

DES Data Encryption Standard. A standard cryptographic algorithm developed by the U.S. NBS.

Digital subscriber line See DSL.

DRAM Dynamic random-access memory. RAM that stores information in capacitors that must be periodically refreshed. Delays can occur because DRAMs are inaccessible to the processor when refreshing their contents. However, DRAMs are less complex and have greater capacity than SRAMs. See also SRAM.

DSL Digital subscriber line. The original name for the physical layer of the Basic Rate Access ISDN channel. Most recently, the term DSL is used as a generic name for any digital subscribe loop system (ADSL, HDSL, and so forth).

Dynamic random-access memory See DRAM.

E

Early deployment See ED.

ED Early deployment. Software releases that provide new features and new platform support in addition to bug fixes. Cisco IOS CTED, STED, SMED, and XED are variations of ED software releases.

End of engineering See EOE.

End of life See EOL.

End of sale See EOS.

Engineering special A subset of a release built specifically by individual engineers to support a critical customer who has encountered a special critical defect. Engineering specials are built by engineers and supported by that engineering group. Images from engineering specials are not shipped through Manufacturing nor posted on CCO. The image banners will clearly identify them as "Experimental Version". Customers should upgrade to a supported release at the earliest availability.

EOE End of engineering. Last scheduled maintenance revision. Engineering will no longer actively apply any defect repairs to the release, regardless of origin or severity (except for security and Y2K defects). The product will still be available through FSO and CCO.

EOL End of life. Software is no longer supported by Cisco personnel and is removed from CCO.

EOS End of sale. The last date for product orderability through Customer Service or Manufacturing. The product will still be available through Field Support Offices (FSO) and CCO.

EPROM Erasable programmable read-only memory. Nonvolatile memory chips that are programmed after they are manufactured and, if necessary, can be erased by some means and reprogrammed.

Erasable programmable read-only memory See EPROM.

F

FCS Date of "First Commercial Shipment" for revenue to customers through any channel.

FDDI Fiber Distributed Data Interface. A LAN standard, defined by ANSI X3T9.5, specifying a 100-Mbps token-passing network using fiber-optic cable, with transmission distances of up to 2 km. FDDI uses a dual-ring architecture to provide redundancy.

Featurette A small, simple feature with minimal complexity such that risk of introducing new defects is near zero and the software management burden is minimized.

Fiber Distributed Data Interface See FDDI.

FIFO First in, first out. A buffering technique.

First Commercial Shipment See FCS.

First in, first out See FIFO.

Flash memory A technology developed by Intel and licensed to other semiconductor companies. Flash memory is nonvolatile storage that can be electrically erased and reprogrammed. It allows software images to be stored, booted, and rewritten as necessary.

FRAD Frame Relay access device. Any network device that provides a connection between a LAN and a Frame Relay WAN.

Frame Relay An industry-standard, switched data link layer protocol that handles multiple virtual circuits using HDLC encapsulation between connected devices. Frame Relay is more efficient than X.25, the protocol for which it is generally considered a replacement.

Frame Relay access device See FRAD.

G – H

GD General deployment. The point at which Cisco declares the release stable on all platforms and in all network environments.

General deployment See GD.

HDLC High-Level Data Link Control. A bit-oriented synchronous data link layer protocol developed by ISO. Derived from SDLC, HDLC specifies a data encapsulation method on synchronous serial links using frame characters and checksums. See also SDLC.

High-Level Data Link Control See HDLC.

I

Integrated Services Digital Network See ISDN.

Interim Build Work-in-process image builds (typically performed weekly) that are built between maintenance releases to integrate the latest round of bug fix commits (for example, 12.0(7.3)). This type of a release is periodically submitted to the Automated Regression Facility (ARF) and the development test teams. ARF will execute a "72 hour" regression test run and post a report with any newly found regressions identified. Since only limited testing is applied to interim releases, images from those releases should be delivered with caution to customers. Interims are designed to provide an integrated fix prior to the release of that fix in the next maintenance release. Images banners for interim build images will display "MAINTENANCE INTERIM SOFTWARE".

Internet Protocol See IP.

Internetwork Packet Exchange See IPX.

IP Internet Protocol. A network layer protocol in the TCP/IP stack offering a connectionless internetwork service. IP provides features for addressing, type-of-service specification, fragmentation and reassembly, and security. This is documented in RFC 791.

IPSEC IP Security. A Cryptographic algorithm used in computer communication.

IP Security See IPSEC.

IPX Internetwork Packet Exchange. A NetWare network layer (Layer 3) protocol used for transferring data from servers to workstations. IPX is similar to IP and XNS.

ISDN Integrated Services Digital Network. A communication protocol (Q.931), offered by telephone companies, which permits telephone networks to carry data, voice, and video traffic.

IXC Inter Exchange Carriers

J – K – L

LD Limited deployment. This phase is the time frame between FCS and GD for main releases. Cisco IOS ED releases only live in limited deployment phase, as they never attain GD certification.

Limited deployment See LD.

L2F Layer 2 forwarding.

L2TP Layer 2 tunnel protocol.

LEC Local Exchange Carriers

M

Mainline branch The branch being used for a particular version of IOS software. For example, 12.0 mainline uses 'connecticut' or 'conn' branch. This branch is used to integrate fixes and to generate weekly interim build images for development test purposes.

Major release The IOS software release vehicles, which transcend internal business units and Line of Businesses boundaries to provide cross-platform features. The new IOS release model has two major releases: the mainline release and the consolidated technology release.

Management Information Base See MIB.

Mature maintenance See MM.

MCM Multimedia Conference Manager. A Cisco service offering that uses H.323 protocol to deliver voice and multimedia services.

Mfg FCS Date that a software release is made available for shipment through Manufacturing with hardware or media orders for revenue.

MIB Management Information Base. A database of network management information that is used and maintained by a network management protocol such as SNMP or CMIP. The value of an MIB object can be changed or retrieved using SNMP or CMIP commands. MIB objects are organized in a tree structure that includes public (standard) and private (proprietary) branches.

Minor release A term not commonly used. It refers to the combined group of specific technology releases (STED), specific market releases (SMED), and X releases as opposed to major releases (grouping of mainline and CTED).

MM Mature maintenance. Under normal circumstances, the release would have reached end of engineering (EOE) at this point. However, customer insistence on keeping the release alive is addressed by transitioning into mature maintenance phase. While in this phase, the release will only receive defect repairs for customer-found severity 1 and severity 2 defects. Internally found problems will be addressed on a case-by-case basis.

Multimedia Conference Manager See MCM.

N

NGRP Next generation of release process.

Nonvolatile RAM See NVRAM.

NRP Network Route Processor.

NSP Network Switch Processor.

NVRAM Nonvolatile RAM. RAM that retains its contents when a unit is powered off.

O – P

Open Shortest Path First See OSPF.

OSPF Open Shortest Path First. A link-state, hierarchical IGP routing algorithm proposed as a successor to RIP in the Internet community. OSPF features include least-cost routing, multipath routing, and load balancing. OSPF was derived from an early version of the IS-IS protocol.

PCMCIA Personal Computer Memory Card International Association (also referred to as People Can't Memorize Computer Industry Acronyms). Created by a Sunnyvale, California nonprofit trade association to standardize the connection of peripherals to portable computers, PCMCIA developed the removable lightweight credit card size module (often called the PCMCIA card), that adds features and/or memory to portable computers, switches, and routers.

Personal Computer Memory Card International Association See PCMCIA.

PIM Protocol Independent Multicast. A multicast routing architecture that allows the addition of IP multicast routing on existing IP networks. PIM is unicast routing protocol independent, and can be operated in two modes: dense mode and sparse mode.

PNNI Private Network-Network Interface. An ATM Forum specification that describes an ATM virtual circuit routing protocol, as well as a signaling protocol between ATM switches. This interface is used to allow ATM switches with a private network to interconnect. PNNI is sometimes called Private Network Node Interface.

Posting The act of delivering images to CCO and the release archive (/release).

Private Network-Network Interface See PNNI.

Protocol Independent Multicast See PIM.

Q – R

QoS Quality of service. A measure of performance for a transmission system that reflects its transmission quality and service availability.

Quality of service See QoS.

RAS Reliability, availability, and serviceability.

rcp Remote copy. A protocol that allows users to copy files to and from a file system residing on a remote host or server on the network. The rcp protocol uses TCP to ensure the reliable delivery of data.

RED Random early detection.

Reliability, availability, and serviceability See RAS.

Remote copy See rcp.

Renumber build A build on the throttle branch that occurs after the throttle build and after regression testing is completed on throttle build images. The renumber build is designed to renumber the software image from an interim notation to a maintenance revision notation (for example, from 12.0(6.6) to 12.0(7)). Renumber builds normally do not contain new bug fixes. The renumber build is the final build on the throttle branch and generates a maintenance revision which is FCSed on CCO and Mfg. Images banners for renumber build images will display “RELEASE SOFTWARE (fc1)”.

Restricted maintenance This is the end of the MM phase. During this phase, release source code is locked to avoid major application of fixes that might adversely affect the quality of the code.

Route Processor See RP.

Route Switch Processor See RSP.

RP Route Processor. A processor module in the Cisco 7000 series routers that contains the CPU, systems software, and most of the memory components that are used in the router. RP is sometimes called a supervisory processor.

RSP Route Switch Processor. This is the same as the Route Processor with switching capability.

S

SDLC Synchronous Data Link Control. An SNA data link layer communications protocol. SDLC is a bit-oriented, full-duplex serial protocol that has spawned numerous similar protocols, including HDLC and LAPB. See also HDLC.

Shadow build A build occurring on the mainline branch in the “shadow” of a throttle branch (in parallel with builds on the throttle branch). Shadow builds occur so that fixes committed into the mainline are built and made available for testing weekly. Shadow builds are not intended for customer consumption, strictly for internal engineering purposes. Image banners from shadow build images will display “CISCO DEVELOPMENT TEST VERSION”.

Short-lived BU release See X release (or XED).

Showstopper Cisco IOS software will not reach FCS if it contains defects (bugs) marked by Cisco’s Customer Advocacy group as showstopper.

Silicon Switching A fast switching mechanism implemented in some Cisco routers.

SIMMs Single in-line memory module. A circuit board that holds random-access memory (RAM) chips. SIMMs can be plugged into sockets on the computer's motherboard to add memory to a computing system.

Single in-line memory module See SIMMs.

SMED Specific market early deployment release. A release of software targeted on a specific market segment that provides maintenance revisions until unification back into the next consolidated technology release. SMEDs usually transcend the LOB boundaries and are managed by the IOS Technology Division.

SNA Systems Network Architecture. A large, complex, feature-rich network architecture developed in the 1970s by IBM. SNA is similar in some respects to the OSI model, but with a number of differences. SNA is essentially composed of seven layers.

Software image The monolithic compiled software binary delivered to customers. IOS images are specific to hardware platforms. For example, 'rsp-pv-mz.120-5.S.bin' is a Cisco IOS 12.0(5)S image for the rsp platforms (RSP7000 and 7500 series routers).

Software rebuild or rebuilds A second build performed on a throttle branch after the renumber build was completed. This happens when a catastrophic defect that significantly impacts customer usage is found on the renumber build. If the renumber images have already been formally posted to CCO, the release numbering for the rebuild will be augmented to clearly identify the rebuild. For example, 12.0(2a), 12.0(1)T1, and 12.0(3)DB1 are rebuilds of 12.0(2), 12.0(1)T, and 12.0(3)DB respectively.

Specific market early deployment release See SMED.

Specific technology early deployment release See STED.

SRAM A type of RAM that retains its contents for as long as power is supplied. SRAM does not require constant refreshing, as does DRAM. Compare with DRAM.

STED. Specific technology early deployment release A release of software with limited platform support, created for strategic business needs and to provide maintenance revisions until unification back into the next consolidated technology release.

Synchronous Data Link Control See SDLC.

Systems Network Architecture See SNA.

T

TCP/IP Transmission Control Protocol/Internet Protocol. A common name for the suite of protocols developed by the U.S. DoD in the 1970s to support the construction of worldwide internetworks. TCP and IP are the two best known protocols in the suite. See also IP.

Teletypewriter See TTY.

TFTP Trivial File Transfer Protocol. A simplified version of FTP that allows files to be transferred from one computer to another over a network.

Throttle branch The branch pulled from the mainline branch to provide a controlled repository just prior to FCS. Typically, only customer critical fixes are allowed in the throttle branch, usually to fix a catastrophic problem or repair software regression. The throttle branch runs parallel to the mainline branch and any fix applied to the throttle branch is also applied to the mainline branch. The use of a throttle branch allows the mainline to remain open to all bug fixes without impacting the upcoming maintenance release.

Throttle build Compiled images on the throttle branch which incorporate "showstopper" critical fixes into images prior to the final regression testing. Throttle builds are considered interim builds except that the physical build is performed on a separate branch from the mainline branch. As such, images banners for throttle build images look similar to that of interim images and will display "MAINTENANCE INTERIM SOFTWARE". See banner section.

Token Ring A token-passing LAN developed and supported by IBM. Token Ring runs at 4 or 16 Mbps over a ring topology. It is similar to IEEE 802.5.

Transmission Control Protocol/Internet Protocol See TCP/IP.

Trivial File Transfer Protocol See TFTP.

TTY Teletypewriter. A device that has a typewriter-style keyboard and built-in printer; it is used to send, receive, and print out signals received over telephone or communication lines.

U

UART Universal Asynchronous Receiver Transmitter. An integrated circuit which is used for transmitting and receiving data asynchronously via the serial port. The UART also has a buffer for temporarily storing data from high-speed transmissions.

Universal Asynchronous Receiver Transmitter See UART.

Upgrade Planner The section of CCO through which Cisco IOS software images can be downloaded: http://www.cisco.com/cgi-bin/Software/Iosplanner/Planner-tool/iosplanner.cgi?

V – W – X – Y – Z

VIP Virtual Interface Processor.

VTY Virtual TTY.

WRED Weighted random early detection.

XDSL Digital subscriber line. A group term used to refer to ADSL, HDSL, SDSL, and VDSL. All are emerging digital technologies using the existing copper infrastructure provided by the telephone companies. xDSL is a high-speed alternative to ISDN.

X release (or XED) A release of software that enables IOS and BUs with critical time-to-market commitments to deliver new features/platforms prior to the release of the corresponding maintenance release of the parent technology release. Often referred to as an X release.

INDEX

Numerics

A

B

C

D

E

F

G–H

I

K–L

M

N

O

P

R

S

T

U

V

W

X–Z

Cisco Career Certifications

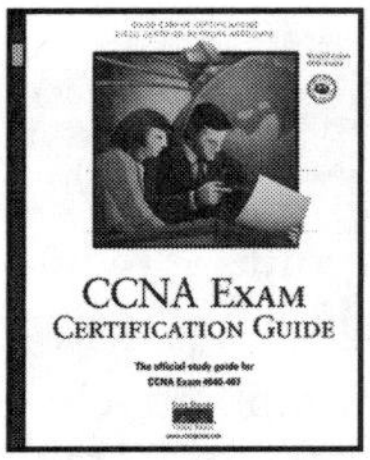

CCNA Exam Certification Guide

Wendell Odom, CCIE

0-7357-0073-7 • AVAILABLE NOW

This book is a comprehensive study tool for CCNA Exam #640-407 and part of a recommended study program from Cisco Systems. *CCNA Exam Certification Guide* helps you understand and master the exam objectives. Instructor-developed elements and techniques maximize your retention and recall of exam topics, and scenario-based exercises help validate your mastery of the exam objectives.

Advanced Cisco Router Configuration

Cisco Systems, Inc., edited by Laura Chappell

1-57870-074-4 • AVAILABLE NOW

Based on the actual Cisco ACRC course, this book provides a thorough treatment of advanced network deployment issues. Learn to apply effective configuration techniques for solid network implementation and management as you prepare for CCNP and CCDP certifications. This book also includes chapter-ending tests for self-assessment.

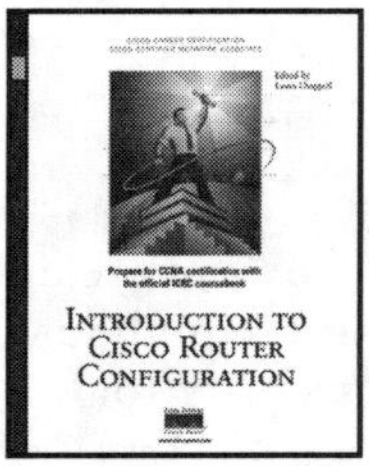

Introduction to Cisco Router Configuration

Cisco Systems, Inc., edited by Laura Chappell

1-57870-076-0 • AVAILABLE NOW

Based on the actual Cisco ICRC course, this book presents the foundation knowledge necessary to define Cisco router configurations in multiprotocol environments. Examples and chapter-ending tests build a solid framework for understanding internetworking concepts. Prepare for the ICRC course and CCNA certification while mastering the protocols and technologies for router configuration.

Cisco CCNA Preparation Library

Cisco Systems, Inc., Laura Chappell, and Kevin Downes, CCIE

1-57870-125-2 • AVAILABLE NOW • CD-ROM

This boxed set contains two Cisco Press books—*Introduction to Cisco Router Configuration* and *Internetworking Technologies Handbook,* Second Edition—and the *High-Performance Solutions for Desktop Connectivity* CD.

Cisco Systems
Cisco Press

www.ciscopress.com

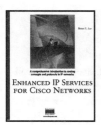

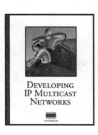

Staying Connected to Networkers

We want to hear from **you**! Help Cisco Press **stay connected** to the issues and challenges you face on a daily basis by registering your book and filling out our brief survey.

Complete and mail this form, or better yet, jump to **www.ciscopress.com** and do it online. Each complete entry will be eligible for our monthly drawing to **win a FREE book** from the Cisco Press Library.

Thank you for choosing Cisco Press to help you work the network.

Name ______________________________

Address ______________________________

City ____________________ State/Province ____________________

Country ____________________ Zip/Post code ____________________

E-mail address ______________________________

May we contact you via e-mail for product updates and customer benefits?

❒ Yes ❒ No

Where did you buy this product?

❒ Bookstore ❒ Computer store ❒ Electronics store
❒ Online retailer ❒ Office supply store ❒ Discount store
❒ Mail order ❒ Class/Seminar
❒ Other ______________________________

When did you buy this product? ________**Month** ________**Year**

What price did you pay for this product?

❒ Full retail price ❒ Discounted price ❒ Gift

How did you learn about this product?

❒ Friend ❒ Store personnel ❒ In-store ad
❒ Catalog ❒ Postcard in the mail ❒ Saw it on the shelf
❒ Magazine ad ❒ Article or review ❒ Used other products
❒ School ❒ Professional Organization
❒ Other ______________________________

What will this product be used for?

❒ Business use ❒ Personal use ❒ School/Education
❒ Other ______________________________

How many years have you been employed in a computer-related industry?

❒ 2 years or less ❒ 3-5 years ❒ 5+ years

Cisco Systems
Cisco Press

www.ciscopress.com

CISCO SYSTEMS
CISCO PRESS

www.ciscopress.com

Which best describes your job function?

- ❐ Corporate Management
- ❐ Systems Engineering
- ❐ IS Management
- ❐ Network Design
- ❐ Network Support
- ❐ Webmaster
- ❐ Marketing/Sales
- ❐ Consultant
- ❐ Student
- ❐ Professor/Teacher
- ❐ Other ______________________________

What is your formal education background?

- ❐ High school
- ❐ Vocational/Technical degree
- ❐ Some college
- ❐ College degree
- ❐ Masters degree
- ❐ Professional or Doctoral degree

Have you purchased a Cisco Press product before?

- ❐ Yes
- ❐ No

On what topics would you like to see more coverage?

____

____

Do you have any additional comments or suggestions?

____

____

Cisco IOS Releases: The Complete Reference (1-57870-179-1)

Cisco Press
201 West 103rd Street
Indianapolis, IN 46290
www.ciscopress.com

Place
Stamp
Here

Cisco Press
Customer Registration
P.O. Box 189014
Battle Creek, MI 49018-9947